NORTH SEA

SKAGERRAK

SCANIA

RÜGEN

DENMARK

JUTLAND

Jellinge

Ribe

Hamburg

SAXONY

FRISIA

FRISIAN IS.

RHINE R.

MAAS R.

FRANCE

FLANDERS

St. Valéry

SOMME R.

SEINE R.

Paris

Orléans

Chartres

Dreux

Le Mans

LOIRE R.

Alençon

NORMANDY

Rouen

Fécamp

Bayeux

Avranches

BRITTANY

Nantes

Tours

ENGLISH CHANNEL

ISLE OF WIGHT

Shoreham

Chichester

SUSSEX

KENT

Dover

THANET

Maldon

ESSEX

London

THAMES R.

Oxford

Gloucester

Hereford

GWENT

POWYS

WALES

Chester

Lancaster

SOLWAY FIRTH

STRATHCLYDE

Dumbarton

Edinburgh

BERNICIA

LINDISFARNE

Jarrow

Durham

DEIRA

York

NORTHUMBRIA

HUMBER R.

TRENT R.

OUSE R.

Lincoln

Nottingham

Derby

MERCIA

EAST ANGLIA

Ely

Norwich

WESSEX

Exeter

N

Miles

0   100   200

IONA

ULSTER

Armagh

IRELAND

Clochachois

Dublin

Wexford

Waterford

N ORTH   S EA

palacios

BY ERIC LINKLATER

NOVELS
White-Maa's Saga
Poet's Pub
Juan in America
The Men of Ness
Magnus Merriman
Ripeness is All
Juan in China
The Sailor's Holiday
The Impregnable Women
Judas
Private Angelo
A Spell for Old Bones
Mr Byculla
Laxdale Hall
The House of Gair
The Faithful Ally
The Dark of Summer
Position at Noon
The Merry Muse
Roll of Honour
Husband of Delilah
A Man Over Forty

FOR CHILDREN
The Wind on the Moon
The Pirates in the Deep Green
Sea
Karina with Love

SHORT STORIES
God Likes Them Plain
Sealskin Trousers
A Sociable Plover

AUTOBIOGRAPHY
The Man on My Back
A Year of Space

BIOGRAPHY
Ben Johnson and King James
Mary Queen of Scots
Robert the Bruce
The Prince in the Heather

ESSAYS
The Lion and the Unicorn
The Art of Adventure
The Ultimate Viking
Edinburgh
Orkney and Shetland

HISTORY
The Campaign in Italy

VERSE
A Dragon Laughed

PLAYS
The Devil's in the News
Crisis in Heaven
To Meet the Macgregors
Love in Albania
The Mortimer Touch
Breakspear in Gascony

CONVERSATIONS
The Cornerstones
The Raft and Socrates Asks
Why
The Great Ship and Rabelais
Replies

PAMPHLETS
The Northern Garrisons
The Defense of Calais
The Highland Division
Our Men in Korea

The Crossroads of World History Series

EDITED BY ORVILLE PRESCOTT

THE CONQUEST OF ENGLAND

The Crossroads of World History Series

THE CONQUEST OF

ENGLAND

Eric Linklater

Garden City, New York

DOUBLEDAY & COMPANY, INC.

1966

Library of Congress Catalog Card Number 66-11730
Copyright © 1966 by Eric Linklater
All Rights Reserved
Printed in the United States of America
First Edition

CONTENTS

MAPS

ILLUSTRATIONS

(From the Bayeux Tapestry)

AUTHOR'S NOTE

In this narrative—complex because of its broad geographical background—there is some repetition. That repetition, restricted to a minimum, is deliberate, and designed to facilitate the reader's awareness, or reinforce his memory, of the continuity or relationship of events.

With some frequency, reference is made to the writings of early chroniclers, and a note on these chroniclers may be found in the bibliography on pages 299–301.

Except where they seem essential, footnotes have been avoided, because footnotes spoil the appearance of a page, and where back reference may be desired, the way to it can be found in the index.

The illustrations are taken from the Bayeux Tapestry, an almost contemporary account-in-pictures of the battle of Hastings and the events immediately preceding it.

The bibliography cites my authority for the description of persons and events in the narrative; for the elucidation of their purposes and inter-relationship I have sometimes relied on my own judgment.

THE CONQUEST OF
ENGLAND

Chapter I

THE YEAR OF THE COMET

For seven nights in April 1066, the sky over England—over much of the known world, indeed—was lighted with sinister brilliance by a star that was manifestly an intruder in the ordered pattern of familiar constellations. It had a flaming head, in which shone an incandescent core, and a long, flamboyant tail. It was a foreign body in the firmament, such as none had ever seen before and no one could explain; but to an age that believed in portents and was quick to recognise in phenomenal occurrences the omens of doom, the comet was widely accepted as a harbinger of catastrophe. When at long intervals in succeeding centuries it re-appeared, Halley's comet always excited fearful speculation, but never did it disfigure the sky with a more apparent significance than in 1066, when the course of English history was about to be violently disrupted and a new growth of enormous potency implanted in its broken soil; and when, to those who had ears for more than the gossip of their own acres, not only in England but in northern France and Scandinavia, the menace of war and murmurs of change were clearly audible.

On the English throne sat the Saxon earl Harold Godwineson, grandson of an upstart but the most powerful man in England and brother-in-law of the late king, Edward the Confessor. Edward had ruled, in name at least, for twenty-four years and had died childless on the 5th January. On the following day Harold went with purposive and what may seem to be improper haste from a weakling's funeral to resolute coronation as monarch of a divided land. His title to the throne had only a doubtful foundation in legality. It was said that on his death-bed the Confessor had named Harold as his heir; and allowing for the possibility of rough persuasion, that is not improbable. But the Confessor had not summoned the Witan to declare his choice and have it substantiated by the approval of his council. There were in London men of influence, of the stature of those qualified for the Witan's elective privilege, and they acquiesced in what a prudent judgment must regard as Harold's self-nomination. Their hasty decision can be justified, as can Harold's own action, by the unquestionable fact that he was the only man in England who could hope to rule the Saxon kingdom, and who might hope to keep it intact. His working title to the throne lay in his own fierce ability and heroic temper, and in the recognition of his quality by a group of Saxon magnates who may be called loyalists.

His assumption of the crown, however, was also an act of open and contumacious defiance. That Edward the Confessor had named Harold as his successor is open to question, but there is no reasonable doubt that in 1051 he had nominated William, duke of Normandy, as his heir. A family connexion between the ducal house and the Saxon kingdom had been established in 1002 when Emma, sister of duke Richard II, who was William's grandfather, married Ethelred II and bore him two sons, of whom the elder was Edward, later called the Confessor. After the death of Ethelred, and the Danish conquest of England, Emma married Cnut the Great, then king of England, and her sons by Ethelred lived in Normandy as protégés of its ruling house. Edward succeeded to the English throne in 1042, and comforted his loneliness in a foreign land by summoning to it Norman clerks, prelates, and noblemen. In 1051 the great earl Godwine and his sons were banished—though they soon returned—and Edward dismissed his wife Edith, Godwine's daughter, whom it is safe to say he had married under pressure. In the brief freedom of that year he obeyed the dictates of sentiment and repaid the hospitality of the Norman court by a promise of his throne to his cousin William.

Thirteen years later Harold, Godwine's son, was forced by foul weather to land from an endangered ship near the mouth of the Somme, and was promptly made prisoner by Guy, count of Ponthieu. Harold was on a mission, the purpose of which is uncertain, though Norman historians agree that it was to confirm his king's bequest of England to their duke. The count Guy delivered his prisoner to William, and according to the historians William of Jumièges, William of Poitiers, and the pictorial evidence of the Bayeux Tapestry, Harold swore on sacred relics his fealty and allegiance to duke William. The possibility that his oath was exacted under duress need not be excluded, but his quick seizure of the throne in the nervous darkness of January, no more than a year or two later, was a repudiation of his word, and of the old king's pledge; and open defiance of William.

But Normandy was not the only danger that now threatened England. Rebellion had driven Harold's brother Tostig from his earldom of Northumbria, and he had found refuge with his wife's brother, the count of Flanders. That he would accept an enforced exile was not to be expected, and in May of the year of crisis he made an abortive attack on the Isle of Wight and the east coast about the mouth of the Humber. Defeated there, he retired to the court of Malcolm III, king of Scots, with whom he had enjoyed long friendship, and from there resumed an association of some sort with Harald Hardrada, king of Norway.

Harald of Norway, a half-brother of St. Olaf, was as formidable a figure as can be found in all the Norse sagas. More than thirty years before he had fought in the great sea-battle of Stiklestad in the Trondheim fjord; he had served under a prince of Novgorod and in the Varangian Guard in Constantinople. He was reputed to have led the Varangians to victory in Sicily and north Africa, and when he returned to Norway, to whose throne he succeeded on the death of his nephew Magnus in 1047, he fought for year after year, but inconclusively, against Sweyn of Denmark. Magnus, his predecessor, is said to have entered into treaty with Harthacnut—son of Cnut the Great and Emma his wife, and for two years, from 1040 to 1042, king of England—by which one would succeed to the kingdom of the other, should the latter die childless. This treaty gave Harald Hardrada inheritance of the dubious claim which Magnus had half-heartedly advanced; and in 1058 he had asserted his claim by sending his son, in command of a fleet reinforced from the Hebrides and the east coast of Ireland, to attempt invasion of England in alliance with a prince of Wales. And now, having patched up a peace with Denmark, Harald Hardrada was again ready for invasion, with the frustrated Tostig to help him; though whether for Tostig's benefit, or primarily his own, the course of history has obscured.

Though Harold Godwineson, as it appears, was openly faithless to his own sworn word and his late king's purpose, the splendid audacity of his policy must be acknowledged, and it may not have been wholly reckless. By his own choice he exposed England to invasion and war from two sides, but he may have counted on the support of all who saw in his action the only prospect of maintaining a Saxon kingdom, and with himself on its throne he may have thought it would appear, to rivals oversea, a stronghold whose native habit of stubborn resistance could neither be ignored nor easily overcome. In the ninth century Alfred of Wessex had defied the great army of the Danes when England lay exhausted by prolonged and ferocious war; and only thirty years before Harold's hurried coronation England had thrown off the remnant authority of a more successful invasion and the last vestiges of Cnut's wide and well-ordered empire. An English king on the English throne was a formidable opponent.

But if, by a pretence to strength, he hoped to dissuade William of Normandy and Harald of Norway from adventure, his hope was falsified. His reign was short, and twice before the year was out he had to fight for the crown he had put on with such determined haste. In the north, near York, he defeated Tostig and Harald Hardrada, and victory there showed the persistence of Saxon courage. But his defeat at Hastings, after a day of most resolute battle, was proof of a decay that could not be patched by courage nor riveted by the military rule of even so swiftly moving and masterful a man as Harold. Saxon England had been battered too long, and while some of its people were still ready to fight for an old cause with traditional valour, many others waited on events with sullen indifference.

The battle of Hastings opened the way to the Norman conquest of England. It was an action so decisive in history—so decisive of history—that there is some temptation to regard it solely as the beginning of a new order of history. There is obvious reward in the survey and assessment of what followed the conquest; less, perhaps, in consideration of the preliminary exercises which made it possible. But the conquest was, in fact, the culmination of many preceding exercises, and it cannot properly be seen in isolation. It cannot properly be measured, nor will its consequences be fully comprehensible, without some examination of the state of England—of the temper and government of the invaded island—or without a comparable analysis of the nature and purpose of those who, in earlier years, had probed and tested and penetrated its defences.

England has always been, and possibly remains, something of an enigma in the history of the western world. Though essentially and often defiantly isolated—though separated from its mother-continent by the decisive waters of the English Channel—it is, and always has been, a related part of Europe: part and parcel of the spiritual, intellectual, or political life of Europe, giving and receiving, preserving or undermining the power of its continental neighbours while paradoxically asserting its basic independence, and cultivating from a European seed-bed its own intransigent, unpredictable, and distinguishing growths, its island blooms and blemishes. It is evident, moreover, that the isolation of its character, if not its destiny, was shaped and established by fundamental paradox: the successive invasion of several alien or semi-alien peoples was needed to form its historic quality which, so far from being native, was induced and cumulative.

The Celtic inhabitants of pre-Roman Britain—of the southern half of the island—accepted under duress a Roman civilization, and England remained a Roman colony for some four hundred years. The consequences of that occupation can neither be measured, nor ignored, for its consequences were obscured by a long period of anarchy and the passage of unrecorded time; but consequences of some sort, and possibly of a profound and influential sort, there must have been.

One obvious consequence was the establishment of a political identity that was dissipated and lost when the Romans withdrew. The governing and middle classes of Roman Britain accepted and may well have been satisfied by the security of their place within the Roman empire; though Roman authority had not wholly subdued the Celtic complaint of anonymous herdsmen and their pagan beliefs. When the last Roman garrison retired to the continent, anarchy remained, and throughout a long dark night England was a confused and distracted battlefield that invading Germanic tribes divided. In obscure alliance with native chiefs they established provincial powers that fought for a shifting hegemony and strangely coalesced into an Anglo-Saxon land from which, out of Northumbrian oases, in its recurrent turbulence, emerged a Christian scholarship that sent its missionaries to the continent from which its torment had emanated. Long before England acquired a political unity there were Englishmen who re-asserted the identity which had been lost when the Romans left, and England began its long career of interference with its neighbours: in the beginning a benign interference, as would sometimes be its interference in the future.

The Romans, the Anglo-Saxons, then the Danes: they were the invaders that made from the Celtic natives of south Britain the kingdom that William the Norman conquered, and some description of it is necessary. Necessary, too, is recognition that William's invasion of England was a gamble which succeeded against odds that would have frightened a lesser man. His motive was obvious—the acquisition of a great prize and a power more certainly independent than that which he enjoyed on the continent—but the adventurous spring of his action, the gambler's instinct in his policy, can hardly be appreciated without reference to his ancestry and the comparable ambition of his neighbours in Norway and Denmark.

What is gratifyingly apparent is that from William's victory emerged a nation that through nine hundred years of intermittent progress has remained, unique in Europe, immune from foreign invasion or any consequent submission other than to internal dissidence. In those growing centuries the off-shore island acquired, by intellect and war, so great a position in the world—for a century, indeed, a dominating position—that all remembrance of earlier defeat receded from the general mind until, in popular apprehension, the story of England had its purposive and practical origin in a union, fortuitously benign, of William's Norman knights with a Saxon society of acquiescent thanes and a submissive peasantry.

That is not a true reading of what happened, but a popular interpretation of history, however erroneous, may not be lightly disregarded, for intuitively it may select for remembrance those deeds, those characters and circumstances, which in fact decided the course of history; and the achievements of William the Conqueror were so productive that his common acceptance as the *fons et origo* of England, and so of the expansion that created an empire, cannot be denied an essential truth. But historic truth has never a simple beginning, and under scrutiny of its backward parts, of the centuries immediately preceding his victory, the Conquest may be seen—without diminution of what William did, or of his place in history—as the conclusion of a process which had begun some two hundred years before.

Before that time there had been sea-borne raids on the coast of England, as on all the western shores of Europe, which had no larger purpose than a pirate's profit, the satisfaction of a thin-ribbed, adventurous people's ardent hunger for money and cattle. Then, for many years, the seas were quiet and the vikings stayed at home. In the course of time they renewed their voyaging, and the pirate raids eventually became a policy, an open and enlarging policy that achieved successes and met defeat. In England periods of fearful crisis recurred, and England survived them; while in northern France a duchy established by the arrogant invasion of a viking called Marching Rolf outlived the hostility of its neighbours and internal revolt. The duchy of Normandy grew in power, developed its separate character, and created something like a constitution; yet retained, like its parents in the north and its founding fathers, a certain flexibility of outlook, a fluidity of intention, that was to let it intervene, in the critical year, as the successful competitor in the continuing rivalry for the great prize which, for generations, had irresistibly allured the more adventurous minds of the viking countries.

The prize was England, the richest kingdom of northern Europe, and infinitely attractive because an island. For him who had the strength to rule and hold it, England could be a fortress within whose rampart of the sea its fields would fatly feed his conquering people, and security from greedy neighbours would bless the fruits of conquest. The viking adventurers of Norway and Denmark had early learnt the advantages of sea-power and strategic harbours; and the earliest purposive invaders of Saxon England had clearly seen the rewards, of more than booty, that the island offered. Sweyn Forkbeard of Denmark had nearly won it; his son, the great Cnut, was more successful. Norway had recurrently maintained its rival efforts, and then, in the last throw of all, William in his French duchy reverted to type, and with a gambler's confidence that no hero of the sagas could have bettered, but with a statesman's intention rare among his predeces-

sors, made his preparation for invasion under the nose of Harald
Hardrada, and defeated Harold Godwineson, an opponent worthy of his sword, in a battle that must take precedence over all
the fabled battles of England and the north: the furious fighting
at Stiklestad, where St. Olaf fell by the Trondheim fjord; the sea-
battle of Svold, off the island of Rügen, where Olaf Tryggvison
died in the shadow of his ship; the nine battles of king Alfred;
the great victory that Athelstan won at Brunanburh—none was
so momentous as that of Hastings, where Harold was killed in
the shield-ring of his housecarls, and William of Normandy—
great-grandson of duke Richard I, who was Marching Rolf's
grandson—won his title to the English throne, and in the year of
the comet began a new volume of its history.

Chapter II

THE NORSE PROPULSION

BEORHTIC, king of Wessex, ruled from 786 till 802, and in his days, according to the Anglo-Saxon Chronicle, 'came three ships from Heretheland' to the Dorset shore. Their crews landed on the Isle of Portland, and when the king's reeve at Dorchester rode down to collect a tax or customs duty, they killed him and his company. 'These were,' says the Chronicle, 'the first ships of Danish men that sought the land of the English race.' But if 'Heretheland' is Hordaland—the accepted identification—the invaders were not Danes but Norwegians; for Hordaland lies about the Hardanger fjord. To early English writers the piratical visitors from Norway and Denmark were all 'Danes.'

In June 793, Holy Island, off the coast of Northumberland, and the priory of Lindisfarne were sacked; Aidan, the sainted monk from Iona, had founded the priory in 635, and St. Cuthbert of Durham had made it famous. But the heathen jeered and asked, 'Where is now their God?' The monastery of St. Paul at Jarrow was spoiled in 794, and the Irish Annals of Clonmacnois say that about this time 'all the islands of Britain were wasted and much troubled by the Danes.' They agree with the Chronicle that this was their first footing in England. The Isle of Skye and the little island of Rathlin were pillaged in 795, when Iona was devastated and 'the Gentiles,' as the Annals of Innisfallen call them, came also to Ireland. Three years later, on the same authority, 'the Hebrides and Ulster were plundered by Scandinavians.' Iona, the heart and centre of the Celtic church, was raided again in 802, and in 806—according to the Annals of Ulster—sixty-eight monks were murdered there. The abbot Cellach escaped and fled to Ireland, where he founded a new monastery at Kells; but Ireland offered no safety. Before the middle of the ninth century the vikings had encircled it, planted colonies, and penetrated far inland. Dublin, Wexford, Waterford, and Limerick grew up as Norse settlements.

The islands of Britain and their monasteries were not the only victims of the Norsemen's expansive fury; there were other shores endangered by that fierce propulsion. As early as the last quarter of the eighth century the Danes—inhabitants of Jutland, the Danish islands, and Scania, the southern part of Sweden—were strong enough to menace the northern marches of Saxony, which by then lay, though somewhat incoherently, within the kingdom of the Franks; and Charlemagne was compelled to strengthen his fleet and look to the defences of the Frisian Islands and the Channel coast from the Somme to the Seine. Aquitaine was raided, as were the islands of Noirmoutier at the mouth of the Loire, and Rhé near La Rochelle.

These early raids on the coasts of France and Britain were pirate forays. The vikings came to plunder, and went home with the loot they had taken. But they also gathered information about the invaded lands, and when their incursions were renewed they showed increasingly an appreciation of their opportunities, and among themselves a spirit of co-operation that let them divide their spoils without internecine conflict. In England the Norse attack, in its first exploratory and piratical phase, was brief; and for forty years after 794 its shores were untroubled, though south Wales endured a harsh invasion. France suffered longer, but for twenty years after 814 France—or, more accurately, the Frankish empire—was also free from viking punishment. The reason for its immunity was, presumably, the disabling effect on Denmark of its internal politics; the succession to its throne was long disputed. But some time after 830 a more or less stable monarchy was established, while simultaneously Louis the Pious, a son of Charlemagne and heir to the Frankish empire, was distracted by domestic revolt; and the Danish offensive was renewed. Both France and England were attacked, and in the second half of the century their assailants made evident a more serious purpose. A movable plunder no longer satisfied them, and they looked for lands in which to settle.

Who, then, were they—these now resolved and daring invaders—and what was the spirit that moved them to such great adventure? From where did they fetch their strength and imagination to steer westward from Hordaland and Jutland, from the Baltic and the Skagerrak, to the shores of Northumbria and East Anglia and the wilder climate of the Hebrides, to the more distant coasts of southern Ireland and France? None before them had sailed the sea so boldly. The Romans had had no reason to leave soundings, and Pytheas of Marseille, who in the darkness of the fourth century B.C. may have seen the hilly isles of Shetland, could have gone so far without losing sight of land. It was the vikings who made a highway of the North Sea.

As to who they were, the Irish had a better understanding than the English chroniclers who labelled them all as Danes. The Irish, who in the early days saw much more of them, distinguished between the Finn-gaill and the Dubh-gaill: the Norwegians, or White Foreigners, and the Danes, or Black Foreigners. In Ireland, Danish attack was, on the whole, unsuccessful; and Ireland, Scotland, and the Scottish isles—the Hebrides, Orkney, and Shetland—fell to Norwegian influence or into Norwegian possession. Under the deep penetration of the new phase, the northern part of Northumbria became Norwegian territory, but the kingdom of Deira, of which the capital was York, was Danish; as were the so-called Five Boroughs of Lincoln, Stamford, Derby, Nottingham, and Leicester in the English midlands, and the kingdom of East Anglia. Both Danes and Norwegians settled in France and the Netherlands: it may have been a Danish host that first sailed up the Seine to Paris, but it was a Norwegian marauder who founded the duchy of Normandy. Swedish adventurers usually confined their interest to eastern Europe, and were more concerned with trade than with battle; though dynastic complications brought members of its ruling family into contact and conflict with the other Scandinavian monarchies. The Baltic shore was largely settled by Swedes, and their trading posts at Kiev and Novgorod were the foundation of a Russian state.

The word 'viking,' commonly applied to all Scandinavian adventurers of this period, comes from Old Norse *vík*, a bay, and primarily meant one who did business in the fjords or sea-lochs which indent the northern lands. To go 'a-viking' was a civil term for piracy, and its extension from coastwise voyaging to the open sea was a natural development.

The viking motive was profit, but the temper which decided

on so dangerous a quest for profit was adventurous, and the spirit
of adventure is not to be discounted by the probability that many
men were persuaded to go to sea by the pressure on land of a
suddenly increasing population. The *Gesta Danorum* of Saxo
Grammaticus, written at the end of the twelfth century, and the
earlier *Historia Normannorum* of William of Jumièges, offer economic explanation of the movement: in both it is said that the
population of Norway and Denmark had become too great to be
supported, and that emigration was enforced by hardship at
home. It is possible, indeed, that refugees from Charlemagne's
imperial advance had added to the indigenous population, but the
degree of pressure is unknown, and it has to be remembered that
the age of barbarian 'folk-wandering,' whose massive migrations
had hastened the dissolution of the Roman empire and continued
after its fall, was not so long past that all memory of it had been
forgotten.

The acceptance of a settled habitation was not yet a compulsive habit, nor the reality of frontiers an established fact. Earl
Rognvald of Möre, a Norwegian potentate in the latter part of
the ninth century and father of that Rolf (or Rollo) who settled
in Normandy, traced his descent through eleven generations from
a king called Fornjot who ruled in Finland. His alleged ancestors
—or most of them—are mythical creatures, but the tale of their
exploits is, quite clearly, a fabulous recital of the discovery and
exploration of Norway; and from such an ancestry an appetite
for discovery, a zest for exploration, certainly survived to ani-
mate the viking age.

But what materially assisted, and may have prompted, the great
Norse propulsion was a technological triumph: the vikings had
learnt how to build and propel swift and seaworthy ships. They
and their ancestors had had the advantage of living, for several
centuries, in heavily timbered countries whose tortuous coasts
and innumerable islands had given them, as almost their only
means of travel, many hundreds of miles of sheltered water. To
go in search of new land—or food, or trade—they felled the
trees and built boats; and their apprenticeship had lasted a long
time. The remains of a boat found at Hjörtspring in Jutland show
that shipwrights of the Iron Age could fashion a canoe-like vessel,
round in the bottom, of five strakes fastened to the ribs by lash-

ings. The earliest inhabitants exercised their nascent skill in the tideless waters of deep fjords or under the lee of protecting isles. They learnt the tricks of coastwise navigation, and presently acquired more skill and knowledge from their southern neighbours.

By the fourth century A.D. they were making iron-fastened, clinker-built boats with upswept bow and stern and a primitive keel consisting of a narrow, thickened bottom-plank.—This on the evidence of two such craft found at Nydam in Schleswig.—These boats were propelled by oars that grommets of raw hide fastened to horn-shaped tholes on the gunwale; but there is no evidence that the oar was a northern invention. The oar, which is a lever capable of more work than a paddle, was certainly known to Homer, and presumably was introduced into northern waters by the Romans: it was an instrument destined to be fully as useful as the wheel. But boats of the Nydam sort were meant neither for sea warfare nor voyaging in the open sea, and the Jutes, Angles, and Saxons who first invaded England probably hugged the coast until, across the Straits of Dover, they could see the white cliffs of their landfall. Gradually, however, the northern shipwrights mastered their craft and made an art of it, till eventually they built long vessels whose swift and lovely lines were the epitome of competence and sea-kindly strength. As their builders' knowledge grew, and experience encouraged their crews, they dared the outer sea. They discovered the limitations of a longship, as well as its uses, and for trade and Atlantic voyaging to Iceland they built other sorts with taller sides and a broader beam. Then all the known seas were theirs, for exploration, for plunder, and a path to conquest. Other men in other lands had invented the wheel to give them mobility; but for the range of their large destiny the vikings built ships.

There may well have been economic pressure behind their voyages, and the loud annoyance of an over-crowded market-place, but the population of all Scandinavia in those early centuries can never have been large, in a modern appraisal of numbers—and what marvels were done by a few thousand, or a few tens of thousands, of wandering people! The churchmen of Northumbria and Iona, those devout and holy men who lived in the bliss of a primitive piety between their golden missals and a simple flock, had good reason to denounce their fearful depredations; but would

their chalices and pyxes have survived the greed of nearer neighbours, though no viking had ever come within the shadow of their
abbey walls? Silver and gold have always been destined for theft,
and the sea-thieves who emptied the coffers of Christianity in Britain brought in return—or their successors brought—the vitality of
a race envigorated by northern springs and dignified by a habit of
mind that set poetry on a level with action; and, indeed, found little
difference between them. He was an Englishman who wrote the
crabbed and heroic tale of Beowulf, but the Norsemen who came
with swords against the English had stories as nobly tempered and
poetry more intricately fashioned.

They were brutal and merciless, but they brought enduring
strength. The early comers were heathen in the gloom of the last
grim generations of heathendom, when no hope was promised for
the best of men but to die with their gods, already doomed, in the
ultimate lost battle of their race; and when their successors took to
Christianity and the miracle of the risen Christ, they embraced
their new faith with as bloody a fervour as had nerved their fathers
to courage when an heroic rage could open, as they thought, the
gates of Valhalla. They were greedy and spendthrift, grasping and
generous; they were masters of the sea, and submissive to drunken
appetite. They were avid of fame, and possessed a curious reverence for the tortuous processes of law. They were compact of
primal energy and original sin, of a lawyer's subtlety and a mari-
ner's skill, and in their faculty of imagination they could see the
relationship between poetry and swordsmanship. Harald Hardrada,
last of the great vikings who invaded England—to be killed at
Stamford Bridge—is somewhere said to have spent the night before
battle in discussion, not only of poetry, but of the correct rules
and better modes of poetry.

Those were the men who, in the ninth century, rowed up the
Thames and the Seine to assault the largest of known towns. They
sacked the lesser towns of Europe where now stand Hamburg,
Antwerp, Seville, and Bordeaux. Their Swedish neighbours
founded Russia and besieged Constantinople. Long before William's
conquest of England they had established a duchy that threatened
the tremulous balance of emergent France; they found and colonised the volcanic desolation of Iceland, and there created the only
literature of that age in Europe: a literature of marvellous variety,

of solid fact and fanciful addition, of heroic memory or vision. They sailed between the Pillars of Hercules, they discovered Greenland and settled a fringe of its coast beneath the ice-cap. They reached the northern shores of America and posted a hopeful colony somewhere, it may be, between the Hudson River and the St. Lawrence. They made England part of a Danish empire that did not survive its gifted, ruthless, and benevolent despot; and their brilliant, if short-lived, conquest of Sicily lay not far ahead.

It has long been a critical habit to esteem the Mediterranean as the source of all that is, or has been, good in the civilization of western Europe, and no one with a particle of judgment would deny or disparage the inestimable gifts of Palestine; the arts and philosophy that a truculent and ingenious Hellas bequeathed; the ordered authority and evangelical expansion of Rome; the medical and mathematic additions to knowledge that an Arab imperialism brought from the southern shores of the inland sea. But all the virtue in the world, and the moral, aesthetic, or administrative products of virtue, are worthless, because inoperative, without a physical ability, a strength of mind and body, to give them action and by example proclaim their value. And to all north-western Europe a prodigious reinforcement of that necessary strength—sometimes an addition to failing strength, sometimes the injection into apathy of a new impulse—came from the vigour of the Norse propulsion; for the singular benefit of that boreal increase was its ability to combine with existing manners and marry its own strength to them.

Though destruction was the first recorded effect of Norse invasion, the destruction of native cultures was not its ultimate consequence. England was roughly refashioned, but not destroyed. The anarchy of emergent France was aggravated, but the feudalism which built it was stiffened and exercised by the challenge of its growing neighbour. And in the western parts of Scotland the remnant fringe of Celtic genius—pushed to its farthest limits—was kept alive by the benign cohabitation of Norse seamen with the compliant widows of the Gaelic warriors they had killed.

It is not extravagant to say that from the sub-arctic parts of Europe came much of the formative, exploratory, and imaginative strength that enabled the rest of the continent to enjoy and exploit its Mediterranean inheritance, and in the course of time to expand that inheritance and by its precepts civilise lands newly found. If the Mediterranean gave wisdom, the vigour of northern seas helped to propagate it.

Chapter III

VIKINGS IN FRANCE

I N the ninth century France did not exist. It is convenient, however, to anticipate history and give its later name to that part
of Charlemagne's empire which, after its division at Verdun in
843, fell to the lot of his grandson Charles the Bald, and corre-
sponded geographically with the mediaeval kingdom of France.
It was an administrative, not a natural, division, and had no stability. Charles was almost constantly at war, with the Bretons who
defeated him, with the people of Aquitaine who defeated him, with
his brother Louis the German, and with Norse pirates and invaders
who extorted large ransoms from him. The empire was re-divided,
parts of it were temporarily re-united. A pretence of Carolingian
unity was maintained, and Charles, unimpressed by defeat, persisted
in a policy of aggrandisement and got himself crowned emperor
and king of Italy. But administration fell into decay as the royal
power declined, and a rival house was founded when Charles in
861 gave the important military command of Paris to Robert,
count of Tours, called Robert the Strong. Robert, who fought
stoutly against the Norse invaders, was killed in battle. His son
Odo was the hero of the siege of Paris in 885, and after the deposi-
tion of Charles the Fat—son of Louis the German—when the
throne became elective, Odo succeeded to it and was followed by
his brother Robert I. A Carolingian restoration returned the crown
to Charles the Simple, a grandson of Charles the Bald and then a
boy of nine, in 888; and Carolingian kings of dubious authority
followed him until the lack of a suitable heir brought in the first
of the Capetians. He, Hugh Capet, a grandson of Robert I, succeeded in 987.

It is obvious that the almost continuous disorder of the fragmented empire gave to Norse fleets and viking hosts the opportunities they needed to raid, explore, and—where they found the

situation advantageous—to settle. Under a weakened throne, local magnates increased their authority, and others, jealous of their neighbours, may have welcomed the invaders who despoiled them. In France there was no Alfred the Great to forge under pressure a national resistance. The empire, indeed, had not merely broken apart, but with the melting of authority had, in a political sense, become fluid. The Scandinavian north was also fluid, though for different reasons, and in its fluidity there was an out-going stream which, when it reached the estuaries of France, often met little or no resistance. In two respects it was the northern stream which eventually began to create, as if by a chemical reaction, the necessary coagulation of France; for Normandy became a solidly resistant province, and the military authority which, to counter Norse attack, was given to Robert the Strong, enabled him to found a family that later acquired a throne which remained a Capet heritage for more than three hundred years.

The earliest record of vikings in France refers to a raid on the coast of Aquitaine in 799; the pirates were probably a Norse company that had wintered in Ireland and there learnt of the trade-routes between the south of Ireland and the Biscay ports. A little while later Charlemagne reinforced his fleet and stiffened his coastal defences, but there were fresh attacks on Noirmoutier, near the mouth of the Loire, and the Ile de Rhé opposite La Rochelle, which may have come from Ireland or from a viking base in the Frisian Islands. From 814 till 833 the empire was free from attack, and then for some years the coast of Frisia was the vikings' main objective. Antwerp was burnt, the longships sailed up the Scheldt and the Maas, and Louis the Pious, son of Charlemagne, gave a grant of land to a Danish adventurer called Harald in return for his promised help against the foreigners. After the death of Louis the division of the empire gave the coast from the Scheldt to the Weser to his son Lothair, who continued his father's policy and bought Harald's allegiance with a grant of the island of Walcheren.

There can be no doubt that the Norsemen had sufficient knowledge of affairs in the empire to let them take advantage of its internal troubles, for now their attack was extended and intensified. From the Elbe to the Guadalquivir, from Hamburg to Seville, their ships spread fear and devastation. In 841 they sailed up the

Seine and plundered as far as Rouen; in 842 a Norse fleet from
England raided what is now the Pas de Calais; in 843 they explored
the resources of the Loire and sacked Nantes. The Garonne took
them farther, and they reached Toulouse. In great numbers their
ships were seen off the coasts of Spain and Portugal; they attacked
Lisbon and Cadiz and took Seville all but its citadel, which the
Moors held against them. The Moors, indeed, stoutly defended
their Iberian shore.

In 845 the Danes were in the Elbe, and burnt Hamburg; and the
legendary Ragnar Lodbrok—Ragnar Hairybreeks—took what was
probably a mixed fleet up the Seine as far as Paris. Of the Norse or
Danish invaders of France, Ragnar is the first to be named, and
the most famous of all viking leaders; though his fame is partly
fabulous. He has a distinguished place in Scandinavian genealogy,
and is said to have been a son of king Sigurd Ring of Denmark, and
through him perhaps a descendant of the remote Yngling kings of
Sweden; on his mother's side a more fanciful pedigree relates him
through Sigurd the Volsung to no less a personage than Odin. Of
larger importance are his descendants, among them Harald Fairhair, the unifying king of Norway, and Cnut the Great, king of
England. Ten years after the attack on Paris three of his sons,
Halfdan, Ubbi, and Ivar the Boneless, led an attack on England
and wintered in the Isle of Sheppey; while another son, Bjorn
Ironside, returned to the Seine. It was in Ragnar's time that some
connexion, intercourse, or relationship between the viking raids on
England, France, and Ireland became evident; and perhaps it was
largely a family connexion.

In the great megalithic tomb of Maeshowe in Orkney there are
runic inscriptions which appear to show that for some time Ragnar
and his sons lived there, perhaps in consequence of domestic strife
that drove them out of Denmark; an inference that may find confirmation in Irish annals. The Irish had made acquaintance with
Ragnar in or about the year 831, when he is said to have sacked
Dublin and either killed or taken prisoner an Irish kinglet; and
Irish annalists refer to a period of exile that he and some of his sons
spent in Orkney. He is reputed to have died in Northumbria, after
his defeat by its king, Aelle. An heroic poem called *Kraku-mal*
purports to record his death-song in a snake-pit where Aelle had
thrown him, and though that clearly belongs to the fabulous part

of Ragnar's story, there may be substance in the tradition that the invasion of England by his sons, who captured York in 866, was undertaken to revenge him. Though Ragnar's course through the angry years of the ninth century cannot be plotted, his recurrent intervention in the affairs of Scandinavia, France, England, and Ireland shows the far-ranging interest and extraordinary freedom of movement of the viking hordes; and his sons sailed farther still, to Spain and Africa.

Ragnar's attack on Paris, in 845, was defeated by an epidemic disease, probably dysentery, that incapacitated the invading army. It was a disaster large enough to provoke a legend of miraculous help and the prevailing strength, against a heathen offensive, of Christian prayer. But prayer could not prevent the Danes' return, nor keep their ships from the Seine and the Somme, the Garonne and the Loire.

In 854 a family quarrel, in which the ruling house of Denmark was destroyed in three days of battle, brought a little respite, but it was in the following year that Bjorn Ironside, Ragnar's son, sailed again into the Seine, and for some years thereafter the valleys of the Seine and the Loire were never secure against attack. Incapable of resistance, Charles the Bald paid Danegeld and encouraged his assailants to return for more. An anarchic, incipient feudalism grew to irresponsible power under an impotent throne, and the magnates of the church and a dismembered realm bought security at the expense of their neighbours. In 859 there was a peasant uprising against the invaders: the peasants, protected neither by king nor barons, rose in desperate assertion—not of their nationality, for they had none, but of a common wish for security and peace—and were defeated somewhere in the valley of the Seine.

That was the year when a viking fleet under Bjorn Ironside sailed southward from the Seine, across the Bay of Biscay, to the Straits of Gibraltar and the coast of Morocco, where it took Moorish prisoners, many of whom were carried to Ireland, where the Moors were known as the 'blue men.' There were forays in Spain and the Balearics, vikings wintered in the Camargue, pulled their boats up the Rhone, and raided in Provence. Next year they sailed to Italy, took Pisa and a town near the mouth of the river Magra, not far from Spezia: it has been suggested that they were looking for Rome, but because they thought one or other of the captured towns was their objective, Rome was spared. They returned to Brittany in 862, and the death of Robert the Strong, in battle at Brissarthe in 866, reflects the sporadic continuance of war against the invaders. A few years later France enjoyed relief when the attack on England was heavily resumed, and measures were undertaken to protect the vulnerable rivers; from the Danes' defended camps their victims may have learnt some lessons in fortification.

In 881, when vikings returned to France, they were sharply defeated at Saucourt, near the Somme, by the brothers Louis the Stammerer and Carloman, sons of Charles the Bald. In 885 they entered the Seine with a very large fleet and a numerous army, and laid siege to Paris. There were, by that time, some defensive works on the river—perhaps fortified bridges—and Paris was skilfully defended by count Odo, son of Robert the Strong. The siege was hotly pressed, but Paris was held, and the invaders pulled some of their light craft overland, beyond the town, to plunder in the upper reaches of the river. Later, by politic arrangement, they were given freedom to take what they could in Burgundy, on condition of respecting the districts of the Seine and the Marne.

They reached Verdun, and were again beaten by Odo, now king in succession to Charles the Fat. The invaders retired to the coast, and in Brittany met new disaster. A large Norse or Danish army had been overwhelmingly defeated by the Bretons. Only a few hundred, it is said, survived from a force of several thousand, and when this remnant was joined by the army of the Seine their combined strength was still no match for the fiery Celts under Alain, count of Vannes. They retreated, some to Flanders, others to the Somme, and in Flanders, near Louvain, they were again repulsed by Arnulf, a bastard son of Carloman who was later crowned emperor, an honor that he did not long enjoy.

The resilience, the sturdy recovery of France, was remarkable. Despite the melting away of central authority, of a general administration, the fragments of empire seem to have been imbued with a new power and will to resist their old enemies, and the last of the Carolingians and the predecessors of the Capetians were alike capable of recruiting and leading resolute forces against them. The leaders of the people of northern France—of what, in the future, was to become France—had been toughened under the hammer, and so far from yielding to punishment, were beginning to return it. It was, however, neither Arnulf nor count Alain who drove the vikings to their ships, but hunger. A cold, wet harvest was followed by famine, and in the autumn of 892 the viking host, embarking at Boulogne and the mouth of the Somme, crossed over to Kent. A fleet of two hundred and fifty ships, it is said, could take the whole army, together with the horses they had added to its strength, though seven years before no fewer than seven hundred ships had sailed up the Seine. These figures may be quite unreliable, and yet show the invaders' proportionate loss. What mattered most to the people of the Frankish empire was that, for the first time in half a century, their land was undisturbed by Danes or Norsemen.

Across the Channel the vikings found no easy conquests, though they were helped—either incidentally or on purpose—by the Danish settlers in Northumbria and East Anglia, who revived their hostile attitude to Alfred of Wessex. But under Alfred and his son Edward the Elder, and Ethelred of Mercia, England was able to defend itself. In their strategy the invaders were marvellously volatile. From Kent they crossed the whole country to the Severn and the Welsh border; and their tactics, as usual, were burly and uninhibited. But their strategy failed to disrupt the kingdom, their tactics were countered by a resistance as stubborn as their onslaught was fierce. The campaign—a fairly continuous series of operations—lasted for four years, at the end of which time the invaders had won no new ground. In England, however, as well as in France, society had not yet stiffened into a uniform or general nationalism—it was still characterised by an accommodating fluidity—and many survivors of the army which had failed to take Paris, and been unable to conquer any parcel of England, found congenial domicile with their settled cousins in Northumbria and East Anglia.

The obdurate, the irreconcilables, and those who could still man and provision their ships, returned to France. If the revival, under pressure, of England and some parts of the Frankish empire is remarkable, no less impressive is the vikings' capacity for accepting defeat in France as the logical preliminary to a fresh attack on England, and defeat in England as the compulsive invitation to a new onslaught at the mouth of the Seine. Whatever the initial springs of action may have been—whether hunger induced by the pressure of an excessive population, or the spur to adventure of a technological superiority in ship-building—it is difficult to resist a feeling that a good deal of viking enterprise, in its not-quite-adult phase, was due to an acquired sense of métier. With a good sea-going ship, and three or four score trained fighting men, the apparatus of conquest was available, and a viking leader's professional instinct was to make use of it.

Many examples could be cited, but the manner of the return to France may be evidence enough. It was a very small force that ventured once more into the Seine, but its audacity quickly won reinforcement from the reservoir of hungry or adventurous professionals of the same sort who were waiting for a fresh initiative to point the way to new fields of opportunity. The little season of peace that had been enjoyed by the Frankish empire—by nascent France—had come to an end, and Norse intruders were again in the lower reaches of the river, they were moving towards the Meuse, and eastward to Burgundy. From Ireland came adventurers who looked for profit in the valley of the Loire; but they were defeated. It was on the banks of the lower Seine that the Norsemen made their abiding foothold.

How initially this came about is not known. There is no record of the early military operations, the local diplomacy, the establishment and reinforcement of a power that proved sufficient to achieve recognition and require royal negotiation to admit and limit its power. All that is known is that in 911 a meeting was arranged between Charles the Simple, grandson of Charles the Bald, and a viking leader called Rolf or Rollo, and at St. Clair-sur-Epte the province later called Normandy was ceded to Rolf on condition that he accept Christianity and pledge himself to defend the kingdom of Charles against further attack.

Rolf was the father of William Longsword and grandfather of duke Richard I, whose son Richard II was the grandfather of William the Bastard who conquered England in 1066. But who was Rolf?

The generally accepted view is that he was a younger son of Rognvald, earl of Möre, a Norwegian magnate in the days of Harald Fairhair, the great king who unified all Norway. Against that opinion rests only a statement of the very unreliable chroni-

cler, Dudo of St. Quentin, that he was the son of a Danish nobleman who, after expulsion from Denmark, travelled to England,
Frisia, and France. His Norwegian ancestry can be accepted, with
reasonable assurance of its accuracy, and the Norwegian story supplies not only a convincing background for his culminating
achievement, but a genealogical tree—already mentioned, but now
in need of amplification—that seems to naturalise or domesticate
his acquisition of Normandy in a family tradition.

His father, Rognvald of Möre, went with Harald Fairhair west
over sea to his subjugation of Orkney, Shetland, and the Hebrides,
a campaign in which Ivar, a son of Rognvald, was killed; in com-
pensation for whose death Rognvald was given the earldom of
Orkney, or confirmed in his title to it. Rolf, a younger son, was a
great viking. He grew so tall that no horse could carry him—but
probably the Norwegian horses were no bigger than an Iceland
pony of to-day—and because he had to go upon his own feet he
was known as Marching Rolf[1]. He offended king Harald Fairhair
by harrying and committing what was called a 'strand-slaying' in
the great gulf south of Oslo, and was outlawed. He followed a
customary viking path to the Hebrides, and remained there long
enough to beget a daughter who later married a Scots kinglet. Rolf
may have adventured in Ireland, England, and the valley of the
Loire, but Icelandic annals say firmly that he won his place in
Normandy in 898; and if that is true he must have spent thirteen
years in establishing the power that Charles the Simple confirmed
in 911. He had served a lively apprenticeship to war, and a distinguished father must, in the beginning, have helped him to enlist
followers whom his own success in arms would later multiply.

According to the *Landnámabók* of Iceland—a directory and
genealogy of the early settlers—Rognvald, earl of Möre, was a son
of Eystein Rattle, son of Ivar, earl of the Uplanders, son of Halfdan the Old. So far his ancestry may be accepted as historical. But
Halfdan is said to have fetched his descent from that remote king
called Fornjot who ruled over Finnland, and Fornjot's son was
Kari, the father of Frosti, the father of Snow the Old, whose
grandchildren were Nor, Gor, and a daughter called Goi. As genealogy this is patently ridiculous, but the exploits credited to Nor

[1] *Göngu-hrólfr.*

and Gor, when their sister disappears and they go to look for her, are unexpectedly realistic. Gor takes ship and in the Gulf of Bothnia searches the islands, the Stockholm skerries and the Baltic isles, and Denmark; while Nor travels through Lapland and down over Norway to the western fjords, to Trondheim and the Sogne fjord, and after some incidental warfare meets his brother, who by then had come north from Denmark. In the Uplands they find their sister, married to the man who had abducted her, and after a battle make peace with him. Thereafter Nor returns to the land he had subdued, and calls it Norway, while Gor, ruling the islands as a sea-king, marries and begets two sons, Heiti and Beiti, who become sea-kings in their turn and fight with the sons of Nor. And Heiti becomes the grandfather of Halfdan the Old, great-grandfather of earl Rognvald, who was the father of Marching Rolf.

Here, in the simplification of a fable, is the story of the discovery, exploration, and subjugation of Norway and the Scandinavian islands, and the political divisions that later occurred. Was it a story current when Marching Rolf first led his seamen to conquest in northern France? It would be strange indeed if some version of it were not known: not the version abridged and quoted here, which has a sophisticated, a literary tone, but a less stylised and more factual version. Tales of their ancestry were assuredly a common entertainment in all noble families of the heroic age, and it would be absurd to suppose they were not believed.

So, then, one may entertain the thought that Marching Rolf, after fighting for some years in Normandy—or what was about to become Normandy—not only formed the intention of making it his own, but felt secure in the knowledge that what he proposed was, for one of his family, nothing out of the ordinary. His ancestors before him had done the same sort of thing. To fortify the strength of his great body he had the example of family history—and *bon chien chasse de race.*

His ambition, moreover, was feasible because, alike in the lands from which he had come and the land where he had arrived, all was flux and motion. The men of the north were not settled in their habitation, but looking for fat fields wherever they could be found—and for another century and a half would still be searching —and the men of a divided, broken empire lived precariously in the dissolution of Charlemagne's over-arching power. Round a strong man islands of authority could coagulate, and might be extended.

The land of which Rolf was in possession, in or before 911, lay on both sides of the Seine above Rouen, with a westward boundary near Evreux and an eastward frontier on the river Epte. But already his influence had begun to spread farther. Within a few years Rouen was his, and before his death his territory had expanded until on the west it reached the river Vire, which flows into the sea at the inner corner of the Cherbourg peninsula, and on the east the Bresle, which meets the coast at what is now Le Tréport. William Longsword added the peninsula and extended his westward boundary to the Couesnon, whose mouth is at Mont St. Michel in the Gulf of St. Malo.

It was an unlikely parcel of land to have acquired and to rule. Except for the coast it lacked a decisive, natural frontier, for the little rivers which marked its landward boundary—the Bresle, the Epte, the Avre, the Couesnon—made no great barrier against aggression. Nor was it a remote, untravelled province, secured by inaccessibility and unimportance. It was, on the contrary, divided by the great waterway of the Seine and crossed by the old merchants' highway from Marseille to the Channel. Its provincial identity, however, was not a new creation, carved from its matrix by the swords of Marching Rolf and his son William. The land they had won had been the Roman province of Lugdunensis Secunda, and within the Christian church's jurisdiction it was an ecclesiastical province comprising the bishoprics of Bayeux, Avranches, Evreux, Seés, Lisieux, Coutances, and the archbishopric of Rouen.

That the church's jurisdiction, in 911, had lost most of its reality, is not to be doubted. The province had repeatedly suffered the full force of Norse or Danish attack during a period of some seventy years, and in the interludes of calm weather between gales of aggression it is more than probable that Normandy, like East Anglia, found room for many pagan settlers. The land that Marching Rolf acquired had almost certainly a population that was, in part, akin to his own followers, speaking the same language, and worshipping—with a diminished reverence that both acknowledged—the same or kindred gods. In these circumstances it may seem surprising that the Christian church survived, and still possessed such influence, if not actual authority, in a province dominated by heathen men, that their heathen ruler had to accept baptism to legitimate his title. But the church in Normandy had a long history, and had learnt the art or developed the faculty of survival. It boasted a missionary bishop of the third century, and despite burnt and abandoned monasteries retained a spirit as hardy and expansive as that of the incomers. The Norman church and the Norman duchy were to grow together, respecting each other's need for power.

As yet, of course, the Norman domain was not a duchy, nor was such dignity accorded to it—and then in a rather haphazard way—until late in the following century. Neither Rolf nor his son William Longsword used any title. The supposed equality of the vikings has little substance in fact, for all their recorded activities show a society dominated by its aristocracy; but its aristocracy lived side by side with lesser men and shared their labours. There was no artificial division, and rank was not created by empty titles. Dudo of St. Quentin, who postures so absurdly as an historian, can occasionally come within measurable distance of the facts, and perhaps one may accept his record of Norse seamen under interrogation: ' "*Quo nomine vester senior fungitur?*" *Responderunt, "Nullo, quia aequalis potestatis sumus." '*—' "What title does your commander use?" "None," they answered, "we're all equal here." '— It was not true, but an absence of difference existed, and neither Marching Rolf nor William Longsword saw any purpose in creating a nominal difference, or any need to stiffen a natural authority with honorifics.

Of their untitled reign over a hazardously defined colony, little can be said with certainty. Dudo, who was born in the tenth century and died before 1043, wrote an inventive account of the founding of the duchy, but he was a fabulist whose purpose was to glorify duke William and magnify all the deeds of his ancestors. He makes his intention clear in the story he tells of the manner in which Rolf did homage for his possessions to his superior, king Charles. He was commanded, says Dudo, to kiss the king's foot. He refused, and delegated the duty to one of his companions, who, instead of bowing to the royal toes, picked them up, lifted them to the level of irreverent lips, and nearly toppled the poor king off his throne.

It is an engaging story—it was designed to show that Normandy and its rulers were, from the beginning, not merely proud, but in-dependent—but it has not the smack of truth. There seems no rea-son, however, for doubting Dudo's assertion that William Long-sword was the son, by Rolf, of a girl with the homely name of Poppa, daughter of a count Berengar, whom Rolf had taken cap-tive on a viking raid into Bayeux. There may indeed be confirma-tion of it in the fact that William, in the course of time, begot a son, Richard, whom he sent to Bayeux, where there was, as it seems, a stubbornly persistent Norse colony, to learn the Norse or Danish tongue.

Rolf may have died, or possibly abdicated, in 925. That he had to fight for the establishment and extension of his domain is not to be doubted; that he was a natural leader, skilled in the use of arms and the disposition of his forces, a man of unusual vigour and posi-tive imagination, is indisputable; and apart from his politic alle-giance to a Carolingian king and the Christian church, nothing more of value, or approved by evidence, can be added.

He was succeeded by his son William, who like his father did homage to Charles the Simple. Before he added the Cotentin, or Cherbourg, peninsula to his domain, he may have had to suppress a Breton rising there, and then a revolt of recalcitrant Danes. It is possible that he invited new Danish settlers to the Cotentin. He is said to have been a just and vigorous man, and in 942 he was mur-dered, at Picquigny on the Somme, by order of Arnulf of Flanders, who had forced a quarrel on him in consequence of personal insult or some dispute about an intervening property.

Richard, his son, was only ten years old when he succeeded, and almost immediately his inheritance was threatened by a new viking invasion. A Norse or Danish fleet under a leader called Sigtrygg sailed up the Seine, and showed enough power or achieved enough success to seduce from their proper allegiance a large number of Normans led by Thormod, a local chieftain. They abjured their nominal Christianity, and may have compelled young Richard to join them in apostasy. This crisis brought to the aid of the Christian party the French king, Louis IV, called Louis d'Outremer because he, a son of Charles the Simple, had been brought up in the court of his uncle, Athelstan of England, grandson of Alfred the Great. Louis defeated the heathen invaders, Thormod was killed, and young Richard, rescued from the rebel faction, was confirmed by Louis in possession of his Norman lands.

Then, as appears—and this is not improbable—Louis decided to remain in Rouen, take advantage of the power and prestige he had won, and substitute for his role as deliverer the more profitable one of a conqueror. The Normans united in opposition, and to their assistance—if not by invitation, by uncommonly well-timed accident—came Harald Bluetooth, son of Gorm the Old, sole king of Denmark. Harald, who later embraced Christianity, was at this time still a heathen; but unless much has been omitted from the story of his intervention, he was inspired by such magnanimity as any Christian might envy. He landed in the Cotentin, made his headquarters at Cherbourg, and advanced to Bayeux. The Normans hurried to join him, and on the banks of the Dives, in 945, he met in battle Louis d'Outremer, defeated him, and took him prisoner. Then, having re-established young Richard as ruler of the land, Harald Bluetooth retired to his own country. It is a puzzling story, but open to explanation. In the forgotten or omitted part there must have been some detail about the payment made to king Harald for his services: a payment possibly augmented by ransom for king Louis. The vikings were always capable of generosity, but it was not the policy of a king to be generous, without recompense, to another power.

In 954 Louis d'Outremer was succeeded by his son Lothair, last but one of the Carolingian kings; and two years later the death of Louis was followed by that of Hugh the Great, count or duke of Paris, and father of the first Capetian king. Hugh Capet was a boy of thirteen, and according to Dudo of St. Quentin his father had asked Richard of Normandy to be his guardian; the association so formed was strengthened when Richard married Emma, sister of Hugh and great-grand-daughter of Robert the Strong who, nearly a hundred years before, had assumed military command against viking invasion and so created the position of authority from which the Capet dynasty eventually emerged. Hugh Capet did homage to Lothair, his king, but the apparent peace of the realm was threatened by a quarrel, obscure in origin—but family dissension, a mere jostling for power, or endemic jealousies may have started it— which broke in spectacular fashion in 961.

In that year Lothair summoned to Soissons a general assembly of his magnates: a rare event in France. To it came Richard of Normandy with an armed force and the intention, which cannot be explained, of dispersing the assembly. The royal troops opposed and defeated him. A certain Theobald, count of Tours, was involved in the dispute, and in Normandy there was severe fighting which cannot be rationalised by any clear division between right and wrong. It is said that Harald Bluetooth of Denmark intervened again; but that story may be doubted. The province suffered heavily—either for its virtue or its folly—and the settlement effected between Lothair and Richard, at Gisors in 965, seems to have been welcomed by both sides; for it was followed by a long season of peace, and closer, more friendly relations between Normandy and the country of its suzerain.

Lothair died in 986 and was succeeded by his son Louis, who reigned for a short and troubled year. The Carolingian dynasty had reached its terminus. Hugh Capet was chosen king, and within a few months his son Robert was accepted as joint-king. In the year of their coronation there was nothing to suggest that a new era had begun; France was not yet a nation, but it had acquired a race of kings who would eventually create from its diverse and dissident peoples a lasting unity. What influence was exercised by the Norman province on Hugh's election is matter for speculation, but the Normans' increasing tendency to talk, think, and worship like Frenchmen which, if it did not begin at the peace of Gisors, was there encouraged and thereafter magnified, must have reflected, in the latter years of the century, the friendly relations of their rulers, initiated in the youth of Hugh Capet and fortified by Richard's marriage to his sister.

The manner in which the descendants of Marching Rolf's men turned their backs to Scandinavian origins and adopted the religion and culture of their new neighbours—the seeming entirety of the change—is very remarkable, but in Norse history not an isolated phenomenon. In Ireland and the Hebrides Norse invaders made no use of military success to impose their own tongue and a faith in their own gods on the people of the lands they occupied, but let their identity vanish in a Celtic ambience. In Iceland a self-sufficient, aristocratic Norse community accepted Christianity, and the

Latin culture which accompanied it, with a welcome that trans-figured their life and created a literature—in its time, unique in Europe—of marvellous range and vigour. And in England, within a few generations, the French-speaking invaders of Norse descent, whom duke William led to conquest, forgot their adopted tongue and continental loyalties, and became Englishmen.

This flexibility, or malleability, in a race of otherwise fierce and stubborn temper, was a consequence of two conditions common to all viking incursion into new territories. The first and more readily comprehensible of these conditions was that the invaders were men: not family parties, but men. Those who settled in the lands they invaded had still to satisfy a need more imperative than their appetite for land or plunder, and to win the favour of women whose fathers or husbands they had killed—or to retain female interest and companionship—they had to learn at least the elements of the language the women spoke. The tongue they had been taught at a mother's knee had to be discarded for that more useful in a foreign bed.

The second condition reveals something that, to modern apprehension, closely resembles innocence. The viking hordes that devastated Europe and re-fashioned its history were unaware of nationality, they had no racial prejudice, their minds were unclouded by patriotism, they were unburdened by political loyalties, and their religion implied no subservience to their gods. To a quite extraordinary extent they were free people, with an almost untrammelled freedom to follow the leaders of their choice and live wherever complaisance or a sword could win them subsistence and room to move.

In this they were not mere creatures of their time, but different from their neighbours, and the difference is very clearly demonstrated in two accounts of the famous battle of Brunanburh that, according to the Anglo-Saxon Chronicle, was fought in the year 937. On the one side was Alfred's grandson, Athelstan of Wessex and Mercia, who styled himself *rex totius Britanniae*—he who fostered Louis d'Outremer—and on the other a strong confederacy of Scots, the Norse of Ireland, and the Welsh of Strathclyde. Athelstan won a major victory, and here is how an Anglo-Saxon poet saw it:

'The foe fell back; the Scots folk and the shipmen sank death-doomed. The field was slippery with warriors' blood from the morning tide of the sun, eternal God's bright candle, till the splendid star went down to rest.

'Many a warrior lay, by spears brought down; many a Norseman was shot through his shield, many a Scot also, weary, war-sated. All the day long the West Saxons, troop after troop, pressed on their foes, hewed runaways from behind with swords sharp from the grindstone. Never did the Mercians grudge their hard hand-play to the heroes, death-doomed, who with Olaf had come aland for battle, over pell-mell of the waves, in the breast of a ship.

'By swords put to sleep, five young kings lay on the field, and seven of the earls of Olaf; of the army, of shipmen and Scots, numbers beyond counting.

'The lord of the Norsemen was put to flight, need drove him with a little troop to the beak of his ship. His keel took the sea, the king fled to the fallow flood, and saved his life.

'Thence too old Constantine ran north to his own country, that hoary warrior. No cause had he to rejoice in sword-play.'

That poem, in the Anglo-Saxon Chronicle, was inspired by patriotism. It is the voice of Wessex that cries in triumph the bravery of its men, and the voice of Mercia glorifies the valour of its soldiers. England was already self-conscious, aware of nationality, and stoutly prejudiced in favour of England.

But fighting on Athelstan's side were a great Icelandic hero, Egil Skallagrimson, his brother Thorolf, and three hundred men under their command; and Egil's saga—one of the major works of Icelandic literature—also commemorates the battle. The saga, admittedly, was written long after the event, but clearly reflects the heroic temper of Norse enterprise in the tenth century; as this short extract shows:

'Then Thorolf grew so fierce for battle that he slung his shield behind him, and taking his halberd in both hands leapt forward and cut or thrust on either side. Men sprang back or away from him, but he killed many. There was no holding him, and he cleared a path in front of him till he came to earl Ring's banner. He killed the man who bore the banner, and cut down the pole. Then he thrust the point of his halberd through the earl's chest, through byrnie and body and out between his shoulders, and heaved him up, high on the blade, and stuck the butt of the halberd down into earth. So the earl died on the spear-point, in sight of all, his own men and his enemies.'

Now between that and the Anglo-Saxon account there is a vast difference: difference of approach, difference of mood. Here is no patriotic or national feeling, but pride and delight in individual prowess. In the saga the story of the battle concludes with the assertion that 'Athelstan got an exceedingly great victory.' To the Icelander the victor was not Wessex, not Mercia or England, but the hero, Athelstan; and though Egil's three hundred were a little Norse contingent in a great English army, the Icelandic author of the saga says nothing whatever to glorify them, to draw attention to Norse bravery, or to exalt them above their English comrades. There is no trace, in the saga, of national or racial feeling, and no exultation over the defeat of powerful enemies. The poet of the Anglo-Saxon Chronicle is fiercely pleased by the death of foes; the saga merely records it.

The Norse—Norse or Danes, the men of the great propulsion —were uncommitted men. Those who settled in Normandy, enjoying the same intellectual or moral freedom as those who fought at Brunanburh, saw the manifest advantages of adopting the Latin culture that flourished beyond the little rivers which drew their boundaries, and being unhampered by prejudice, adopted it as easily as those little rivers could be crossed.

It appears, however, that in the opinion of their neighbours they did not slough their Norse characteristics, or all the habits bred in their abandoned hinterland of dark hillsides and dancing fjords. To the annoyance of England the Francophile Normans still gave help and shelter to vikings on their way to an English harvest, and even as late as the eleventh century a heathen army that had been plundering in France was received with friendship under the Christian roofs of Rouen. The death of Richard himself—Richard I of Normandy died in 996—was recorded by a monk of Rheims in words, of little charity, that deliberately recalled his viking origin. 'Richardus pyratarum dux apoplexia minore periit.'—'The pirates' leader died of the lesser apoplexy.' So wrote Richer, the monk of Rheims.

Chapter IV

THE MATTER OF ENGLAND

THE Norse assault on Lindisfarne, in 793, fell upon the Northumbrian coast with the shock of a tidal wave that rises from a smooth sea, breaks without warning, and with the cold unconcern of the sea retires from its casual destruction to leave behind not only present misery, but fear of the future. That fear was justified when, in the following year, the vikings came to the Tyne, some fifty miles south of Lindisfarne, and the rich monastery of Jarrow was sacked; but there the invaders were stoutly opposed. Then, for forty years, the sea remained calm and England was untroubled by the long dark ships. The first attack had been premature. It did indeed foretell the war that was to come, but in the manner of a herald who rides forward to declare hostilities before his country has mobilised. It may also seem premature to describe those early raids as a threat of war against England, for in the last decade of the eighth century England was not a united kingdom; its nationality was neither manifest nor assured. But despite the angry divisions of the island, a man of learning and authority had seen it whole and proclaimed its essential oneness.

The attacks fell on that part of England where already there had been a premonition of unity, and where there existed a concept of unity that depended not on political agreement but on unanimity of faith. The Christian church had established a pattern for the future, and a churchman, widely renowned for patient scholarship, had declared the existence of the English nation. The Venerable Bede had foreseen what history was about to disclose.

Of the ten royal families—most, if not all, claiming descent from tribal deities—who ruled over their several parts of England towards the end of the sixth century, two shared Northumbria, the country beyond the river Humber. There was the older kingdom of Deira, in the middle and east of what is now Yorkshire, and north of it the larger kingdom of Bernicia. They were presently united, and within the first quarter of the seventh century Edwin of Deira was recognised not only as king of all Northumbria, but as overlord of southern England. He married a Christian princess of Kent, and with her took to his northern kingdom Paulinus, newly consecrated a bishop, who had followed Augustine to England in the mission ordered and equipped by pope Gregory the Great in 597.

Augustine's mission had been a failure—he was arrogant, Celtic monks were stubborn, native princes thought his religion would make men too mild—but in the north Paulinus won a multitude of converts. His first task was to gain the favour of the king; then Edwin summoned a council at which his chief men and the archpriest of their pagan faith argued with Paulinus: that was the occasion which Bede, when he wrote his history, made memorable with the simile he recorded from the speech of an unnamed warrior. What is the life of a man? said the heathen chief. It is like a sparrow flying from a winter night into the warmth of a lighted hall, and out again into the darkness. In the discussion that followed the archpriest himself was converted, and when a wooden church had been built in York, Edwin was baptised; and in the river Trent Paulinus baptised his obedient people. That was in 627.

Edwin's supremacy over England did not last long. He invaded north Wales and provoked a counter-offensive by Cadwallon, king of Gwynedd, and the heathen Penda, a nobleman of the great midland kingdom of Mercia. Edwin was killed, Northumbria ravaged, and Paulinus fled in ignorance of the Roman missive which, had it reached him, would have brought papal authority for his appointment as archbishop of York.

But Christianity and Northumbria were both rescued—and Cadwallon killed—by Oswald of the royal house of Bernicia, who reigned till 641 and re-established the authority previously claimed by Edwin over the English kingdoms of the south. During Edwin's rule Oswald had lived in exile and received baptism in Iona, where that princely figure Columba—born of the royal blood in Ireland and nurtured in its piety—had established his autocratic and adventurous mission in 563. Now Oswald sent word to Iona that a new bishop was needed for Northumbria, and the ascetic evangelist Aidan, with a company of monks, came to Lindisfarne and estab-

lished a monastery where they lived in the barest poverty, but from
a humble centre exerted great authority. Under Oswald of Bernicia and Aidan of Iona, Northumbria became a nursery of learning and the Christian faith.

Other monasteries were founded, boys were trained for the service of the church, piety and scholarship created a literature in
which miracles jostled the theme of salvation. Cuthbert, a Border
shepherd's boy, was moved by a vision to accept monastic discipline in Melrose; during long years of devotion at Lindisfarne he
established a rule of gentle care for birds and animals; and achieved
the reward of sanctity when his bones were translated to the new
cathedral at Durham. Hilda, a princess of Deira, founded at Whitby
a famous monastery for both men and women: it became especially
famous because it was there that Caedmon, first of English Christian poets, wrote his hymn of the Creation; and there, or in some
neighbouring monastery, was nurtured the poet who wrote *The
Dream of the Rood*.

Northumbrian missionaries carried their message to the kingdoms of the south of England, and to the pagan peoples of Europe.
Willibrord was the apostle of the Frisians, and opened a way for
the West Saxon Boniface, the apostle of Germany, and Alcuin, of
the school of York, who became adviser and mentor to Charlemagne. The Venerable Bede died in 735, the year of Alcuin's
birth, but by then there was substance in his belief that he and his
predecessors had spoken, not for a province, but a nation.

Bede was not a travelling teacher. His fellow-Northumbrian,
Benedict Biscop, who went six times to Rome and brought back
enough books to form a library, had founded the monasteries of
Wearmouth, between the Wear and the Tyne, and Jarrow; and in
one or the other Bede spent his scholarly life. So far as is known,
he never went farther than Lindisfarne or York, but his fame was
carried abroad. So far as the conditions of his time allowed, he was
a scientist, an historian, and a theologian; as historian he was
scrupulous in his treatment of material, he respected the difference
between prime and secondary sources, and he wrote in vigorous,
unaffected Latin. His masterpiece is the *Historia Ecclesiastica Gen-
tis Anglorum*, the ecclesiastical history of the English nation.

In 731, when he finished his great book, there was, on the surface of life, hardly more reason for the amplitude of his title than

there had been ninety years before, when Oswald, the king of Northumbria, asserted his suzerainty over England. There was a new claimant to political supremacy, and perhaps a stronger one; but no more stability. In the affairs of the church, however, a major contest had been resolved and a unifying authority established. The Celtic discipline that Columba brought from Ireland to Iona, that woke Northumbria to missionary enterprise and by Northumbrian fervour kindled the Christian faith in southern England, had encountered the stronger discipline of Rome, and after much dissension it had been admitted that he who kept the door of heaven was St. Peter, not the Irish saint. The papal mission of St. Augustine had failed to coerce into union the stubborn Welsh and Irish churches, but later the Irish had accepted the Roman computation of Easter—which for long had been a cause of offence— and in the south and east of England continental teachers had strengthened a general obedience to Rome. The much-travelled Benedict Biscop brought home, as well as books, relics, vestments, and stone-masons, the Benedictine rule for the monasteries he founded; and his fellow-Northumbrian, Wilfrid of the stormy soul—saint and bishop of York—saw in the church that ruled Rome and Gaul a power that over-rode all earthly kingdoms. He saw, too, how greatly unity would strengthen the power of the church, and at the synod of Whitby, summoned by Oswy, king of Northumbria, in 664, he led the Roman party to victory.

Three years later Oswy of Northumbria and Egbert, king of Kent, sent a priest called Wighard to Rome for consecration as archbishop of Canterbury. Wighard and most of his companions died of the plague, and pope Vitalian chose instead of him an elderly native of Asia Minor, Theodore of Tarsus. At the age of sixty-six, Theodore had a distinguished reputation as a scholar and philosopher, but he had been brought up in the teachings of the eastern church, and as a mentor in his western charge he was accompanied to England by a learned African, the abbot Hadrian. Theodore arrived in Canterbury in 669, and within three years the improbable pair had so far succeeded in their unlikely task of establishing ecclesiastical order that Theodore, archbishop of Canterbury, could call a general council of the whole English church. For seventy years that church acknowledged the authority of Canterbury as its only archbishopric, and by its example of unity set the pattern for a nation.

Secular power moved from Northumbria to the midland province of Mercia where Penda, the heathen who had killed Edwin, became king and in a later war killed Oswald, the Christian king who had been taught in Iona and by the time of Bede was advanced to sanctity. Penda in his turn was killed by Oswald's brother Oswy in a decisive battle in what is now the West Riding of Yorkshire. The enmity between Penda and Oswy was complicated by their domestic relations, for a son of Oswy was married to Penda's daughter, and another son and a nephew were living at Penda's court. Penda, with reinforcements from East Anglia and north Wales, marched with a formidable army, and Oswy is said to have tried in vain to buy peace at a great price before, in desperation, he committed his cause to God and won a victory that made him overlord of England: *Bretwalda* is the title used by Bede. Like Oswald his brother he is remembered as a Christian king, devoted to the church, but after three years his supremacy was broken by revolt in Mercia. In 670, when he died, the greater part of southern England acknowledged as overlord Wulfhere, a son of Penda, and in 678, after renewed warfare, a battle on the Trent resulted in victory for Mercia, and the Northumbrian domination of England disappeared for ever.

Under Ecgfrith, the son of Oswy, the Welsh of Strathclyde and the Scots of Argyll were probably tributaries of Northumbria, and the Picts were certainly its enemies, their enmity enforced by Northumbrian expansion. But Northumbria's power in the north was broken, as it had been in the south, when Ecgfrith rashly invaded Scotland—or what is now Scotland—and was utterly defeated by Brude, king of the Picts, at Nechtansmere near Forfar in 685. The northern frontier of Northumbria was then in danger, but the province was saved by the last of its notable kings, an illegitimate son of Oswy called Aldfrith. A man of learning who had been taught in Ireland and Iona, he was also a statesman, and though the frontier which had once been held beyond the Firth of Forth had to be withdrawn, and his hold on Lothian was curtailed, he established within his diminished kingdom a peace of sufficient endurance, a rule of adequate authority, to permit that growth of spirit and scholasticism which gave his land its lasting fame.

Aldfrith died in 704—Bede and Alcuin both revered his memory—and after his death there was no dynastic stability in Northumbria. Aldfrith's son was murdered, the physical nature of the land assisted the tendency to anarchy prompted by a native spirit of independence, and Alcuin regarded the vikings' sack of Lindisfarne as a judgment on the evil living of Northumbrian kings. Charlemagne himself, who listened long to Alcuin's teaching and advice, was moved to fierce denunciation of Northumbria's people. He called them traitors, worse than heathen. But Northumbria, its kings and its scholars and its missionaries, had done by then their essential work.

The history of Mercia was less troubled than that of its northern rival. Wulfhere, son of Penda, who brought to an end Northumbrian supremacy and was briefly recognised as overlord of England, was followed by two kings who retired into religious life and one who went mad. But Ethelbald, grandson of a brother of Penda, called himself *rex Britanniae* and ruled a federation of kingdoms between the Humber and the English Channel of which Wessex, soon to be of major importance in English history, was no more than an appanage of Mercia, and London, divorced from the kingdom of Essex, seems to have been Ethelbald's personal property.

He ruled for over forty years with military authority and generosity to the church, but his private life gave rise to scandals which included personal violence and disrespect of nunneries so blatant as to invite reproof from Boniface, the English apostle to Germany. He excused his sins with further benefactions, but was murdered by his bodyguard in 757, and after a brief period of civil war was succeeded by Offa, a descendant of the family of Penda. He re-established the supremacy of Mercia, and that is the dominating fact in the history of England in the second half of the eighth century. The ancient dynasty of Kent was extinct, Sussex became a Mercian province, Wessex after a brief revival was divided by internecine war and its emergent king acknowledged dependence on Offa; who further asserted his authority by ordering the execution of a king of East Anglia. By 774 he styled himself *rex Anglorum*, and sometimes *rex totius Anglorum pa-*

triae, though there is nothing to show that his authority reached beyond the Humber.

The genealogies of the Dark Ages are suspect tales, but it is probable that some of them are substantially true, and it is not without interest that the kings of Mercia claimed descent from Woden through a king of Angel—which is probably that part of Schleswig-Holstein overlooking Kiel Bay—who, a hero of Teutonic legend, was called Offa. In English history the later Offa's enduring memorial is the great dyke he built, one hundred and twenty miles in length, to mark his western frontier against the untamed Welsh of Gwynedd, Powys, and Gwent. The remains of that prodigious earthwork, straddling the hills from the Wye to the Dee, are evidence of a good general's eye for country, and with unconscious piety its name preserves the name of a great-grandsire of one of England's fierce founding fathers: Offa's dyke, that divided England from Wales, is a linguistic link with England's Baltic origin.

Offa's power was recognised abroad. In Rome there was a rumour that he was engaged with Charlemagne in a plot to depose the pope, and Hadrian I wrote anxiously to the emperor to say that he put no trust in the story and had no doubt of Offa's loyalty. Papal legates came to England in 786—the first since Augustine—and travelled widely through the country to enquire into the state of the church and to reiterate, to clergy and laity, the canons of their faith and such necessary commandments as obedience to bishops and the punctual payment of tithes. They were everywhere received with deference—the authority of Rome was now indisputable—and having fulfilled their major tasks they listened to Offa's request for the establishment of a new archbishopric in Mercia. He was jealous of the power of Canterbury, whose archbishop, Jaenberht, with a round dozen suffragans under him, supported Egbert, king of Kent—of a new dynasty—whose unwillingness to acknowledge Mercian supremacy was becoming more evident. The growth of his kingdom was the reason that Offa put forward to justify his request, but hostility to Kent was his true motive; and policy—the recurrent policy of yielding to strength—was presumably the cause of the legates' compliance. The bishop of Lichfield received from Rome the pallium they recommended, and Lichfield became the site of an archbishopric.

In his relations with Charlemagne, the Mercian king insisted on his equality with the emperor. It was Charlemagne who, about the year 789, proposed that one of his sons should marry one of Offa's daughters; to which Offa replied that he would consent only if Ecgfrith, his son, got Charlemagne's daughter Bertha in marriage. Ecgfrith's lineage, through Offa, king of Angel, to the god Woden, may have been older and more distinguished than that of the emperor, but Charlemagne resented the proposed alliance, and showed his dudgeon by prohibiting trade with England. —Had it not been for his displeasure there might have been no knowledge that England, at this time, enjoyed any trade with the continent.—Alcuin of York was then obliged to descend to politics, and some years later a formal treaty was concluded between the two monarchs, and the English export of woollen garments was regulated.

That commerce was beginning to be of national importance under Offa is shown by the good coinage minted in his time. Mercia, indeed, may have blessed posterity with the once-useful word 'penny,' which is probably derived from the name of the heathen Penda; and under his greater successor its coinage dominated English trade. At the beginning of the eighth century there existed a somewhat haphazard local coinage, unmarked by the name of its issuing king and mint, but Offa's money, in the earlier years of his reign, bore an admirable portrait, and in later years his name was boldly displayed on the one side of his silver pennies, the name of the mint on the other. He also struck gold coins that copied those of the caliphs of Baghdad: on the obverse the Arabic inscription was reproduced by a Mercian craftsman who did not know its meaning, but on the reverse *Offa Rex* was inscribed; and presumably the coins were designed to encourage a trade emanating from Spain and Africa, those shores that the Arabs dominated.

Offa was a great king. At the end of his reign he was supreme in England, and by policy and trade he had compelled a continental recognition of England's status. The island that was known for its piety and scholarship, for such missionaries and teachers as Willibrord and Boniface and Alcuin, had now won recognition of its secular power; but its power had no stability, no permanence.

Offa died in 796, his only son a few months later, and Kent rose in rebellion.

The next king, Cenwulf, engaged in a two years' war with Kent, and set his brother on its throne. The king of Wessex, who had married one of Offa's daughters, died and was succeeded by Egbert, whom Offa had forced into exile; and Egbert did not recognise Cenwulf as his overlord. The king of Northumbria, also a son-in-law of Offa, was murdered; and Mercian influence in the north died with him. In East Anglia, Essex, and Sussex, Mercian authority was still recognised, and on the Welsh border Cenwulf resumed a policy of aggression. But his major problem appears to have been church politics, and his most significant reverse the loss of the newly established archbishopric of Lichfield. The church's interest was not confined to dogma and the cure of souls. It had acquired large properties, and was concerned with privilege and power. Augustine's see had been divided, but the primacy of Canterbury was rooted in tradition, and Cenwulf's revengeful effort to win papal approval for the re-establishment of a single archbishopric for southern England—but with its seat in London, not in Canterbury—was unsuccessful. Lichfield lost its brief authority, and Canterbury was confirmed in the lonely supremacy ordained for it by Gregory the Great.

The focus of power was moving gradually to the south, from Northumbria to Mercia, and next in turn was the country of the West Saxons. In 825 Egbert of Wessex brought Mercian supremacy to an end by his decisive victory in the debatable land which lay south of the modern town of Swindon in Wiltshire. Moving swiftly to exploit success, Egbert sent an army into Kent under his son Ethelwulf, who drove out a Mercian puppet-king and received the submission of Kent and Essex, Sussex, and Surrey; the men of East Anglia, already in revolt against Mercia, also acknowledged Egbert's supremacy, and the frontiers of Mercia shrank around its midland isolation.

A few years later Offa's diminished kingdom was unable to resist Egbert's aggressive policy. The proud line of Offa was extinct, and Egbert, the new man of power, with a distinguished ancestry to enhance the prestige of success, was able to enlist widespread support. Mercia was conquered, and on coins minted in London, the port of Mercia, Egbert proclaimed himself its king. Northumbria was threatened with invasion, but came to terms and acknowledged him as *Bretwalda:* Northumbria, surviving internecine war, had preserved its tradition of scholarship and still comprised nearly all England beyond the Humber and much of what is now Scotland.

Under Egbert Wessex became, in effect, the south of England—Kent, Surrey, and Sussex were permanently added to its realm—but Mercia rebelled and recovered a substantial independence that included its recapture of London and a large part of Berkshire. Egbert fought in Devon and Cornwall, and so far made himself master of that wild British peninsula that its aspiration to independence was finally defeated, though its unwillingness to acknowledge defeat long remained. Egbert's policy of expansion was curtailed by Mercia's stubborn revival, but he created in the south the kingdom that was to be foremost in resistance to Danish invasion when viking aggression became a purposive policy and sought possession of England; and the royal house of Wessex established in the south a moral and social ascendancy that would strangely survive conquest by Cnut, by William of Normandy, and all the subsequent shifting of political and economic strength in England. Egbert of Wessex created a visage of England that was to live through all its history. The social supremacy of the south of England—which antagonised but without visible effort dominated through the industrial revolution the money-spinning north of England—was Egbert's benefaction, bought in the first instance by resolute warfare, to all those rich and comely shires which lie south and west of Oxford Street.

Before he died he had to face one of those viking onslaughts that now seem preliminary to the two hundred years' war which was to begin in earnest when the sons of Ragnar Lodbrok took York in 866. After the early raids on Lindisfarne and the Dorset coast the longships did not return till 835, when they came disastrously to Sheppey at the entrance to the Thames. Three years later a viking host found allies in the Britons of Cornwall, and attempted the invasion of Wessex. They were met and defeated by Egbert at Hingston Down, north of Plymouth. After this final benevolence he died and was succeeded by his son Ethelwulf, who reigned for twenty years, and in a period of history tormented by recurrent raids or invasion, distinguished himself by a great victory over the northern heathen, and the strange indulgence, during a time of peril for his kingdom, of a lengthy pilgrimage to Rome.

In the thirty years after the assault on Sheppey there were at least a dozen attacks on the south and east coasts of England by Norse or Danish raiders. Kent was hard hit and in 850 a viking host wintered in Thanet, another in Sheppey in 854. East Anglia, and Lindsey between the Humber and the coast, also suffered. Southampton was pillaged, and the extraordinary mobility of the pirates, on land as well as on the sea, was demonstrated in 855 when they raided part of Shropshire. There was a battle in Northumbria, and in the first English naval battle Athelstan, the son of Ethelwulf, defeated a Danish fleet off the east coast of Kent. Another Danish attack was repelled on the north shore of Somerset, and in 851 Ethelwulf of Wessex defeated a great army which had taken by storm both Canterbury and London, and is said to have entered the Thames with a fleet of three hundred and fifty ships. Such numbers are always suspect, but it is safe to assume that by mid-century viking invasion was well organised, and the intrusive force might number several thousand men. It had also become obvious that a local defeat had no deterrent effect on the viking offensive.

Ethelwulf's battle was fought somewhere south of the Thames, and four years later he left his kingdom to the care of his eldest living son, and went on his leisurely pilgrimage to Rome, where he remained for a year and then spent some holiday months at the French court of Charles the Bald. His apparent irresponsibility roused adverse criticism in Wessex, and to avoid trouble he agreed to give half his kingdom to his son Ethelbald; who, on his father's death, married his widow: a young girl, the daughter of Charles the Bald, whom Ethelwulf had wed during his vacation abroad. Ethelbald did not live long and was succeeded by his brother Ethelbert; who died childless in 865. A third brother, Ethelred, came to the throne, and in his reign the purposive war began.

The political structure of England had been much simplified since the previous century, and in its southern half there were now only three kingdoms: dominant Wessex, a diminished Mercia, and a vaguely recorded, shadowy East Anglia; while, beyond the Humber, Northumbria filled a great area to which only a

strong tradition and uncertain authority gave coherence. But simplification—or a process of identification—had gone further than
jealous policies admitted, and the nationality or one-ness that
Bede had proclaimed is now visible, by the telescopic magnifica-
tion of hindsight, through the shifting boundary-lines of Anglo-
Saxon regalities. The church had established the powerful unity
of faith, and a network of temporal authority that its increased
possessions gave it; and England had begun to find a native voice.
In the centuries to come it would win pre-eminence by its
poetry and its wars, and very early in life it laid steps for the
future by growing inured to war and beginning to make a literature.

The material of the epic poem *Beowulf* is a legendary mutation
of ancient Scandinavian history, but the poem is English, and
probably—though scholars are at variance about its origin—the
work of a Northumbrian in the creative years that followed the
introduction of Christianity from Iona. Some of its principal
episodes are the wild stuff of primitive story-telling: Beowulf,
the hero of gigantic strength, fights with the monster Grendel,
and in darker, more desperate conflict in a sea-cave, with Grendel's
hideous mother. But it is not a barbaric poem. The story is told
with a grave and noble courtesy, and much of the background is
furnished with a sombre splendour. The king's hall is hung with
tapestry, there is treasure in a dragon's lair, and as well as the
killing of the dragon there is ponderous war with a king of Sweden. Christian sentiment goes with sword-play, and heroic melancholy frames the warrior's valour. It is not the poem of a simple,
emergent people, but rather the stiff and solemn utterance of a
man encumbered by too much finery.

Beowulf makes it very difficult to imagine the nature of life
in England in the seventh, eighth, and ninth centuries, and the
discovery of the great funeral-hoard at Sutton Hoo, in Suffolk,
adds to the difficulty by substantiating the incidental truth of the
poem: not the truth of Beowulf's fight with Grendel's mother,
but the verity of its rich and elaborate background. The treasure
of Sutton Hoo was unearthed in 1939, when a barrow was
excavated and the remains of a ship, or open boat, some eighty
feet long, was revealed. It was not the burial-place but the cenotaph of a dead king, whose importance had been such that a

wealth of magnificent gold ornaments, lavishly bejewelled, of silver vessels and splendid weapons, had been buried for his comfort in the after-world. This fantastic hoard has been described as 'the final flower of pagan Saxon art. But it is not decadent. The gold jewellery is full of new and daring ideas; it shows an overflowing exuberance, and displays the highest possible level of craftsmanship, excelling anything that has preceded it in Saxon archaeology. . . . It is difficult to repress the feeling that the standard of perfection set by the Sutton Hoo master-goldsmith, the infinite pains taken, for instance, in the minute cloisonné work on the pair of hexagonal plaques or the purse-lid, reveals a spirit directly connected with that expressed in the work of the exacting and indefatigable Northumbrian illuminators. It seems likely that further study may establish that this final phase of pagan Saxon art made more substantial contributions than was hitherto thought possible to the Northumbrian renaissance.'[1]

The king so signally honoured has tentatively been identified as Ethelhere, an East Anglian ally of Penda of Mercia, who died in or about 656. The art of the Northumbrian illuminators, mentioned in the paragraph above, is magnificently preserved in the intricate decoration, the ornate splendour, and bold text of the Lindisfarne Gospels, a work of the next half-century. Here, then, in the illuminated Gospels, in the Sutton Hoo treasure, and in *Beowulf* is evidence of a rich and formal culture that seems oddly out of place in a land where wolves still harboured in great forests, and rivers crawled through impenetrable marshes to a hostile sea. It was a land in which the vast majority of people lived within common knowledge of primitive poverty and hunger —though most of them probably ate much better and lived longer than any continental peasants—and where local warfare could easily break the tenuous structure of its laws. But domiciled in its rude monasteries and heavily mannered courts was the double wealth of jewelled ornaments, brought in trade from the eastern Mediterranean or fashioned by native smiths in meagre, nearby cottages, and of minds that could devise the enamelled illumination of the Lindisfarne Gospels and forge the resonant, elaborate poetry of *Beowulf*.

[1] *The Sutton Hoo Ship Burial:* Trustees of the British Museum.

There are two shorter poems, of the eighth or ninth century, called *The Seafarer* and *The Wanderer*, and they—more clearly than the remnants of improbable splendour—offer a clue to the mood and temper of English life in those Dark Ages. They are skilful, mannered works that reflect their authors' solemn wonder at the world they live in—that expose a troubled fascination by the majesty and cruelty of the sea—and are infused with a noble melancholy. Life is a tyrant, and its tyranny must be endured. Once upon a time life was good, there was warmth in the hall, and hearts were high; but all that was long ago.

Such, perhaps, was the temper which united the struggling peasant in his unhedged field and the noble in the rude luxury of a small king's court. Almost certainly it was the temper which received with ecstasy the Christian promise, and fortified by Christian faith awoke the imagination of him who wrote *The Dream of the Rood* to see the Cross as a living tree now bright with treasure, now stained with ebbing blood, and endowed with speech to tell of resurrection. But it was also the temper which, in the last years of the tenth century when most of England was corrupt and sick at heart, inspired Byrhtnoth of Essex to engage the Danes in hopeless battle at Maldon: a battle fought by pessimism raised to the pitch of valour:

> 'Thought shall be the harder, heart the keener,
> Mood shall be the more as our might lessens.'

England's face to the world has often been enigmatic, and in the latter half of the ninth century its expression—on that part of it which is faintly visible—may hide as much as it reveals; but there is no discernible hint of the temper that would later create a legend of 'merry England.' There is sadness on its brow, patience in its eyes, and behind a stubborn, arrogant head the intermittent light of faith. One can see nothing at all of the earthbound peasants whose labour fed their betters and nourished in them a capacity for thought and action, an appetite for rich furnishings, and the dignity of imaginative and jealous kings. It was a hardy, enduring peasantry, and, except when the harvest failed, well-fed—of that there can be no doubt—and blessed with a folk-memory that may have been haunted by tales of Arthur and a lost civilization.

Much of the land of England was still clothed in forest or encumbered by swamps, but its wealth was so notorious—the wealth of its churches and its rulers, but especially the wealth of its fields—that its greedy and bolder neighbours in the harsh lands of Scandinavia now saw it as the greatest prize within their reach, so for generation after generation they poured their ever-renewed attack upon the ever-reviving resistance of its stubborn shores. They had seen as much of France and northern Europe as its great rivers could show them, from the Elbe to the Garonne; they had searched all Ireland, and looked dubiously at Scotland; and their considered choice—apart from those who had settled in Normandy—was England. Ruthlessly, and with a persistent re-iteration of their intention, they fought to conquer and possess it; and until it was twice conquered England preserved its identity, and behind an often-yielding battlefront retained a spirit capable of revival. There were many casualties, and its native scholarship almost died. But out of tribulation emerged the sublime figure of Alfred the Great, who rescued and miraculously restored to English life its humane interests. From sore perplexity Alfred engineered an English renaissance, and it was the ultimate defeat of what he had fought for, and created, that gave to the conquest of England the dignity of tragedy.

Chapter V

THE SPLENDOUR OF WESSEX

THE two hundred years of Norse and Danish aggression that culminated in William of Normandy's conquest of England were not centuries of continuous war, but centuries so inundated by war that their periods of peace are like the scattered islands of an archipelago in an angry sea. The purposive tide broke on East Anglia in 865, and the invaders soon made their intention clear. Their immediate predecessors had learnt a great deal about the geography of England, and the newcomers had the advantage of the knowledge thus painfully garnered. Their leaders were three sons of Ragnar Lodbrok who, when they took York in 866, are said to have explained their motive as revenge for the death of their father; who is supposed to have been killed there by Aelle, king of Northumbria. That may be so; what is certain is that the invasion led by Halfdan, Ubbi, and Ivar the Boneless brought about the permanent occupation of large tracts of England by the Danish seamen who followed them, and for most of what they won they had to fight.

English historians have stressed the heroic resistance offered to rough opponents—which, indeed, can hardly be overpraised—and there used to be a fairly general belief, for which historians could not deny all responsibility, that England was a peace-loving, inoffensive land that lay wide-open to aggression. That, however, is not a view substantiated by history. England was as closely accustomed to war as any of its Scandinavian assailants, and had many advantages unknown to them. Its intellectual superiority was manifest. The riches which invited attack gave it resources far beyond those available to the foreign seamen in their scantily burdened ships. Its kingdoms had a coherence and a discipline of law that vastly exceeded—or should have exceeded—the arbitrary or *ad hoc* loyalties of their invaders. The

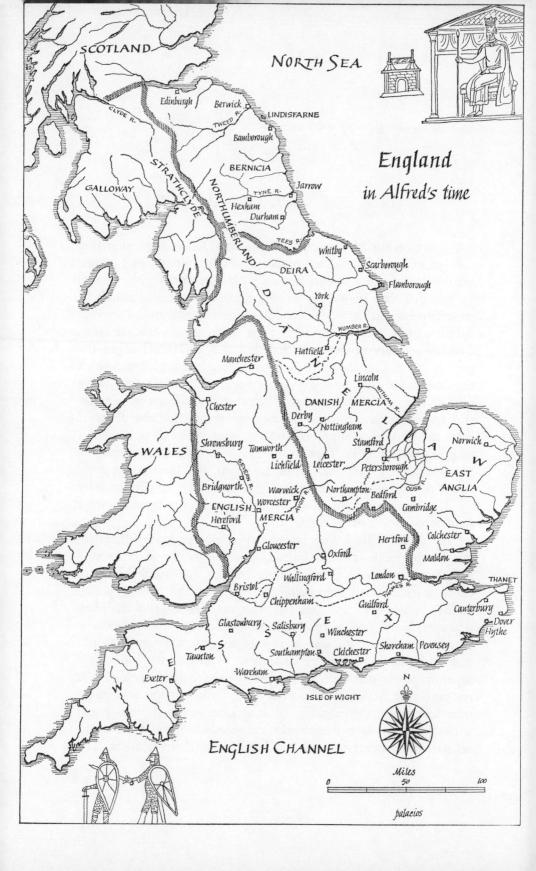

SCOTLAND

NORTH SEA

England in Alfred's time

CLYDE R.
Edinburgh
Berwick
TWEED R.
LINDISFARNE
Bamborough
BERNICIA
STRATHCLYDE
GALLOWAY
NORTHUMBERLAND
TYNE R.   Jarrow
Hexham
Durham
TEES R.
Whitby
DEIRA
Scarborough
Flamborough
York
D
A
HUMBER R.
Hatfield
L
Manchester
Lincoln
Chester
DANISH MERCIA
WITHAM R.
Derby
E
Nottingham
L
WALES
Shrewsbury
Tamworth
Stamford
A
Norwich
Lichfield
Leicester
Petersborough
W
Bridgnorth
Warwick
Northampton
EAST
SEVERN R.
Worcester
AVON R.
Bedford
OUSE R.
ANGLIA
ENGLISH
Hereford
MERCIA
Cambridge
Gloucester
Oxford
Hertford
Colchester
Maldon
Bristol
Wallingford
London
THAMES R.
THANET
Chippenham
Guilford
Canterbury
E
Glastonbury
Salisbury
S
X
Dover
S
Winchester
Shoreham
Hythe
E
Taunton
Southampton
Chichester
Pevensey
W
Wareham
ISLE OF WIGHT
Exeter

ENGLISH CHANNEL

N

Miles
0   50   100

palacios

English were vulnerable because their coast-line was long and they had no defensive navy or an over-all military command that held in reserve a mass of manoeuvre to meet attack; but they had a nobility dedicated to war, a peasantry instructed in war, and a local knowledge of the country that was fought over, which, in combination, could provide a formidable defence. It is possible, indeed, that if the valour and pertinacity of each side could be weighed exactly in a balance—the dogged resistance of England against the indefatigable recurrence of Scandinavian attack—the weight of approval would fall on the northern side. England suffered, and suffering has usually had a loud, protesting voice. But the Norse refusal to acknowledge defeat—the persistence of attack on a redoubtable stronghold that again and again rebuffed assault—compels the admiration of an objective critic, though such a critic will undoubtedly admit that the greatest figure to emerge from the war was Alfred of Wessex.

It was in 865 that Ethelred I succeeded his brother Ethelbert, 'and the same year,' says the Anglo-Saxon Chronicle, 'a great heathen army came into England and took up winter quarters in East Anglia; and there they were supplied with horses, and the East Angles made peace with them.' Six years later, when the Danish army fought at Ashdown, the Chronicle says it was drawn up in two divisions, the one commanded by the heathen kings Halfdan and an unknown 'Bagsecg,' and the other by 'the earls'; of whom five, who are named, are said to have been killed. The army, it is clear, was something more than a viking host, and the invasion of England was on a larger scale than private venture. Its known leaders were the sons of Ragnar, but to call the whole army Danish is probably a simplification. It is more likely that recruiting had been wide-spread—in the Norwegian fjords, in the nearer parts of the Baltic, in the Frisian islands, as well as in Denmark itself—and the mobility of the army implies the organisation and discipline of, at least, a semi-professional force: a force, that is, of men who had some experience of war and were bound by articles of association. But for several years it had no obvious plan of campaign, no strategic purpose; it wandered from one part of England to another as if it had come only in search of subsistence.

Its first year was spent in East Anglia, and from a defended site mounted men rode out to forage and levy blackmail on the surrounding country; local peace became a commodity that, like other commodities, could be bought. Then, in the autumn of 866, the army advanced on York and occupied it.—An accompanying fleet presumably found convenient anchorage in the river Ouse.—There was civil war in Northumbria, and its king, Osbert, had been ousted by the usurper Aelle, a man with no hereditary claim to the throne. If, as seems probable, Aelle had only recently driven out Osbert, it is difficult to see how he could have put Ragnar Lodbrok to death; it is possible, however, that Ragnar had been killed by Osbert, and together with his throne the usurper acquired the reputation of having done that famous but perhaps only legendary deed.

For several months the Danes remained in York, untroubled by attack, but by March of the following year the rival kings had agreed to join forces for an assault on the city. They broke in, through its outer defences, but failed to capture it. The Northumbrian army suffered heavy losses, both kings were killed, and the survivors made peace.

In the autumn the Danes set up a tributary king in York, and marching into Mercia established winter quarters in Nottingham. The king of Mercia was Burgred, who had married a princess of Wessex. He sent a plea for help to Ethelred, king of the West Saxons, who with his brother Alfred led an army that laid siege to the town. The Danes showed no wish to come out and give battle, and Ethelred had no means of breaking through the walls. There may have been skirmishing, but there was no general engagement, and the siege was broken off when the Mercians decided to buy peace. The Danes returned to York and spent another year there.

In 869 they rode across Mercia into East Anglia and took up winter quarters at Thetford. The king of East Anglia was Edmund, who is said—but on doubtful authority—to have been born in Nuremberg of 'old Saxon' stock, and to have been summoned to his throne, while still a boy, in 855. He offered battle to the Danes at Hoxne, twenty miles from Thetford, and was defeated. Edmund was killed, perhaps on the battlefield, but according to stubborn tradition in a savage sequel to the heathens' victory. It is alleged that he refused to abjure his Christian faith, and died a martyr. The date of his canonisation is unknown, but he has lived in history as St. Edmund.

In the following year the Danes marched south, and in Wessex raised a defensive earthwork between the Kennet and the Thames near their confluence at Reading. Three days later a reconnaissance in force, under two earls, was defeated at Englefield, some miles to the west, and four days after that an English army under king Ethelred and his brother Alfred gave battle to the Danes and was defeated with heavy losses to both sides. The English army broke contact, the Danes moved forward to the chalk-ridge of Ashdown, on the West Berkshire downs, and a few days later there was another general engagement. Ethelred faced that division of the Danish army which two kings commanded, but would not attack until he had heard mass; so Alfred led the way against the Danes' second division. His biographer, the Welsh monk Asser, later bishop of Sherborne, says the Danes had the higher ground and Alfred led the charge with the fury of a wild boar: *aprino more*. On the ridge was a single thorn-tree which Asser had seen with his own eyes—'*quam nos ipsi nostris propriis oculis vidimus*'—and round it the battle raged till nightfall, when both sides retreated from the ridge. But the Danes, who had lost five earls and the king called 'Bagsecg,' must have had the worse of it.

A fortnight later they had their revenge at Basing, and two months after that, in a battle at an unidentified place called 'Meretun' the English had the better of it till late in the day, when the Danes re-grouped and won back their lost ground. Behind them the Danes had the advantage of sea-power—their fleet could bring reinforcements to make good their heavy losses—and in April 871, their ships came up the Thames to Reading with a new army. In that month king Ethelred died, and his brother Alfred was at once recognised as his successor.

Defeat marked the opening of his reign. The English lost in a small encounter at Reading, and Alfred himself, after a delusive prospect of victory, was defeated at Wilton near Salisbury. In the year of his accession he fought in nine general engagements, all south of the Thames, and there were, in addition, uncounted skirmishes. It became necessary to buy a temporary peace from the enemy, and that having been done, the Danes took up winter quarters in London and exacted heavy tribute from it.

Halfdan was now, it seems, the single leader of the Danes; and coins bearing his name were struck in London. Ivar the Boneless appears to have gone to Dublin, and though Ubbi, the third of the brothers, was in East Anglia at the time of the death of Edmund the Martyr, there is no mention of him in later years unless he can be identified with the unnamed brother of Halfdan who fought in Devon in 878.

Revolt in Northumbria provoked Halfdan to a northward march in 872. The puppet-king he had set up was driven out, and with the archbishop of York took refuge with Burgred of Mercia. The Danes made no move to subdue Northumbria— apparently the revolt had collapsed—but went into winter quarters at Torksey in Lindsey; and for several years the North- umbrians enjoyed, presumably by consent, a precarious indepen- dence under their own elected king. Mercia was less happy, for presently the Danes marched into Repton and drove out king Burgred; who, after a reign of more than twenty years, found refuge in Rome. The kingdom of Mercia was given to one Ceolwulf, a foolish thane, says the Anglo-Saxon Chronicle, who 'swore oaths to them and gave hostages, that it should be ready for them on whatever day they wished to have it, and he would be ready, himself and all who would follow him, at the enemy's service.'

For ten years the Danish army had fought and marched and been ruled as a single force: an astonishing achievement for which Halfdan must be given the credit. But in 875 the unity of command was broken, and while Halfdan with his followers went again into Northumbria, and took up winter quarters on Tyneside, the remainder of the army under Guthrum and two other so-called 'kings' marched to Cambridge and for a year established themselves there. From his base on Tyneside, Halfdan plundered beyond the English border into the lands of the Picts, and the Welsh or Britons of Strathclyde; and later divided Northumbria—or that part of it which is now Yorkshire—among his followers, and encouraged them to plough the land and settle down there. He himself appears to have left England, and may have gone into northern Ireland.

But Guthrum's army undertook an extraordinary march from Cambridge to Wareham in the south of Dorset, where, according to Asser, they found very secure quarters in a nunnery; and there chose to negotiate with the West Saxons. They gave hostages and took a great oath to leave Wessex; and promptly broke their oath. The Danes were mounted, and under cover of night they rode past the West Saxons towards Exeter. Alfred pursued them, but failed to prevent their occupation of the town. They were, however, gravely handicapped by disaster at sea, for a fleet of a hundred and twenty ships, sailing with reinforcements, ran into a wild storm off Swanage and suffered heavy loss; and again they gave hostages to Alfred and swore to keep the peace. In harvest-time they marched away, and returning to Mercia compelled the puppet-king Ceolwulf to surrender half his realm, which was divided among those in the army who chose to settle on the land. The eastward shires of Lincoln, Nottingham, Derby, and Leicester became a Danish colony.

But Guthrum still had a useful army, and in the early days of 878—moving, contrary to custom, in mid-winter—he marched from Gloucester to Chippenham, and settling down there enforced submission on all the surrounding country, though many fled 'across the sea,' says the Chronicle: meaning, presumably, across the Severn into Wales. Alfred, with only a small force, had to retreat before him, and found a hazardous refuge somewhere among the woods and fens of Somerset. There, says Asser, he was forced to live on what he could take by raiding the enemy's country, and when he could not rob the heathen he had to rob Christian households that had yielded to them. That was the period when he came nearest to defeat, and in later years the peril in which he lived was decorated with much romantic adventure.

Guthrum's winter march had achieved what must have seemed, for some while, overwhelming success; and taken by surprise, many of the West Saxon leaders yielded to him. But a major calamity befell the Danes when they lost more than eight hundred men in battle. A fleet of twenty-three ships had crossed over from south Wales, under command of a brother of Halfdan, who was probably Ubbi. According to the Chronicle he carried a magical raven banner of a sort that is mentioned more than once in the sagas. Ragnar Lodbrok is supposed to have had one, as had earl Sigurd of Orkney; by the magic woven into it the raven would flutter before victory, but in Ubbi's last battle in Devon its wings must have hung despairingly; for that was how it foretold defeat. The English leader was apparently a Devon chief called Odda, otherwise unknown.

At Athelney in Somerset Alfred built a stronghold, and more boldly, as it seems, began to move outwards from it. His refusal to accept defeat renewed courage in those about him, and seven weeks after Easter he was able to ride to 'Egbert's Stone,' an unidentified place east of Selwood, where he mustered all the men of Somerset and Wiltshire and the west of Hampshire. They marched towards the Danish camp at Chippenham, and at Edington, to the south of it, met the Danish army and inflicted on it a decisive defeat. The remnant Danes retreated to their camp, followed by Alfred, who seized their horses and cattle and killed all who strayed beyond the perimeter. For a fortnight he besieged them, and then, suffering from cold and hunger, the despairing Danes surrendered. They gave what hostages Alfred demanded, they swore great oaths to leave his kingdom, and promised that king Guthrum would submit to baptism. That he did, and with thirty of his chief men came to his christening near Athelney, and Alfred stood sponsor to him. In the autumn Guthrum led his still considerable army out of Chippenham and marched to Cirencester in Mercia; and the following year he went to East Anglia and there established his kingdom. There were now three Danish armies occupying permanent settlements in England: one in East Anglia, one in eastern Mercia, and one in Northumbria. Master of the south was Wessex, but elsewhere the men of the Danelaw exercised a dominating influence.

The country was not yet immune from viking enterprise, but a fleet which entered the Thames in 878 soon put to sea again and sailed to the continent; while a small invasion of Kent was driven out by Alfred. The Danes of East Anglia gave support to new raiders, and Alfred sent a punitive expedition to the Essex coast which destroyed sixteen viking ships before it met a larger Danish fleet and was defeated. It became evident that Guthrum's baptism had not committed him to the cause of peace, and East Anglia was still a menace.

What happened next is not precisely known, but Asser says that after towns had been burnt and people massacred, Alfred 'occupied' London. Presumably he had to fight for it, but there is no record of a battle, and the Danish garrison may have withdrawn. His capture of the city, however it was achieved, was recognised as an event of general significance, and thereafter, declares the Chronicle, 'all the English people that were not under subjection to the Danes submitted to him.' Alfred of Wessex was recognised as England's overlord, and he showed acceptance of his larger responsibility by restoring London to Mercian government. The Danish puppet Ceolwulf had disappeared, none knows how, and for some years western Mercia had been ruled by an Ethelred, not of the royal house, who acknowledged Alfred and was later to marry his eldest daughter. Mercian dignity was flattered, and the safety of Wessex guarded by a loyal governor in London.

In a treaty made between Alfred and Guthrum there was provision for the control of trade and movement between the two kingdoms, and English inhabitants in the Danelaw were assured of equality before the law. It was a great tract of land that Guthrum ruled, for as well as East Anglia, Essex and the southern midlands were in his domain; his western boundary lay on Watling Street—roughly on the line from St. Albans to Shrewsbury— with his northern frontier between Northampton and Leicester. But in 890 he died, and two years later England had to face new invasions.

In France the Danes had suffered their major reverse near Louvain, and there was famine in the land. The defeated army, under an unnamed king in a fleet of two hundred and fifty ships, crossed over to the estuary of the Lympne in East Kent and rowed upstream—through country whose appearance has changed utterly since then—to the end of the great forest called the Weald, and established itself in a half-built fortress at Appledore, which lies a dozen miles or so north-west of Dungeness. And a little while later a second army in eighty ships, commanded by Hastein, a viking of great renown, sailed into the estuary of the Thames and either captured or built a fortress at Milton Regis near Sittingbourne in the north of Kent.

But now England was better prepared for defence, and the

half-finished fortress at Appledore—in which the Danes found only a few peasants—was one of many that Alfred had built in the southern counties. He had built ships which were half as long again as the average longship of twenty rowing benches, and these were a useful protection against raiders from East Anglia and Northumbria. He had, moreover, created an army that was capable of rapid movement and able to keep the field for an appreciable time. A peasant militia was never willing to serve outside its own district, but Alfred devised a scheme by which half the levy stayed at home while the other half took the field; and he seems to have imposed some obligation of military service on his nobility that gave him a mounted arm.

There was need for all this preparation. The arrival of the invading armies stirred old ambitions in the Danes of East Anglia and the north, and England was again a country torn and perplexed by war. Alfred's first move was to station himself between the two armies, and he soon won a diplomatic success by persuading Hastein to abandon his stronghold and cross the Thames into Essex. The other army, after pillaging the immediate neighbour-hood, set off on a raiding march into Hampshire and Berkshire that gave them a great booty which they hoped to carry into Essex, where some of their ships had gone. They were, presumably, driving cattle they had taken, and their march was slow. An English army commanded by Alfred's son Edward intercepted them at Farnham, and having beaten them in battle drove them northward in confusion to the Thames. The Danes tried to cross it where there was no ford, and took refuge on an islet in the Colne, a tributary that runs in at Staines. Edward confined them there till his own army grew restless—his men were short of food and their term of service was up—and then, from London, Ethelred of Mercia brought welcome reinforcement. The Danes were unable to fight their way out because their king had been badly wounded; the English, as it seems, were still not strong enough to attack. So terms were arranged, and the Danes marched to their ships and sailed to Mersea Island in Essex.

Alfred, who had been advancing from the west, was compelled by news of unexpected attack to turn about and march to Exeter. The Danes of Northumbria and East Anglia had mustered their ships in two fleets, and while the one, it is said, went north-about round Scotland to attack the north coast of Devon, the other, a hundred strong, sailed down Channel and laid siege to Exeter. Inconclusive operations kept Alfred in the west country for the next six months, but over the rest of England there raged an extraordinary war of movement.

In Essex the two invading armies had concentrated at Benfleet, near the modern town of Southend, and while Hastein was leading a raid into Mercia his fortified camp was attacked and captured—with its ships and booty and the women who were there—by an army consisting of the London garrison troops and the militia of east Wessex. The English returned with their trophies to London, and when Hastein came back from his Mercian raid a new camp was built at Shoeburyness, and the Danes, with few resources after the disaster at Benfleet, resolved on a fantastic progress across the breadth of England. They received large reinforcements from Northumbria and East Anglia, and marched up the valley of the Thames, and westward still until they came to the Severn; then upstream again till they reached a place called Buttington, near Welshpool in Montgomery. Ethelred of Mercia followed them with the nobility of his own country, of eastern Wessex and Wiltshire and Somerset, and somewhere on the Severn he was joined by the Welsh princes whose country was threatened. At Buttington, where they had built a fortified camp, the Danes were besieged, and stood the siege for many weeks in despite of increasing hunger. Those of their horses that did not die of starvation were killed and eaten; but when, in desperation, the hungry army made a sortie to the east, it broke through the English lines and marched back to Essex. The English claimed a victory, but the remnant army of the Danes was sufficient, both in numbers and morale, to plan another reckless enterprise.

In Shoeburyness they summoned to their help fresh reinforcements from a seemingly inexhaustible Danish stock—or, more realistically, the viking stock of mixed origin—in Northumbria and East Anglia; they made arrangements for the safe-keeping in East Anglia of their ships and women and movable property, and again marched across England, moving by day and night, to Chester, which they are said to have found deserted. Its inhabitants may have abandoned it when they heard of the Danes' approach,

for measures were immediately taken to make Chester untenable. An English army had followed, and the neighbouring country was systematically laid waste to prevent the enemy from
foraging. The English army was mounted, and what corn was
not required for its horses was burnt, cattle were driven away,
and the enemy's reconnoitering parties were cut off. But again
the Danes were able to break through the investing army, and
marching into Wales they found sustenance there on which they
lived, for the better part of a year, till the summer of 894. Then,
with the booty they had taken, they marched eastward into
Northumbria, and southward from there through East Anglia to
Mersea Island on the Essex coast. It was a fantastic achievement,
and reveals a mobility on land as astonishing as the vikings' freedom of the sea.

In the west the Danish army which had established itself near
Exeter was at last defeated and driven back to its ships; in large
numbers it raided Sussex, but was defeated with heavy loss near
Chichester. In early winter the Danes on Mersea Island rowed up
the estuary of the Thames, up river and up the river Lea, and on
the Lea, some twenty miles above London, built a fortified camp.
They beat off one serious attack, and maintained themselves till
harvest-time in the following year. King Alfred had taken up a
nearby position to protect the neighbouring fields, and after
reconnoitering the Lea discovered a place where it could be so
obstructed that the Danes would be unable to bring their ships
down; and having contrived the obstruction, built a fort on
either side of it. But once again the Danes showed their ruthless
logic, their capacity for prudence, and their wonderful elusive-
ness. They sent their women back to East Anglia, decided to
abandon the ships that could no longer be used, and marched
westward over the midlands to Bridgnorth on the Severn, some
fifteen miles south-east of Shrewsbury. Again they fortified a
camp, and lived on the country throughout the winter. No
attempt was made to bring them to battle, and in the summer of
896 they split into two parties, one of which returned to East
Anglia while the other marched into Northumberland; and some,
who had no resources, put off to fresh adventure in France.

'By the grace of God,' says the Anglo-Saxon Chronicle, 'the
army had not on the whole afflicted the English people very

greatly'; though manifestly it had lived on the country and enriched itself by plunder. Alfred's failure to defeat the invaders
seems a little odd, and it is difficult to avoid the impression
that in his later years his military policy lacked decision. The
Chronicle suggests a certain fatalism, a pious acceptance of the
calamities inseparable from life, as if a Danish army was no more
to be avoided than debt and domestic crisis and the death of
friends; and one had cause for gratitude if Danish depredation
was not too bloodily destructive. But the balance of power between Wessex and the Danelaw may have been so dangerously
level that it would have been unwise of Alfred to press too hard
and compel his enemies to fight for survival; at sea his policy
appears to have been entirely defensive.

The south of England suffered frequently at the hands of
raiding-parties coming from the east coast, and the longships that
Alfred built for its protection seem to have had little deterrent
effect, though in the summer of 896 the Danes lost a score of
vessels. The English ships were built 'neither on the Frisian nor
the Danish pattern,' but to Alfred's own design, that gave them
more freeboard as well as greater length. There is no record,
however, of their having attempted any offensive operation
against Danish shipping in the harbours of Essex and East Anglia.

The 'wild boar' who had led the uphill charge at Ashdown
had become a profoundly thoughtful man, full of resource in
regions of the mind remote from war, who had seen that
England's losses lay deeper than material devastation, and the
survival of its soul needed books as well as a resolute militia. In
his youth he had mobilised fighting men to save the land, and in
maturity he gathered about him the most learned of his clergy to
rescue and revive the sad remains of its scholarship. In the eighth
century learning had flourished in England, but Latin was not
the least of the casualties of war, and when Alfred opened his
campaign against ignorance there was hardly a parish priest or
clerk who could turn the Latinity of his church into English.
What Alfred proposed was the translation of those books which
he and the bishops of his choice had decided were 'the most
necessary for all men to know'; and all free-born boys whose
parents could afford to send them to school would, from those

translations, be taught to read English. Those who wished to enter the church could later learn Latin.

Scholars imported from the continent, from Wales and Mercia, were set to work. The bishop of Worcester translated the *Dialogues* of Gregory the Great. Alfred himself learnt to read Latin, and with the help of his scholars translated Gregory's *Pastoral Care*, for the benefit of his clergy, and wrote a preface to it in which he described the illiteracy it was meant to combat. The *Universal History* of the fifth century Spanish historian Orosius and Bede's *Historia Ecclesiastica* were next translated; and by the liveliness of Alfred's mind—because of his wide interests and a truly scientific curiosity—the former became a new and original work. He added much that he had learnt from experience, and a geographical treatise on the countries of northern Europe which was based upon his conversations with two remarkable seamen who came to his court. The Norseman Ohthere, who lived in the north of Norway, knew all the coast from the White Sea to the south of Denmark, and the other, called Wulfstan, had sailed from Denmark into the Baltic as far east as the mouth of the Vistula. With their stories, and his own notes, Alfred brought Orosius up to date.

His most ambitious translation was Boethius' *Consolation of Philosophy*, the difficult but most popular philosophical work known to the Middle Ages. Boethius, 'last of the Romans and first of the schoolmen,' had sought to reconcile Plato and Aristotle, and prove their philosophy compatible with Christianity. His life was exemplary, his end was violent, and to an heroical conception of man's duty to be virtuous—that would not have seemed strange to a saga-writer with his conception of good behaviour—he added Christian optimism: 'It is not in vain that we put our hope in God, and pray to him.'—Alfred's translation is free, and he underlined the Christian teaching of his original. His own voice may be heard in the sentence, 'My will was to live worthily as long as I lived, and after my life to leave to them that should come after, my memory in good works.'

He inspired the collection of English annals that formed the basis of the Anglo-Saxon Chronicle, and his last work he called *Blostman*, or 'Blossoms.' It begins with a preface in which Alfred sees himself as a man gathering wood in a great forest where there is timber for all manner of building; it proceeds to translation of the *Soliloquies* of St. Augustine, and continues with passages about immortality—interspersed with workaday illustrations—and the search for God. His piety is evident, and equally clear is his appreciation of the scholarly discipline essential for the understanding of Christian teaching. His purpose was instruction, the creation of a lettered class, and only incidentally did he lay the foundation of English prose writing; a foundation which was obscured, after his death, by a return to Latin scholarship.

Not long before his death he issued a code of laws which may be described as rigidly conservative but coloured with a new humanity. The old statutes of Wessex and Kent and Mercia, pruned and amended where they had become obsolete, were reiterated, and added to them were emphatic injunctions about a man's duty to his lord, restriction of the blood-feud, and measures for the protection of the weak against the strong. It was a code for all England that lay beyond the Danelaw, and it created a tradition that, in time to come, both Cnut the Great and William the Conqueror would respect.

When Alfred died, on the 26th October, 899, the menace of the Danes had not been dispelled, but the body of England had been saved, and the spirit of England revived, by a warrior-king who in his youth had fought manfully for his people, and by most rigorous application in his later years had restored the primacy of intellect. In those turbulent centuries that preceded the birth of modern Europe, none save Charlemagne can dispute his supremacy among men and the rulers of men.

Chapter VI

THE MATTER OF SCANDINAVIA

THE Scandinavian countries which, by aggression, were encouraging a sense of identity in France and England, were themselves without firmly drawn frontiers. It is commonly said that of the three northern kingdoms Sweden played no part in the westward propulsion because Sweden found more profitable exercise in piratical excursions into the eastern Baltic, in colonial enterprise in some parts of what is now Russia, and in commerce that included a profitable trade in slaves with the eastern empire. But if that is accepted it must be remembered that the southern corner of modern Sweden, the rich province of Scania, was then a part of Denmark; that royal alliance or royal dissension often involved Sweden in the affairs of its neighbours; and that the essentially Norwegian settlement of Iceland included some Swedish adventurers. Norway and Denmark were certainly the countries that refashioned so much of Britain, but for long years Norway, Denmark, and Sweden fed upon each other, scoffed their neighbours' territory, and vomited it again under pressure. Ruled by a king of exceptional ability, any one of them could extend its frontiers and wear a look of stability; but under his heir might lose all it had gained and tremble for its independence.

As a single realm Norway came into being under king Harald Fairhair, whose father, Halfdan the Black, had done something to prepare the way for unification. Halfdan had succeeded to some part of the small kingdom of Westford beside the Oslo fjord, and quickly added to his possessions much land in the south-east. When he died he left the memory of a good king and a wise administrator as well as the solid foundation of power on which his brilliant son was to build so large a dominion.

The date of Halfdan's death is uncertain. It used to be said, with confidence, that Harald, when only a boy, succeeded to his father's throne in 860, and won the conclusive battle of Hafrsfjord, that made him lord of the whole land, a dozen years later; but recent scholars[1] have found reason to believe that his reign began in 875, and the deciding battle was not fought until the last years of the century. There is no doubt, however, that strife attended the very beginning of his reign, and the nobles who had been his father's leading men were loyal to the young king and so decisively routed his enemies that Harald was confirmed in his possession of lands north of the Oslo fjord and acquired much of the coast east of the Skaggerak. That this early success was enough to encourage ambition in the growing boy may also be accepted, and regretfully one discards the old story that Harald was inspired to achieve greatness by the taunts of the girl Gyda, daughter of a king of Hordaland, who refused to marry him until he ruled all Norway. 'It seems strange to me,' she is supposed to have said, 'that there is no one in Norway who wants to make the whole land his own, as king Gorm has done in Denmark, and king Eric in Uppsala.' Whereupon, the story goes, Harald swore neither to cut nor comb his hair until that splendid purpose had been achieved; and so won his fame, a wife, and his nickname.

It is probable that Harald, a highly intelligent young man as well as a gifted warrior—a young man whose brain was a step or two ahead of his generation—saw the advantage of ruling a united kingdom whose northern districts were rich in produce for which there was a ready market in the east, and whose southern shores controlled the trade-route from the North Sea to the Baltic. Long years of warfare followed, of which there is no certain record, but the people of the west coast, of Rogaland in the south and Hordaland to the north of it, were vikings attuned to battle, and to conquer them Harald must have used diplomacy, the skill of winning allies, as well as hardy tactics and a shrewd strategy. But allies he found—notable among them Rognvald, earl of the lands of Möre, a province south of the Trondheim fjord—and at Hafrsfjord, not far from Stavanger, against a confederacy that included the kings of Rogaland, Hordaland, and Agdir in the south, he won the decisive victory. It was a savage affair—

[1] Notably Professors Halfdan Koht and Haakon Shetelig.

'Roared there the berserks,
Battle-wood was the host,
Loud howled the wolf-coats
And clattered the iron'—[2]

and thereafter Harald's supremacy was beyond dispute, though to consolidate his power he had to fight other battles, and many who refused to accept the intolerable authority of a single throne emigrated to Sweden or sailed west over sea to Orkney, Shetland, the Faeroes, and Iceland.

There is evidence of the fine impartiality of the vikings in the fact that from their strongholds in Orkney and Shetland they plundered not only the Hebrides and Ireland, but also their native country; and so great was their menace that Harald found it expedient to launch a great expedition against the Scottish islands. His initial purpose was to destroy the pirate roosts, but when he had dealt with Orkney and Shetland, the viking habit appears to have led him farther, and he is said to have continued his voyage southward through the Hebrides as far as the Isle of Man, pausing en route to harry adjacent parts of Scotland. This was the voyage that gave to Norway suzerainty over the Scottish islands— though often without much substance in it—till 1263 in respect of the Hebrides, and in the matter of Orkney and Shetland until 1468.

Harald's unification of Norway consisted only in compelling all parts of it to acknowledge his authority. In the many different folk-lands he installed earls of his own choice, or men of approved loyalty, and upon them and the lesser nobles called *hersirs* he laid certain obligations of service, and exacted heavy taxes from the many small landowners. He did not give Norway a constitution, or a political stability that would survive his death. It was his own strength that won general obedience, his severity that enforced it. That even his most staunch supporters could not claim exemption from the harshness of his judgment is shown by his treatment of that son of earl Rognvald of Möre who was known as Marching Rolf. When Rolf was guilty of the gross indiscretion of plundering in the Wick, king Harald at once declared him an outlaw. Earl Rognvald had long been his friend,

[2] *Heimskringla*, trans. Morris and Magnusson.

and Rognvald's wife pleaded for her son, but pleaded in vain. Marching Rolf was banished, and from his banishment sailed westward through the Scottish isles to Normandy and his historic task.

Harald was a polygamist and begot a numerous progeny of undisciplined, violent, overbearing sons who threatened to tear in pieces the realm he had patched together. Several of them met an early death, however, and danger was further averted when Harald divided some parts of his kingdom among those who remained. A child of his old age, called Hakon, was sent to England where he became the fosterling of king Athelstan, grandson of Alfred the Great; and in Norway Eric Bloodaxe was recognised as the heir to a troubled throne and his father's favourite. Eric's mother was a Danish princess, Ragnhild, for whose sake Harald is said to have put away nine wives of whose company he may have tired. Eric's sobriquet was acquired from his having killed, at an early age, one or more of his brothers; or, at a later date, from his successful warfare in England. His life was eventful, and for much of its vigorous unrest he was indebted to his wife Gunnhild, a sister of king Harald Gormson of Denmark.

Eric held the throne of Norway for a few years only, and then—not later than 945, and perhaps earlier—was thrown out by indignant subjects who resented his brutality and found the arrogance of his queen insupportable. In the sagas a strange tale is told of her early years, which were spent, it is said, in the study of witchcraft in Finnmark, where she was found by Eric when he was returning from an extraordinary cruise into the White Sea. He was hard-hearted and greedy, valiant and imprudent; Gunnhild was greedy too, grim of temper and fair of face, an insolent little woman with a ready tongue and a quick mind. They fell in love, they married, and did harm to many.

He who succeeded to the Norwegian throne when Eric was driven off it was his half-brother Hakon, who had been brought up in England at the court of king Athelstan. In a land no longer united under a strong king, Hakon soon found support; his character was amiable, and he relieved the small landowners of the heavy taxes that his father had imposed. His brother fled to Orkney, and may have spent some years on the usual viking exercises. But by 947 he had learnt of conditions in Northumbria that promised a reward for enterprise, and got himself accepted as king in York. He played his small part in English history, of which something will be said in a later chapter, and after his death Gunnhild and her children returned to Orkney. Either there or in Denmark she found a poet to write an ode on Eric's death, and, as if to perpetuate her own wicked memory, married her daughter Ragnhild to the reigning earl's son. Ragnhild had him killed as a preliminary to the death of others with whom she was involved; and Gunnhild went home to Denmark, where her brother Harald Gormson ruled.

Harald Gormson—Harald Bluetooth, as he was known—was the son of Gorm the Old, who may have been descended from Ragnar Lodbrok. There is little profit, however, in trying to disentangle the line of Danish kings before the time of Gorm, for though the kingdom may have been united more than once, it was certainly splintered again and again. In the far distant past it must have enjoyed an epoch of great splendour in the Bronze Age, and in the heroic darkness of the time of Beowulf, Denmark and Sweden were the background of a war that now seems to have been waged with ponderous deliberation and hieratic state-liness. When Charlemagne carried his conquests to the north, the impact of his unexampled strength, and rumours of a purpose beyond understanding, must have shattered any sense of stability that may precariously have formed, and when his empire began to loosen and fall into fragments under his sons and grandsons, the opportunists in the Danish mainland and its islands took advantage of what was offered by disintegration, and in the presence of a ready spoil had no thought for the larger rewards of a central authority. During this period there was a Swedish invasion that won territory of considerable importance in Schleswig, and for a long time the Swedes held the town of Hedeby on the old Frisian trade-route.

Of Gorm the Old very little is known except that he was the last of the heathen kings of Denmark, and in the *Landnámabók* of Iceland he is associated with other rulers of the time: 'Then Harald Fairhair was king of Norway, and Eric, Eymund's son, of Sweden, and Bjorn, his son; and Gorm the Old in Denmark. Alfred the Mighty in England, and his son Edward; Kjarval in

Dublin; Sigurd the Mighty, earl in the Orkneys.' Additional to that is the undoubted fact that Harald, his son—with whom it is possible to say that real history begins, though dates are still uncertain—thought so well of Gorm that he had him laid to rest under a great barrow at Jellinge in Jutland, where the throne of the kingdom then was, and a little way apart raised a cenotaph to Thyra, his mother. Between them he set up an intricately sculptured stone bearing the inscription in Runic writing that he who raised the memorial was 'Harald who won for himself Denmark and Norway and gave the Danes Christianity.'

But the history of countries—or of large territories which intermittently looked like national entities, and then did not—is still the history of dominating men who combined native ability with the influential blood of a ruling family, to establish for a few years a brief superiority over their neighbours. The whole tale of Scandinavia, in this period, is a revelation of incidental strength that stands in high relief against a background of constitutional impotence, and Harald Bluetooth's bold assertion of power did not establish a continuing state, though it created a persisting idea of Denmark. The prolonged failure of the incessantly repeated Scandinavian onslaught on England was due to the fact that, although it became locally purposive, it never acquired the impetus of policy until the last years of Sweyn Forkbeard.

In Norway king Hakon, Athelstan's fosterling, lived to be known as Hakon the Good, and may well have achieved much of his reputation soon after his arrival from England; for one of his earliest decisions was to restore to the 'bonders'—the farmers, the small landowners—the odal, or freehold rights, they had lost to Harald Fairhair. According to the saga of the kings, he had left England with an appreciable force of men and ships that Athelstan had given him, and it is not improbable that policy moved Athelstan to be generous. It is possible, however, that the English king's parting gift was an expression of real friendship, for Hakon appears to have been a most likable man—blithe of temper, well-spoken, and wise—and Athelstan had had him christened.

Hakon's earliest task was to drive out Danish pirates from the southern shores of Norway, and he carried his preventive warfare into Denmark without, as it seems, provoking any immediate reprisal. In his own country there was a short season of peace, of fair weather and plenteous harvests, and Hakon re-established the old laws of the country and pushed his influence into parts of Sweden. He sought means by which to establish Christianity, and sent to England for teachers and a bishop; but Norway was not ready for so drastic a change. Churches were built and consecrated, but there was wide-spread, fierce resistance to the new faith, and at a great *thing* convened at Lade, north-east of Trondheim, Hakon, for the sake of peace, consented to take part in the heathen ritual of the blood-offering and the cup dedicated to Odin.

It was, perhaps, as well that he did so; for now came word that the sons of Eric Bloodaxe—who, with their mother, had come from Orkney into Denmark—were in the Wick with a great force, and harrying its shores; and the stubborn heathen, who had humiliated Hakon at Lade, rallied quickly to his side and somewhere on the coast of Agdir the aggressors were soundly beaten, and Guthorm, one of Eric's sons, was killed. Again there was an interval of peace—possibly of some duration—for when Harald Bluetooth furnished the surviving sons of Eric Bloodaxe with more ships and a new army, and Hakon had to decide whether to confront them at once or discreetly retire and look for reinforcements, he was rebuked in notable fashion by an old bonder called Egil Woolsark. 'Your father,' he told Hakon, 'never sought advice on how to retreat, and no such advice will you get from me.' So Hakon turned towards the enemy, and in great relief the old man admitted, 'With all this long peace I've been afraid of dying of old age in a straw-bed, though what I had hoped was to fall in battle fighting for my lord. And now it looks as if I'll get what I want.'

Egil Woolsark had his wish and died after fighting, not merely with courage, but with great cunning in a fierce battle north of Trondheim, where another of Eric's sons was killed and Hakon again had the victory. But war continued, and on the island of Stord, at the mouth of the Hardanger fjord, Hakon was surprised by a Danish fleet under Harald, son of Eric Bloodaxe; and there, after fighting against heavy odds, Hakon the Good was killed. According to the saga of the kings he had reigned for twenty-six years, and in his last battle carried the sword Quern-

biter that Athelstan of England had given him. After his death
the remaining sons of Eric ruled the middle parts of Norway—
with their irrepressible mother to give them advice—but in the
south there were semi-independent earls or kinglets, and in the
north the powerful earl Sigurd of Lade dominated all the folk-
lands of Thrandheim. Too strong for direct attack, Sigurd was
defeated and done to death by conspiracy, but his son Hakon who
succeeded him was a greater warrior than his father, and for
many years Norway was torn by strife between him and the
sons of Eric, the oldest of whom, and nominally the king, had
now acquired a nickname and was known as Harald Greycloak.
In his impotent and partial reign internecine war brought wide
distress, and Norway was stricken by famine.

Denmark showed greater promise. While the sons of Eric prevented the growth of Norway, Harald Bluetooth extended and
consolidated his kingdom, and by his conversion to Christianity
may have hastened its progress towards civilisation. His boastful
inscription on the Jellinge stone was both overstated and premature, for it cannot truly be said that he ever ruled all Norway,
even indirectly, and it is impossible to suppose that Denmark was
unanimous in acceptance of the new faith; but his missionary
enterprise was vigorous, and parts of Norway were subject to
him. His kingdom included lands about the Wick, especially on
its eastern side, and in Sweden perhaps the coast of Halland as
well as Scania; the Danish islands, and Jutland as far south as
the great protective earthwork called the *Danevirke*, that marked
his frontier against the German empire. The efforts he made to
extend his dominion farther were bold, imaginative, and unscru-
pulous.

When earl Hakon of Lade, his strength exhausted by war, fled
from Norway, Harald Bluetooth made him welcome at his court;
where he was also entertaining his nephew, a grandson of Gorm
the Old, whose viking voyages had been so well rewarded that
he was known as Gold-Harald. Then there followed—if the
saga of the kings can be trusted—plot and counter-plot of black-
hearted duplicity. Earl Hakon, from the safety of Denmark, fostered resistance in Thrandheim to Harald Greycloak, and Gold-
Harald demanded from Harald Bluetooth a share of his Danish
kingdom. In great anger king Harald refused to contemplate such

a division, and Gold-Harald threatened civil war. So, on Hakon's advice, the king offered Gold-Harald the neighbouring realm of Norway. That he proposed to acquire by inviting Harald Grey-cloak to visit him with the promise of restoring certain lands that Greycloak—sometime his ally, but now his enemy—had previously ruled; and if Greycloak accepted the invitation, Gold-Harald could deal with him.

That part of the plot went according to plan. Harald Grey-cloak came with three ships to Limfjord in Jutland, and Gold-Harald met him with nine. Greycloak was killed, but Gold-Harald did not live to enjoy his victory or his promised kingdom. For earl Hakon and king Harald had decided that Gold-Harald was too ambitious to be trusted, and Hakon, leading a larger fleet into Limfjord, gave battle and took him prisoner; and Gold-Harald was hanged. Then the king and earl Hakon led a great expedition into Norway, and met no resistance. Hakon was made earl over all the lands in the west and north, and another Harald who had lately joined the Danish king—Harald the Grenlander, a great-grandson of Harald Fairhair—became king in the south of Norway. He who gained most from plot, counter-plot, and invasion was earl Hakon; for he, secure in a great dominion, declined to pay king Harald Bluetooth the taxes that he owed.

But Hakon came to the king's assistance when the German emperor, Otto II, marched against him to take reprisals for Danish raiding into the country beyond the Elbe.—Otto the Great was lately dead, and it seems that Harald Bluetooth thought the time propitious for a southerly enlargement of his lands.—Hakon came from Norway with a great host, and in Schleswig at the Danevirke there was a battle in which the emperor's army was repulsed. Supposing that a conclusive victory had been won, Hakon re-embarked his army to sail north again to Norway, but was held by adverse winds in Limfjord; and when the emperor launched a new attack, the Danes were defeated and king Harald had to sue for terms.

According to the saga, it was at this juncture that Harald Bluetooth and all his army accepted Christianity; and the king, in his new-found enthusiasm, is said to have insisted that earl Hakon, before leaving Limfjord, must also be baptised and take with him to Norway priests and other learned men to convert the northern kingdom. If it is true that Hakon submitted to baptism under duress—and it would be a gross error to disbelieve everything in the sagas that to a modern mind may seem improbable—the water of baptism merely inflamed his temper, and a pretty picture follows of the explosive mood in which he put to sea. No sooner had he left Limfjord than he cast ashore all his Christian passengers, and in a heathen fury harried in Scania, and wherever else he found it convenient to land, and defiantly reverted to heathen ways by making a blood-offering to Odin. Harald Bluetooth, though now a Christian, was still as liable to militant indignation as any heathen, and followed with a punitive host that wasted the land of Norway as far as the Sogne fjord; but earl Hakon re-established his authority, and still refused to pay Harald tax or tribute.

This violent story of upper-class manners—which explains so much of early Scandinavian history—now approaches a climax of domestic rebellion, and the death of Harald at the hands of his son Sweyn; who later became famous as Sweyn Forkbeard and fathered a son, Cnut the Great, whose fame would be even larger.

Sweyn, like Gold-Harald, demanded his share of the Danish realm, and Harald Bluetooth again refused to contemplate division. Then Sweyn mustered a fleet, and found a potent ally in Palnatoki, a lord of the redoubtable viking confederacy in Jomsburg. They attacked Harald—who was about to renew his war with Norway—in Ise fjord in the north of Zealand, and though Harald was too strong for them, he got his death-wound in the battle, and Sweyn succeeded him as king of Denmark. But his alliance with the vikings had unforeseen consequences, and by their leader, earl Sigvaldi, he was constrained to go to Jomsburg, which lay on the south side of the Baltic, east of Rügen, and perhaps on land now lost to the sea near Peenamünde, in the country of the Wends; who were a Slavonic people resident there since the seventh century. The Jomsburgers were a pirate horde of whom inflated stories were later told. It was said of them that they were dedicated to war, and in a fierce, maritime way lived monastic lives and held all goods in common; but probably they were professional freebooters like Algerian corsairs in a much later century, and Jomsburg may have been established by Harald Bluetooth himself as a Danish out-post. The Jomsburgers were evidently dependent on the goodwill of the Wends who lived on either side of them, and their alleged purpose in kidnapping Sweyn was to force him into marriage with Gunnhild, daughter of king Burislaf of Wendland, and persuade him to give in marriage to Burislaf his sister Thyra. It is difficult to accept this story with perfect confidence, but it may be noted that genealogists name Gunnhild as the mother of Cnut the Great; though she is sometimes said to have been the sister of Boleslav, king of Poland.

There follows, in the saga of the kings, another story that cannot be presented with a guarantee of literal truth. In a scene of ritual drunkenness, however, it exposes the temper of braggart daring that must have accompanied or instigated the inception of many a viking enterprise; so the story may be true in a general or impressionistic way. King Sweyn, it is said, held a funeral feast or 'grave-ale' for the father he had killed, to which the Jomsburgers and the chiefs of Scania were bidden; and at the feast men drank deeply and made wild promises. Sweyn drank to the memory of his father, and pledged himself to invade England and kill its king. Then, because Denmark was nominally Christian, the Jomsburgers had to drink, in the largest of beakers, to Jesus Christ; and earl Sigvaldi, having drunk also to his father, pledged himself to go into Norway and kill earl Hakon. His brother Thorkel took the same oath, and others followed suit. A little note of realism intrudes—the evidence of increasing drunkenness—when it is recorded that a man named Vagn swore to go into Norway and not return until, having killed an otherwise unknown person called Thorkel Leira, he had lain with Thorkel's daughter Ingibjorg. And realism continues into the following morning, when the Jomsburgers are said to have had doubts about the wisdom of their behaviour, but to have decided to bring matters to a conclusion as soon as possible.

Earl Hakon's son Eric was now grown to manhood, and he and his father made such hearty preparation for battle that they met the Jomsburgers with a fleet of nearly two hundred ships off the coast south of Romsdale, and decisively beat them. Eric was merciful to some of his captured enemies, who pleased him by a display of courage while they awaited execution, and set them free; thus allowing a romantic conclusion to the tale, for

Vagn, who had sworn to kill Thorkel Leira and lie with his daughter, did both. But Hakon got little credit for his successful battle, because the rumour spread that to ensure victory he had made a sacrifice to Odin of his son Erling. Yet he ruled well over the western parts of Norway, and kept peace in the land until, in his latter years, he gave way to uninhibited sensuality and made enemies of the many men whose daughters he took for brief, unmannerly satisfaction. His conduct provoked rebellion, he was forced into flight, and was shamefully killed while hiding in a pig-sty. His greatness in battle, his generosity and wisdom in peace, were forgotten, and he was remembered as Hakon the Evil.

Sweyn Forkbeard had neither joined the Jomsburgers in their attack nor fulfilled his promise to give Thyra, his sister, to Burislaf of Wendland. He had, indeed, repudiated his queen, Gunnhild, Burislaf's daughter. After the battle in which the Jomsburgers were defeated, their leader, Sigvaldi, who had escaped the slaughter, came again to Denmark, and insisted that Sweyn should keep his word and send Thyra to Wendland. She went reluctantly, unwilling to wed an old heathen man, and got no comfort from a promised dowry consisting of the lands in Wendland that the unhappy Gunnhild had been given for a jointure. She would neither eat nor drink, and after several days made her escape, with those who had escorted her, and fled into Norway; where there was now another king.

Olaf Tryggvison, who ruled for five explosive years from 995 to 1000, stands out even among so many untrammelled figures as though his life were illuminated by a light of absolute though slightly insane heroism. Christian missionaries have often been set apart from the ordinary run of mankind by a dedication built upon bravery and humility; but Olaf's dedication to the Christian cause was made of courage and total arrogance. A great-grandson of Harald Fairhair, his mother had fled from the sons of Eric Bloodaxe after her husband's murder, and Olaf had been born while she was in hiding. He spent his childhood in Sweden and his youth in Russia, where for some years he was a slave, but rose to favour under king Vladimir of Novgorod. Service in Wendland, where he married a daughter of Burislaf, was followed by service under the emperor Otto II; and then he took to seafaring and war in England, France, and Ireland.

While his ships were harbouring in the Scilly Isles he met a Christian hermit from whom he received baptism, and in Ireland, some little time later, he got news from Norway that earl Hakon in his old age had lost favour with his people, who would welcome a king of Harald Fairhair's blood. Olaf, with five ships, sailed north and east, by the Hebrides and Orkney, and came into Norway near Trondheim, where he found the country in open rebellion against Hakon. The great earl was killed; Eric, his son, fled into Sweden; and Olaf was acclaimed as king. He travelled fast and far through the land, and was accepted everywhere, even in the south where Danish rule had been established. Then, having gathered friends about him and persuaded them to his purpose, he declared his intention to christen all Norway. East of the Wick, where Harald Bluetooth's missionaries had preceded him, he met no resistance, but north of the Wick there was opposition, and Olaf at once let it be seen that he was utterly determined to promulgate the faith, and in his own way. In the words of the saga: 'Those who gainsaid him he mishandled sorely. Some he slew, some he maimed, and some he drove from the land.'

As he had begun, so he continued. His kingly rule became a single-hearted mission, his zeal never flagged. From the Wick he went west to Agdir, north to Rogaland, and in Hordaland, where the bonders were prepared to resist, he won their compliance by giving his sister Astrid in marriage to a local magnate. Near the Sogne fjord he dominated a great assembly by a show of force, and secured wholesale conversion by the superiority of his strength. At Lade he burnt a famous temple, and provoked a rebellion so serious that he had to retire to the Wick. There he entertained the idea of marriage to Sigrid the Haughty, queen of Sweden, who appears to have regarded the proposal with some favour until he insisted that her baptism must precede their nuptials. To which Sigrid answered that although she would not abandon the older faith in which she had been brought up, she had no objection to his worshipping whatever god he chose. Whereupon, if the saga can be trusted, Olaf exclaimed, 'What would I be doing, marrying a heathen bitch?', and struck her on the face with a glove. After which there was no more thought of a wedding.

When spring came he mustered a large army and went north again to deal with the stubborn people there, who for the second time faced him with an armed and rebellious multitude. They would have nothing to do with baptism, but said that he must join them in the older ritual of a blood-offering to the gods. He temporised, and promised to meet them at Lade on the south shore of the Trondheim fjord, in the season proper to blood-offering. There he went with thirty ships, and on the first day there was a great feast, 'and men were very drunk,' and all slept peacefully. But in the morning, after mass, Olaf summoned the multitude to hear him. He was willing, he said, to make a blood-offering with them, if that was what they wanted; but it would be the greatest blood-offering ever known. For he would sacrifice, not beasts, but men; and not slaves or criminals, but the greatest in the land. And name by name he pointed to a dozen of their chiefs.

The rebels admitted defeat—he had thirty ships in the fjord —and when they had obediently submitted to baptism, Olaf took hostages for their good behaviour. There was fighting before the conversion of the north was completed, and Olaf celebrated success by establishing a market that became the town of Nidaros, and building there a great ship of thirty benches called the *Crane*. To Nidaros came ships from Iceland, where Thangbrand, the Saxon priest, had been reaping converts with a sword, and the Iceland sailors also accepted the Christian faith; among them was Leif, son of Eric the Red, who later found a new land beyond the Atlantic.

For nearly five years Olaf continued his violent and compulsive mission, and in the second half of his short reign Thyra, the sister of Sweyn Forkbeard, arrived in Norway as a fugitive from the heathen court of old Burislaf of Wendland. She sought help from Olaf, and being, as the saga says, both handsome and 'smooth-spoken,' she soon married him.—He had had several wives before her.—They spent a winter in Nidaros, and before spring she had persuaded him, against his better judgment, to undertake an expedition to Wendland to claim the lands, or their equivalent, that she had been given as a dowry. He built another ship, the

Long Serpent, even larger than the *Crane*, and Thyra bore him a son who, to their grief, died in infancy. Before leaving Norway he sent two missionaries to Iceland, to complete the task that Thangbrand had failed to accomplish, and Leif Ericson went to Greenland, charged with the same duty. When Olaf, on Thyra's behalf, sailed to Wendland, he had a fleet of sixty longships.

His reception was friendly. There appeared to be no great difficulty in coming to agreement with king Burislaf, and Olaf settled down to spend an idle summer. But while he had been busy with the christening of Norway, a change had occurred in the political balance of the northern countries. Sweyn Forkbeard of Denmark had married Sigrid the Haughty of Sweden, and Sigrid—or so the saga says—remembered her abominable treatment at the hands of king Olaf, and urged the Danish king to take revenge: a revenge that honour also demanded, because Olaf had married Thyra without seeking her brother's approval. There was a Norse proverb, 'Women's counsel is ever curst,' and if the saga tells a true story, the proverb was then given new substance. For Sweyn Forkbeard sent messengers to his son-in-law, Olaf of Sweden, and to earl Eric, son of Hakon the Evil—now married to Sweyn's daughter Gyda, a friend of the Swedish king, and a man of power in the Baltic—to tell them of Olaf Tryggvison's expedition and bid them join him in war against Norway. They did as they were told, and between them mustered a great fleet. Then Sweyn commanded Sigvaldi of Jomsburg to go to Wendland, to spy on Olaf Tryggvison and lead him into a trap.

Sigvaldi used guile to prevent Olaf from sailing westward till he had heard that Sweyn and his allies were ready for battle, and then, by displaying a pilot's knowledge of the shoal waters off the coast of Wendland, persuaded Olaf to divide his fleet and let the greater number head out to sea while he, with eleven ships only—but they were of the largest sort—followed Sigvaldi through shoreward channels which the Jomsburger said were safest for vessels of deep draft. But when Sigvaldi was off the island of Svold he rowed to shelter behind it, and Olaf's ships faced battle against the great fleet of Sweyn Forkbeard and his allies. Of his largest vessels—the *Long Serpent*, the *Little Serpent*, and the *Crane*—Olaf made a fortress by lashing them together, and awaited the onslaught.

It was a fierce and bloody fight that followed, with conclusion in sight from the very beginning, but no thought of yielding in the mind of Olaf of Norway. Slowly but inevitably all his ships were taken save only the *Long Serpent*, which remained, a stubborn stronghold, in the midst of fearful defeat. Spears and arrows flew thickly into the doomed vessel, but its indomitable crew were drunk with battle, and from its bulwarks swept with their swords all boarders back.

Foremost among those who pressed upon the *Serpent* was Eric Hakonson, and beside king Olaf, in the main-hold of the ship, was an archer of great note called Einar. Einar, in quick succession, shot two shafts at earl Eric. The one sank into the tiller above his head, the other went between his arm and his ribs. Then, to a Finnish bowman beside him, earl Eric said, 'Shoot that big man in the hold.'

The Finn shot, and as Einar was bending his bow for the third time, the Finn's arrow struck his bow in the middle and burst it asunder.

Said king Olaf to Einar, 'What broke so loudly?'

'Norway,' said Einar, 'out of your hands.'

There, in that answer, lie both the virtue and the perplexity of the sagas. If Snorri Sturluson, who in the early part of the thirteenth century gathered old stories and wrote the saga of the kings, invented what Einar said, then Snorri—for a moment, at least—was a poet akin to Aeschylus and Dante and Shakespeare. For such a compression of imagination as lies implicit in that simple statement is possible only to genius of the highest poetic order. But it is also possible to a very good man of the ordinary sort whose mind and vision are magnified by danger, and whose faith, loyalty, and determination are concentrated by that danger on a fine but narrow purpose. Did Snorri invent it, or did Einar speak it and someone within hearing escape to remember, for all time's remembering, the perfection of his heroic epigram?

None can reply with any certainty, but perhaps the genius of literary invention is more rare than was heroism, and its native voice, in the age of heroism; and the odds may be that Einar's recorded answer is the true voice of a man who fought in his last fight for Olaf Tryggvison.

Olaf fought till the swords of his men were too blunt to bite, and then, with his shield above him, leapt into the sea and was drowned beneath his ship. And Norway was again divided, but Eric Hakonson, who ruled in the north, had the greater share of authority.

Chapter VII

THE FOREIGNERS IN SCOTLAND AND IRELAND

W HERE history fails, geography may offer explanation. There is no record of the vikings' first arrival in Scotland, but a map will show the course and manner of their early forays.

The parts of Scotland nearest the Norwegian mainland are the archipelagos of Orkney and Shetland—Lerwick in Shetland is only two hundred and twenty miles from Bergen in Norway—and before Norwegian pirates found the profit of an Irish voyage they must have discovered the islands; and probably used them as a forward base.

Until recent years it was commonly supposed that Orkney was settled in the reign of Harald Fairhair by those chieftains who would not submit to his despotism and sought refuge in the islands west over sea; but that is an opinion which cannot now be entertained. The evidence of Norse graves and the nature of Orkney place-names have persuaded both archaeologists and philologists that the islands were occupied by Norwegian immigrants as early as 800; and as Skye, and Lambay Island near Dublin, were invaded in 795, it is safe to assume that Orkney and Shetland had been visited before that. The islands were probably discovered, as Iceland was, by some lone adventurer who went home and told his neighbours that there was fertile land for the taking —a land almost unoccupied—no more than two or three days' sailing to the west; and restless or land-hungry men went out to settle it.

It is almost certain that the earliest Norse immigrants were not warriors, but a simple people intent only on making a living by cultivation of the soil and taking what they needed from an easy harvest of the sea. The islands, it appears, were thinly inhabited, and that may have been the consequence of punitive war by a Pictish king of northern Scotland. The Norse population was replenished by the successive tides of viking enterprise, and in the time of Harald Fairhair was rapidly increased by the flight of intransigents who found his radical assumption of authority intolerable. Because these lately arrived incomers retaliated with predatory raids on Norway, Harald found it necessary to mount an expedition and subdue the islands, and after warfare in Orkney and the Hebrides it is probable that he confirmed his great supporter, Rognvald of Möre, in the *de facto* earldom of the islands which the family of Möre had already established.

That seems the likeliest explanation of the establishment of a Norse power, on the farthest fringe of Britain, which maintained its existence till the fifteenth century. After its incorporation into Scotland, the importance of Orkney vanished utterly, but for a couple of hundred years, under its Norse earls, it either dominated or disturbed all the northern parts of Scotland, extended its warring influence into Ireland, and occasionally pin-pricked parts of England.

The earldom of Orkney was the earliest foundation of a disciplined Norse power in Britain, and the most enduring except for William the Conqueror's achievement in England. Mention has been made of Ragnar Lodbrok's probable occupation of the islands, but the first of their rulers, known within the scope of history, was Sigurd, a brother of Rognvald of Möre. He formed an alliance with Thorstein the Red, a son of Olaf the White, king of Dublin, and Aud the Deep-minded, who was a daughter of the powerful chief Ketil Flatnose. Ketil appears to have established himself in the Hebrides—presumably by conquest—before 857; and Aud, his daughter, lived in her widowhood for some time in Scotland before going to settle in Iceland where her family acquired riches and great distinction. As early as this there was apparently a nexus of kinship that spread across the western sea from Dublin to the Denmark Strait.

Sigurd and Thorstein the Red added much of the northern end of Scotland to the Orkney earldom, and both died in their wars. Sigurd was succeeded by Turf Einar, a son of earl Rognvald who had the misfortune to be one-eyed and base-born —his mother was a slave—but who ruled with great vigour, and in the high manner of the north was a poet as well as a warrior. His first task was to rid the islands of two Danish vikings who had made their home there, and he lived to revenge the murder of his father. Halfdan Longlegs and Gudrod the Splendid, two of Harald Fairhair's trouble-making sons—he begot far too many —killed Rognvald of Möre, and Halfdan retired to Orkney with sufficient strength to drive out Turf Einar. But quickly the earl returned with ships from Caithness, and gave battle to Halfdan who, when darkness fell, jumped overboard and swam to the nearest shore. In the morning search was made for him and other fugitives, and Halfdan was discovered on the small, flat island of North Ronaldsay. He was killed, and Einar, with a deliberate ferocity for which no explanation can be offered, cut a blood-eagle on his back. To this mutilation he added verses that express a defiance, equally deliberate, of the Norwegian king; and the uneasy suspicion remains that Harald Fairhair had connived at the murder of his old friend. Einar was forced to pay a fine of sixty gold marks, but he lived thereafter for many years, and from him were descended all the earls who ruled in Orkney till the thirteenth century.

The history of the Hebrides was very different. That they were occupied by the Norse, and became a Norse dominion, is evident from their Norwegian name, the *Sudreyar*, or southern isles: they lay south of Orkney, some of whose earls claimed title to them. They appear to have been occupied without much fighting. Iona was plundered in 795, and twice again in 802 and 806; and in that decade Skye was invaded. It is admittedly difficult to believe that Ketil Flatnose established himself by friendly negotiation, and there were others who settled in the islands about the same time; but there is no record of a battle—though farther south, in Ireland, battles were frequent—and the probability is that the Hebrideans had no social coherence whatever: no trace or shadow of a political structure from which a leader could appeal, even to local feeling, and summon a local resistance.

That the islands, unlike Orkney, were thickly inhabited is certain, and the Norse invaders never so dominated and conclusively fashioned their dominion in the Hebrides as they did in Orkney and Shetland. The evidence of place-names is sufficient proof of that. In the northern isles almost all the names are Norse. But in the Outer Hebrides—in the long island of Lewis— the proportion of Norse to Gaelic names is four to one; in Skye it is three to two; and farther south, in Arran and the Isle of Man, only one to eight. The impact diminished as it travelled south. It is significant that after the discovery of Iceland there was a considerable exodus from the Hebrides; for the Celtic minority that acquired much influence in Iceland came either from Ireland or the Sudreyar. And gradually thereafter the remaining Norse behaved as they did elsewhere, in France and Ireland and eventually in England: they abandoned their early ferocity and disclosed adaptability. They put on the local colour of their new surroundings, and disappeared into a native populace which they had invigorated. In their later history the people of the Hebrides became the last intransigent and most stubborn defenders of the old Celtic habit of Scotland; and the Celtic wombs that bore a race of fighting men who found their pleasure in noble music and melancholy song were assuredly the daughters of wombs that had been impregnated by viking fathers.

The incoherence of life in the Hebrides, the lack of any formative social structure, was obviously the consequence of a Celtic revulsion from the discipline and co-ordination of effort—from the co-ordination of thought and temper—that are essential to a large and purposive community; for in the much greater and more populous country of Ireland the same sort of revulsion existed and governed its manner of living. It cannot be said that there was no social structure in Ireland, but its society was so fragmented that its units were too small and numerous to find a common course or common authority when the whole country became a prey to purposive aggression. The unit of society was a little rural community ruled by a petty king and called a *túath;* there may have been a couple of hundred of them, but until the Foreigners came and settled, there were no towns in Ireland. From the example of Wales and Ireland and western Scotland it is manifest that the pressure and organisation and commercial diligence inseparable from urban existence were profoundly repugnant to the Celtic mind. It was the Norsemen—mercantile in habit as they were warlike in temper—who built Dublin and Wexford, Waterford and Cork and Limerick.

The little kings of the Irish *túatha* did acknowledge, or tend to acknowledge, local over-kings, and eventually the over-kings came together in the confederations that created Ulster in the north, Connaught in the west, Munster in the south-west, Leinster in the south-east, and Meath in the middle. The possibility of combination was recognised when the Norsemen came; who, from an early stage, had to fight for anything they wanted. As the years went by, and the Norse invasion became more serious, the aggressors had to fight more bitterly and on a larger scale; for aggression, as it seems, persuaded the Irish to acquire a habit of association with their fellows from which, in isolation, they had been averse. The Irish, when they had learnt how to associate, inflicted on the Foreigners many grievous defeats; and the persistence of the invaders, in contempt of humiliation and disaster, can hardly fail to excite admiration. There is, indeed, some evidence, or apparent evidence, that defeat could inspire new effort; though a historic obscurity covers the nature of such inspiration. In a local sense it may have been political or economic; but it may have been due to nothing more than a sense of heroic responsibility that would now be called romantic. The Scandinavian kingdoms were themselves fragmented, and policy—if such it can be called —depended on individuals and their unpredictable moods.

In the early years of the Norse invasion of Ireland there were two outstanding men who left names to be remembered; of whom the elder, as it seems, came of the blood of the royal house of Westford, the little kingdom beside the Oslo fjord. He was called Turgeis by the Irish annalists—his name may have been either Thorgest or Thorgisl—and by the time of his arrival, in or about 834, Ireland may have seemed ripe for conquest. The longships had shown themselves on all its coasts, there were alien fleets on the Boyne and the Liffey, the vikings had penetrated far inland. Monasteries in Ulster had been plundered, there had been raids on the south coast, and Norsemen had sailed up the Shannon; forays had been made into Connaught and Leinster. Turgeis, it is said, came with the intention of asserting his sovereignty over all the foreigners in Ireland, and with him, or closely following him, fell new tides of invasion upon a land whose domestic circumstances were such as to give the invaders great advantage.

The native king of Munster was also an ambitious man, and in his attempt to secure the high-kingship made war upon his neighbours as ruthlessly as any viking. Into the chaos of civil strife came the unrelenting invaders, and Turgeis brought his ships into Lough Neagh. He captured Armagh, the ecclesiastical capital that St. Patrick had founded, and having driven out the abbot acquired the abbacy and its revenue. In a limited sense he may be said to have won the north of Ireland—he had quelled, that is, his immediate opponents—and in a bold attempt to extend his conquests he sent a fleet up the Shannon to Lough Ree in the very heart of the country: on the one side Connaught was menaced, on the other, Meath. He sacked the great monasteries of Clonmacnois, famous as a centre of pious art, and Clonfert that Brendan the Navigator founded. The peril to all Ireland seemed very great, but Turgeis is said to have thrown away all his gains with a gesture of savage arrogance. He let his wife, Aud, or Ota, parade as a heathen priestess before the high altar at Clonmacnois, and if the story is true this gross impiety so enraged the men of Meath and their king Maelsechlainn, who was later king of Tara, that they rose against him, captured him by a stratagem, and in 845 drowned him in Lough Owel.

It is possible that Aud, his high-spirited and demonstrative wife, has also a place in an Arab history that tells of an embassy dispatched by the emir of Cordova to protest against viking depredation on the coast of Spain, where the longships had lately been swarming 'like dark-red sea-birds.' The emir was Abd-ar-Rahman II, and his ambassador was sent to the king of the *Madjus*—the magi, or heathen—who lived on an island distant from the mainland, a three days' voyage. From what part of the mainland the ambassador set sail, history does not record; but close to where the heathen king lived were other islands, and the mainland too. It may be that the ambassador went to Denmark, but the court of Turgeis is a not improbable destination, for the hostilities about which complaint was made occurred in 844, and that was the year before Turgeis died. The heathen queen, moreover, was called by the Arabs *Noud;* and conceivably a foreign ear would so have altered an unfamiliar name. She showed the ambassador so much favour that his companions took fright and begged him to be discreet. He went less often to court, and the queen asked him why. She laughed at his reason, and told him that among the *Madjus* there was no jealousy, because divorce was easy; and that may be the voice of queen Aud who postured so brazenly before the high altar at Clonmacnois.

The year of Turgeis' death was the year when Ragnar Lodbrok led his fleet up the Seine to Paris, and the Irish annalists speak again and again of the great armadas that came about their coasts in that decade. All Norway and all Denmark appear to have put to sea, like lemmings, and it was probably the weakening of both countries by those warlike migrations that made possible the unifying rule of Harald Fairhair and Harald Bluetooth. But Scandinavia had great resources of ships and men, and in the years that followed the death of Turgeis the towns of Dublin and Wexford, Waterford and Limerick were founded in despite of hard fighting in which the Norse invaders were often beaten.

Until 850, or thereabout, aggression came mostly from Norway, but in that year a Danish fleet of a hundred and forty ships launched a great and prolonged attack on the Norsemen; who are said to have been taken by surprise and defeated with a heavy loss of life, goods, and the women they had acquired. The triumphant Danes plundered Dublin and Dundalk, and in Carlingford lough, north of Dundalk, gained another victory after initial reverse and a battle lasting three days. The annalist declares that fortune was reversed, and victory secured, by the Danish leader's timely decision to ask help of St. Patrick, who had been deeply offended by the Norsemen's evil deeds; and with a carefully measured justice explains that 'the Danes were a people with a kind of piety; they could for a time abstain from meat and from women.' Their manners, however, were abominable, for after the battle they boiled meat in cauldrons resting on the bodies of the dead; or so it is alleged in what some may choose to dismiss as a fine flight of Gaelic fancy.

What did occur was an alliance between Danes and Irish that introduced a new element into the struggle which was to torture Ireland for many years to come. The Danes went to the assistance of a local king who was fighting against the Norse in Munster, and the Irish learnt how to profit from the opposing interests of the Foreigners; but, on the other hand, there were Irish recreants, or the sons of mixed marriages, who saw advantages to be got by joining the Foreigners. The original, clean-cut distinction between native defender and foreign aggressor was progressively obscured, and it cannot be doubted that men and women of uncertain parentage became ever more numerous. Among those of sufficient distinction to be mentioned in Irish annals and Norse sagas there are well-known examples of mixed marriage; many Gaelic names occur in Icelandic genealogies; and it is not to be supposed that the humbler sort were immune from the passion that moved their betters. This is not to suggest that Ireland was losing, or would lose, its sense of identity; but it does appear that in a new and larger flux of interest the Irish were given a chance to develop their political genius.

The Danish triumph was short-lived. A newcomer restored the *status quo*, and like Turgeis a few years before, bequeathed a name to history. Olaf the White, a 'war-king' as *Landnámabók* calls him, came with another great fleet in 853 and quickly asserted his strength. There is good authority for saying he was descended from a king of the Uplanders in Norway, and may at some time have ruled in the Hebrides, or over part of them. A distinguished ancestry helped him to establish in Dublin an authority to which Danes, Norsemen, and some native Irish submitted; though not all the Irish were acquiescent. At least one victory over the new invaders is positively recorded, and there is a story—interesting if not wholly convincing—of a king in Leinster who won so many battles that his own subjects grew jealous of his success and expelled him. Of greater moment is the behaviour of the Danes, most of whom left Dublin for renewed war in England; though some entered Irish service.

Olaf, who was married to Aud the Deep-minded, daughter of Ketil Flatnose of the Hebrides, left Dublin not long after his conquest—his purpose unknown, but viking enterprise is a likely explanation—and when he returned was joined there by Ivar, a Dane, who was probably Ivar the Boneless, son of Ragnar Lodbrok. They engaged in war, as it seems, in the middle parts of Ireland, but were repulsed by Aed Finnlaith, the high-king, and prudently withdrew to the seaward state of Dublin. It is possible that Olaf ratified a treaty with Aed by marrying his daughter; but to accept this one must also believe that Olaf the White is the same man as the Olaf of whom Irish annals tell; and that is not certain. Lack of certainty, indeed, haunts all the chronicles of these dark and furious times, for chronology is often vague, and one account may contradict another; genealogy is ever suspect, for genealogists often enhanced a pedigree by fastening great names to its stem; and where all action depends upon the will or fancy of an individual —where there is no visible policy against which to judge the likelihood of a reported action—it is difficult to estimate the probability of its having occurred. It is fairly certain that many of the tales of dauntless war that characterise the Irish annals are much exaggerated, and that so-called battles were, in fact, often concluded, after a preliminary skirmish, by arrangement rather than a fight à outrance; and it is equally probable that some battles—a few, but enough to colour imagination and haunt men's memory—were fought with great bitterness to a bloody conclusion.

The extreme mobility of the vikings also creates difficulty. They used the sea with a contemptuous freedom, their vessels were swift and not dependent on fair winds. Many were small enough to navigate rivers and reach far inland—to sail the sea-lochs of Scotland and the broad inland loughs of Ireland—and sometimes their captains had such open minds, such a brutal innocence and so wide a knowledge of geography, that if the banks of the Seine offered no profit, they would try their luck in the Shannon, and failing to find booty there, turn about and look for fortune in the Thames. When the Moors repelled them they returned to Ireland, and when the resources of the Hebrides looked thin and scattered they provisioned their ships and sailed to Iceland. But few of their younger sons remained in Iceland. When the days lengthened and the air grew mild, they set out again for Norway and England, for the Baltic and Byzantium; or coldly to Greenland. It is not surprising that the ancient chroniclers sometimes confused the actions and the voyages of an Olaf or a Thorlief with those of a contemporary Eric or Ivar; and the difficulties nowadays of deciding who was who, when was when, and where was where may be insuperable.

It appears that Olaf the White used his Dublin stronghold as a base for sea-borne warfare rather than as a centre from which to extend his power in Ireland. He made voyages to the south-westerly parts of Scotland, against the Welsh of Strathclyde and the people of Galloway, and in 870 he and Ivar—or so say the Annals of Ulster—laid siege to the great natural fortress of Dumbarton on the north bank of the estuary of the Clyde, and after four months of patient warfare took and plundered it. From Scotland they returned to Dublin, in a fleet of two hundred ships, with not only the riches of the fortress, the capital of Strathclyde, but a great spoil of English, Welsh, and other captives to be kept for profitable service, or sold with greater profit into slavery. If the Ivar of this story is Ivar the Boneless, he too was a persistent wanderer, for he must have left Dublin to fight against Alfred in England, before returning to join Olaf in war against Strathclyde. And if, as another story relates, Olaf had married, for the third time, a daughter of Kenneth MacAlpine, king of Scots—who united under one throne the two kingdoms of the Picts and Scots—then Olaf, on previous, unknown excursions had had larger dealings with Scotland than anyone has recorded. It is entirely appropriate that a man of whom so little can certainly be told—beyond an importance that none disputes—should have died in a place that no one knows and in an unremembered year. He probably died in Ireland, but possibly on some distant viking cruise.

In the Hebrides, about this time, there were several viking leaders whose names survive, and whose reported activities do something to illustrate the hazardous freedom of the western sea. One of them was Onund, who with three companions led a fleet of five ships through the islands, plundering as they went, till they reached Barra at the southern extremity of the Hebrides. There they found the redoubtable Irish king Kjarval, who captured Dublin after Olaf's death, and as Kjarval also had five ships it appears that his purpose was the same as Onund's: one was a Norse viking, the other Irish, and that was all the difference between them. There was a battle that Kjarval lost, and in his one remaining ship he fled southwards; but Onund and his companions shared the spoils of battle and settled down to winter in Barra, on whose north shore there is an admirable harbour for longships. For three years they used the island as a base for summer voyaging—they plundered impartially in Scotland and Ireland—and then returned to Norway.

There they joined the great host of those who were still opposed to Harald Fairhair, and fought against him in the decisive battle of Hafrsfjord. In the Icelandic saga of *Grettir the Strong* it is said that Onund's ship lay in the very middle of the battle, and Harald himself, having cleared another, was preparing to board when Onund was wounded. He stood on the forecastle, one foot on the gunwale, and warded off a spear-thrust; but in so doing he leaned backwards, and one of the king's forecastle-men struck hard and cut off Onund's leg below the knee. He was carried to a nearby ship belonging to a man called Thrond, and in the general flight which then began, his life was saved.

He recovered from his wound, he was fitted with a wooden leg, and acquired the nickname of Onund Tree-foot. With Thrond and others he debated the feasibility of renewing the war against Harald, but decided that the king was too strong for them; and Thrond and Onund returned to the Hebrides where, says the saga, they met many of their friends. Their intention was to go to Ireland, where Thrond had a brother in Irish service. The brother was called Eyvind Eastman—which suggests that he and Thrond were of Swedish birth—and he had married a daughter of the Irish king Kjarval, or Cearbhall in the Irish spelling. The marriage, and the alliance it betokened, appear to be authenticated by the birth of a son, called Helgi the Lean, who became well-known.

Kjarval's capture of Dublin had been facilitated by a Norse exodus from Ireland into northern England where it was thought, presumably, there would be richer reward; but Eyvind had remained and accepted responsibility for defence of the east coast. He did notable service, it appears, in defeating two formidable Hebridean vikings—Norsemen 'gone native' or sons of Norse fathers and Celtic mothers—who had harried in Ireland with a fleet of eight ships until Eyvind's discouragement of their activity; whereupon they had returned to the Sudreyar and plundered Scotland instead. In their old quarters in Barra, Onund and Thrond had some communication with Eyvind—but without meeting him —and undertook the task of eliminating the Hebrideans. They followed them, again with a fleet of five ships, to the island of Bute at the head of the Firth of Clyde, and in a very fierce battle, in which the Hebrideans were defeated, Onund survived a hand-to-hand conflict in a singular manner: to stiffen his hold on a lurching deck he stood with a log of wood to shore up his lost leg, and when with his shield he warded off a sword-stroke, his opponent's sword bit into the log and stuck there, giving Onund an easy chance to lop off his arm. Or so the saga has it.

Before going to Ireland Thrond and Onund wintered again in Barra. In Dublin Thrond's brother Eyvind recognised Onund as the man who had fought against king Kjarval in the fleet action off Barra, and but for Thrond would have treated him roughly. They were reconciled, however, and after returning to the Hebrides, and living there for some time, Thrond and Onund sailed away from Scottish waters and made their home in Iceland.

There appears to be substantial truth in the story of Onund—it has a likely look—but once again chronology presents a difficulty, for Kjarval is said, by the Irish annalists, to have died in 888, and it is improbable that the battle of Hafrsfjord was fought before 890. An adjustment of dates is not impossible, however, and the account of Onund's voyaging may well be realistic though not accurate in all respects. His warlike engagements are modest in comparison with those reported of king Kjarval, who is alleged to have undertaken sixteen campaigns in just over forty years: against Dublin in 846; in support of the foreign Irish in 859; against the Norse in 860, 861, and 862; against Leinster in 853, 864, 870, and 871; against Meath in 859; against Munster in 864, 871, and 879; against Connaught in 871 and 873; and against Decies in 874.[1]

While Norse and Danes were busily occupied in France and England, Ireland had some respite from war—though there was civil war in Dublin—but in 914 Rognvald, a grandson of Ivar the Boneless, took Waterford, and two years later his brother Sigtrygg recaptured Dublin. Against the new menace the high-king Niall Glundubh mustered the forces of twelve petty kings and gave battle to the Foreigners near Dublin; but died in a great defeat. Then for half a century there was confused and inconclusive fighting, and though in the south the Foreigners' towns of Waterford and Wexford, Cork and Limerick, grew stronger, there were Irish victories to counter them, and Muirchertach 'of the Leather Cloaks,' a son of Niall Glundubh, emerged as a tireless and often successful leader. Olaf Sigtryggson, who came into Ireland after having been driven out of York in 945, was for many years the most powerful of Norse rulers, but in 980 his son was killed in a great battle at Tara in which the high-king Maelsechlainn broke the power of the Dublin Foreigners.

They recovered, and Dublin was ruled by Sigtrygg Silkbeard, a son of Olaf and the Irish princess Gormflaith, sister of a king of Leinster. But in Munster two remarkable brothers had made themselves masters of their native province and taken Limerick.

[1] A. O. Anderson, *Early Sources of Scottish History*.

One of them died, and the survivor, Brian Boru, was acknowledged king of Munster. He advanced victoriously into Leinster,
and captured Dublin. He made peace with the defeated Norse, and
after negotiation with Maelsechlainn was recognised as high-king.
There followed a dozen years of peace, but then Leinster rebelled
and Sigtrygg of Dublin, in alliance with its king, went over sea to
Orkney to ask support from earl Sigurd. In April 1014, Brian
was killed and the Norse alliance defeated at the momentous battle of Clontarf; and because the battle may have had larger impli-
cations than conflict between Norse and Irish usually had, it will
be discussed at some length in a later chapter. Here it is enough to
say that no major attempt was thereafter made to establish Norse
supremacy in Ireland, but Sigtrygg continued to rule Dublin for
another twenty years—apparently a good and able king, it was he
who struck the first coinage in Ireland—and gradually the process
of inter-marriage and its products obliterated differences between
the Foreigners and the natives, and Norse and Dane forgot their
origin and became Irish.

In Scotland, in addition to the early loss of the islands, there
had been some infiltration into the south-west from Norse settlements in Ireland. The *Gall-gael*, or Foreign Scots, gave its name to
Galloway, and coastal parts of Argyll were colonised. Occasional
raiders from Ireland penetrated far inland—as far as the upper
Forth and Dunkeld—and Olaf the White, who captured Dumbarton, may have established some connexion with Kenneth Mac-
Alpine. But only in the north and the west was the Norse impact
productive of material change and lasting result, and the earldom
of Orkney, its outstanding achievement, became a power which
played its part in the shaping of Scotland.

Turf Einar, the earl who avenged his father's death by killing a
son of Harald Fairhair, was succeeded by his son, Thorfinn I; who
fortified the Norse blood of his family by marrying a grand-
daughter of Thorstein the Red, who was the son of Olaf the
White and Aud the Deep-minded.—The ruling families of the
northern world lived in a network of blood-relationship.—Thorfinn's son married Edna, a daughter of the Irish king Kjarval, and
their son was the earl Sigurd who fought and was killed at the
battle of Clontarf. He had married a daughter of king Malcolm
II of Scotland, and their son was earl Thorfinn II, called the

Mighty, who extended his dominion far into Scotland and created in the north an unassailable power.

By policy or war he was involved with kings of Norway and Scotland, and his life is the more interesting because it shows alike the strength of a man and the weakness of a system. By his grand-father the king of Scots Thorfinn was given the earldom of Caith-ness, though it is doubtful whether Caithness, which then covered the north of Scotland as far south as the Dornoch Firth, was really within Malcolm's gift; and his earldom of Orkney he shared, in his early years, with his two brothers. This awkward division brought him into conflict with Olaf the Stout, then king of Norway—and after his death more splendidly known as St. Olaf—who as an adjudicator seized the opportunity to assert his superiority over the islands. It was a short-lived superiority, for presently Olaf was driven out of Norway by Cnut of Denmark, and Thorfinn's habit of life was governed only by his own inclinations and the rude cir-cumstances of his time. Because the islands of Orkney lay on the sea-road from Norway to Ireland they had constantly to be guarded against passing vikings; and after the death of king Mal-colm, Thorfinn was deeply engaged in war in Scotland.

Malcolm II was succeeded by his grandson Duncan, to whom Shakespeare gave the larger gift of immortality—'After life's fitful fever he sleeps well'—and Duncan, as it appears, resented the fact that Thorfinn occupied so much of northern Scotland. In 1018 the late king had won a great victory over the Northum-brians and pushed his southern frontier forward to the Tweed; his successor, perhaps, was tempted to complement Malcolm's suc-cess by extending his kingdom to the Pentland Firth. There are, unfortunately, no Scottish records, and the war that ensued is de-scribed only in the saga of the earls of Orkney. In a general way the saga is convincing—it shows a knowledge of the country, and the strategy of the war is made very clear—but in some respects it is garbled, and in others it is probably guilty of exaggeration. There is, however, no doubt that Thorfinn was the victor, and there can be little doubt that his victory so weakened Duncan as to make it easy for Macbeth to supplant him.

In Norway Olaf the Stout tried to regain his kingdom, and was defeated in the great battle of Stiklestad by the Trondheim fjord. His half-brother Harald Hardrada—he who was to be killed at

Stamford Bridge—was wounded, but escaped death or capture with the help of a handsome, fair-haired young man called Rognvald, who was Thorfinn's nephew. Rognvald and Harald Hardrada went east to the court of king Jaroslav in Novgorod, and after some years of lively adventure Rognvald sailed west over sea to claim his share of the earldom. He and Thorfinn made a very friendly agreement, and went into partnership: a partnership in well-organised piracy.

Their base was secure, for Thorfinn commanded the northern end of Scotland and the Hebrides, while Rognvald took care of Orkney and Shetland. In the summer—this was the pattern of their life for about eight years—their longships sailed to the south for plunder in Ireland and the southern parts of Scotland, the Isle of Man, and northern England. After a sea-battle off Man Thorfinn spent the better part of a summer in England, and fought two pitched battles there. Then, when autumn threatened gales, they would return to their twin earldoms in the north to repair their ships and drink away the dark months of the year. Being men of equable and generous temper they had no quarrel until a kinsman of Thorfinn's was driven out of Norway, and with a large retinue came into Scotland to live at his expense. Rognvald objected to paying his share of their entertainment, and sailing to Norway won support from king Magnus, called the Good, who was his foster-brother. War broke out—a tragic and most regrettable war—between Rognvald and Thorfinn, and after several changes of fortune Rognvald was killed, with many of the men whom Magnus of Norway had given him.

Thorfinn again ruled his great realm alone, but thought it expedient to make his peace with king Magnus. He sailed east to Norway, and found Magnus preparing for war against Denmark. There was some hardy conversation between them, and their dispute was still unsettled when Thorfinn turned about and went back to Orkney. His luck held, for Magnus died in Denmark, and with his successor, Harald Hardrada, Thorfinn was on friendly terms.

It is evident, too, that in Scotland he enjoyed friendly relations with Macbeth, whose realm may have been only a fraction of the Scotland that modern maps enclose. Macbeth ruled for seventeen years, till 1057, and there is no record of dispute between him and Thorfinn. Peace lay upon the north—a peace imposed by Thor-

finn's strength—and in or about the year 1050 both he and Macbeth were able to make a pilgrimage to Rome. For some twenty
years Thorfinn, ruling from his court in the West Mainland of
Orkney, dominated a great part of Scotland: in the saga he is said
to have ruled nine earldoms, all the Hebrides, and a realm in Ireland; and a much later authority[2] thought it probable that he held
all the northern provinces down to the river Tay, the Hebrides,
and the Celtic parts of Galloway. For a score of years he held
them in untroubled peace, but when he died, in 1064 or 1065, his
conquests fell away, because his rule was personal and there was
no system or established pattern of government to maintain it.

Except for Cnut in England and the dukes of Normandy, he was
the greatest of the Norse or Danish rulers over-sea, and perhaps
the most prudent; for having won a large dominion he made no attempt to push his luck towards excess. In the saga of the Orkney
earls there is a description of him that, by its lack of compliment,
seems to be realistic. He was, it is said, 'the tallest and strongest of
men, ugly, with black hair, sharp features, a big nose, and a somewhat swarthy countenance. He was a man of great energy, and
greedy both for wealth and honour. He was lucky in battle, skilled
in the arts of war, and of dauntless courage.'[3]

[2] W. F. Skene, *Celtic Scotland*.
[3] *Orkneyinga Saga*, trans. A. B. Taylor.

Chapter VIII

TRIUMPH AND DECLINE

I N the two preceding chapters it appeared convenient to carry the tale of Norse or Danish enterprise and development so far, in the one case, as the decisive sea-battle of Svold; and in the other to the middle years of the eleventh century. The history of Norway and Denmark and their many incursions into parts of Britain is manifestly relevant to the story of England, and Scandinavian history is incomprehensible without some discussion of those who dictated it. The apparent effort to surround and enclose Britain by occupation of the Scottish islands and parts of Ireland was begun by hazard, but in the course of time may have acquired so obvious a pattern that completion of it seemed to offer strategic advantage; and this possibility will be considered in the following chapter. But the focus of the story is England, and now it is necessary to return in time to the final year of the ninth century and the death of Alfred.

He was succeeded by his son Edward, in whose time most of the Danelaw was subjugated, and the great inaugural work of king Alfred seemed to be moving to triumphal conclusion. The new reign, however, made an inauspicious beginning, for Edward's cousin Ethelwold—son of Ethelred I—abducted a nun, and seizing the royal residences at Wimborne in Dorset and nearby Christchurch in Hampshire, declared his intention 'to live there or die there.' When Edward moved against Wimborne, however, the atheling abandoned his nun, made his escape in darkness, and rode to Northumbria where he was made welcome by the local Danish army. In 901 he arrived with a fleet on the coast of Essex, and the following year led a raiding Danish force out of East Anglia into Mercia and part of Wessex. Edward retaliated, harried in East Anglia as far north as the fens, and successfully withdrew the greater part of his army; but the Kentish men, indifferent to discipline, lingered and were caught by the Danish army. In a battle where losses on both sides were heavy a Danish king, so-called, and the atheling Ethelwold were both killed.

For half a dozen years there was peace in the land, and there is some evidence that the relationship between Danes and English was growing easier. The Danish acceptance of Ethelwold as an ally and a leader presumes a diminution of the original antagonism between Scandinavian foreigners and Anglo-Saxon natives; and when Englishmen were able to buy land from Danish owners— as in two cases they certainly did—there is a probability that commerce had begun to cross the frontier and offer an alternative to war. But still the final argument was war, and in 909, for no recorded reason, Edward mobilised an army in Wessex and Mercia and for five weeks harried in Northumbria. He imposed a peace which the Northumbrians broke in the following year. While Edward was in Kent, waiting for a fleet of a hundred sail which he had summoned from the ports of Wessex, the Northumbrians invaded English Mercia, and having pillaged as far south as the Bristol Avon, turned about and crossed the Severn, and plundered along its western bank till they came to Bridgnorth in Shropshire. Then they headed east, and were caught near Tettenhall in Staffordshire. They had undertaken their great raid in the belief that the main part of the English army was with the fleet in Kent, but Edward had moved swiftly and at Tettenhall won a decisive victory in which three Danish 'kings' were killed, and the power of Northumbria was broken. In the same year a Norse or Danish fleet from Brittany sailed up the Severn and did some damage; but most of the ships were either wrecked or destroyed.

Ethelred of Mercia died in 911, but his death did not weaken its military strength, for he was succeeded by his widow Ethelflaed, who was Edward's sister and who, as Lady of the Mercians, led their army with gusto and great ability for the next eight years. Ethelred had held London, but after his death both London and Oxford, 'and all the lands which belonged to them,' passed into Edward's possession; who, having ordered forts to be built on his northern border at Hertford, on either side of the river Lea, crossed to Maldon in Essex and camped there while a great earthwork was raised at Witham on the Roman road from London to Colchester. He received the submission of many of the Danes of

East Anglia, while in Mercia his redoubtable sister was protecting her frontier, and preparing for an advance beyond it, by building forts at Bridgnorth and Tamworth and Stafford. Northumbria was no longer a menace, and Edward could now make plans for a conclusive war against the eastern Danelaw without fear of interruption from the north.

In 913 there was some minor fighting in the midlands when the restless Danes in Northampton and Leicester attacked their neighbours to the south, but in the following year a more serious situation hindered the projected war against East Anglia. Another fleet from Brittany, either Norse or Danish or a mixture of both, appeared in the Severn estuary, and plundered on either side. A bishop was captured near Hereford, who had to be ransomed for forty pounds, and the invaders were so persistent as to offer a battle to an English army drawn in the main from Hereford and Gloucester. But the Danes were soundly beaten and then agreed to give hostages as a guarantee of their promised departure; and still Edward had to keep watch on all the south side of the estuary from Cornwall to Avonmouth, for twice again they tried to break inland. Hunger finally defeated them, and from the Severn they sailed to Ireland in the hope of finding easier provender.

Now Edward resumed his war against the Danelaw, and the high-spirited Lady of the Mercians built more forts. She built ten in all, for protection against west and north and east, and all were shrewdly sited to take tactical advantage of the lie of the land. Edward, moving north to Buckingham, threw up earthworks on either side of the Ouse, between Oxford and Bedford, and earl Thorketil, who commanded at Bedford, submitted to him, as did some from Northampton. In 915 the English king occupied Bedford, and having built another fort there, marched into Essex and fortified Maldon to protect the earthwork at Witham against sea-raiders. Earl Thorketil, and those who followed him, took advantage of the peace he had made with Edward to leave England and seek better fortune in France.

Resumption of the English advance in 917 provoked strong resistance. When a fort was built at Towcester on Watling Street, and another nearby, the Danish armies of Northampton and Leicester and the country farther north made a determined attack on Towcester but were driven off; and other armies from Huntingdon and East Anglia built a new base at Tempsford on the river Ivel, from which they advanced on Bedford; but failed to take it. A third attack was also rebuffed, but the Danes were left in possession of Tempsford. In the meantime king Edward's valiant sister had led her Mercians against Derby, and taken it; and when, before autumn, the assault on Tempsford was renewed, its ramparts were stormed, its garrison put to the sword, and the Danish king of East Anglia fell among his men.

It cannot be supposed that the dead king had had much authority, for in their summer campaign the Danes had shown little evidence of a unified command; but stubbornly they fought on, and in Essex were defeated at Colchester and Maldon, despite seaborne reinforcement in the second battle.

King Edward maintained the offensive and led half the Wessex militia to Towcester, where the army of Northampton submitted to him 'and sought to have him as their lord and protector.' The militia was relieved by its second division, the advance continued to Huntingdon, and there the people of that district submitted. Then he marched south-east to Colchester again—avoiding Cambridge where a Danish army lay—and in Essex, where he was acclaimed by many Englishmen who had been under Danish rule, the remnant of the East Anglian army swore to keep peace 'with all with whom the king wished to keep peace.' Then the army at Cambridge submitted.

There remained Danish forces in strong positions at Leicester, Stamford, Nottingham, and Lincoln, but in 918 the Lady of the Mercians took possession of Leicester, and there was offered the allegiance of York; which by this time was in danger from the Norsemen of Ireland, who had begun to visit the uneasy parts of northern England. But Edward's warlike sister died in Tamworth before she could bind York in a Mercian alliance, and her death roused in Edward's mind some doubt as to the continuing loyalty of Mercia. Advancing against those Danes who stood beyond the Welland, he had a fort built south of the river opposite Stamford. The Danes surrendered, and Edward was about to move against Nottingham and Lincoln when he heard of his sister's death, and marched instead to Tamworth. There he was reassured, for the Mercians acknowledged his authority, and the three kings of west Wales accepted him as their over-lord. Nottingham and Lincoln, isolated now, surrendered without resistance; and Edward of Wessex was king of all England as far as the Humber.

The Danes were a practical people. They had fought fiercely for land which was manifestly worth the trouble of fighting, and having won it they had quickly settled down to work it. They had retained the habit of arms, and could mobilise a local army for the protection of their property and that custom of living which they preferred; and on occasion their local leaders had shown themselves capable of great audacity, their armies of extraordinarily rapid movement. But they had never sought the power of permanent combination, they had not united to establish a sovereign state in England. They had been satisfied with the independence of small autonomies, and when they were faced with a choice between the sacrifice of their independence or the loss of their good land, they sensibly decided to keep the latter. But in the north of England there were less prudent people on the move, and the Anglo-Saxon Chronicle records the fact that in 919 king Edward led an army to Thelwall on the Mersey and there built a fort which was to be occupied and manned, and sent another army, also from Mercia, to repair the walls of Manchester and garrison the town.

The Norsemen of Ireland—White Foreigners or Black Foreigners and the sons of viking fathers and Irish mothers—were overflowing from the Scandinavian settlements and looking for new land in the north-west of England. There is no certain record of their arrival, but the antiquarian and the philologist can show proof that the Wirral peninsula was colonised in the earliest years of the tenth century, and it is almost certain that before the century was half a hundred years old there were settlements not only on the coast, but far inland, from the Mersey to the Solway. Between Dublin and York there was much coming and going, and very little, as it appears, to obstruct the passage of adventurers.

The history of the north of England is, at this time, very obscure; but after the Danes' destruction of the Northumbrian kingdom—which had reached the Solway—the king of Strathclyde may have taken advantage of confusion to extend his rule into north-west England, and against the threat from Ireland the

king of Scots and the king of Strathclyde seem to have made
common cause with the English of northern Northumbria, whose
ruler exercised an uncertain power from Bamburgh on the coast
opposite the Farne Islands. There was a viking chief called Ragnald who, on the authority of the chronicler Symeon of Durham,
defeated Constantine, king of Scots, and Aldred of Bamburgh
at Corbridge in or before the year 915; and two or three years
later—years of which nothing is known—the Annals of Ulster
record an expedition led by Ragnald, 'king of the Black Foreigners,' from Waterford in Ireland to the river Tyne in Northumbria where a Scottish army, having routed the main body of
the invaders, was defeated by Ragnald himself, who had waited
in ambush till he could attack the Scots from the rear. And
Symeon of Durham says that in 919 Ragnald took York and was
accepted as its king.

In the following year there was an Irish invasion of Cheshire,
led by Sigtrygg of Dublin, and in response to the new challenge
that he and Ragnald offered, king Edward mounted the penulti-
mate expedition of his remarkable reign and achieved his final triumph. He marched first to Nottingham, where he ordered the
building of a bridge across the Trent, and from there to Bakewell
in the Peak district. At Bakewell, says the Chronicle, there came to
him the king of Scots and Ragnald, Aldred of Bamburgh, and the
king of Strathclyde, to acknowledge him as their over-lord; and
according to the Chronicle of Melrose, Sigtrygg of Dublin also
did homage. If Sigtrygg submitted it can only have been to superior strength—Edward must have caught him in an untenable
position—but for the others a nominal acknowledgment of Edward's superiority was manifestly sound politics. It left them in undisputed possession of their several lands, it imposed on them some
slight obligation to live at peace with each other, and it paid tribute
to Edward's guardianship of the Irish gateway: his three forts on
or near the Mersey, at Runcorn, Thelwall, and Manchester, were
their protection against new invaders from Ireland.

Ragnald of York died in 921 and was succeeded, without opposition, by Sigtrygg: they were evidently related, and may have been
grandsons of Ivar the Boneless. The aging king saw no occasion to
interfere, but three years later he undertook a punitive expedition
into Cheshire, to suppress rebellious Mercians and their Welsh al-

lies; and in July 924, he died at Farndon on the Dee. He had reigned for twenty-five years and created a kingdom such as no Anglo-Saxon had ruled before him. He had been prudent and patient in preparing his war against the Danelaw, and in its prosecution had shown an imaginative strategy for which, in part, he may have been indebted to his sister, the Lady of the Mercians. Both of them built fortresses, which appear to have been earthworks of great extent, possibly surrounded by a ditch and able to accommodate an army of considerable strength; but who first devised such a stronghold, and then perceived the strategic importance of a system of fortresses, is not known. But Edward the Elder was imaginative in other ways, an innovator in administration, and the division of England into shires was the consequence of his extension of a West Saxon practice into English Mercia, and its imposition on the established divisions of the Danelaw. He could be ruthless in asserting his will, and though he had nothing of his father's interest in literature, he may have had an eye for good design; for he minted an elegant coinage.

He was succeeded by his son Athelstan, who had been brought up at the Mercian court of Ethelred and Ethelflaed, and was said to have been king Alfred's favourite grandson. Independently of his succession in Wessex, Athelstan was recognised as king in Mercia, and his unquestioned authority in the midlands was acknowledged by the overtures for an alliance that Sigtrygg of York was quick to make. They met at Tamworth in January 926, and a pact was sealed by the marriage of Sigtrygg and a sister of Athelstan. But Sigtrygg died in the following year, and when the Danes of York accepted as their king his son by a previous wife, Athelstan promptly revealed an aggressive temper and his royal ambition. The boy, Olaf, got support from his uncle Guthfrith, a Norse king in Ireland, but Athelstan drove them out of York—the boy escaped to Ireland, Guthfrith to Scotland—and, as his father had done, exacted recognition of his supremacy from Constantine, king of Scots, and Owain of Strathclyde, from two Welsh kings and Aldred of Bamburgh. Guthfrith, eluding capture, led an attack on York, but was defeated and surrendered. Athelstan pulled down the fortifications which had been built within the walls of York, and having imposed his peace upon the north, turned his attention to Wales. The Welsh princes submitted without the formality of battle, agreed to pay him tribute, and recognised the river Wye as their frontier with the shires of Hereford and Gloucester.

In the Anglo-Saxon Chronicle the record of Athelstan's reign is deplorably thin. There are fewer than a dozen entries, and several refer to events of minor or domestic interest, such as the death of a bishop and the drowning at sea of Athelstan's brother Edwin. But the chronicler says that in 934 he 'went into Scotland with both a land force and a naval force, and ravaged much of it'; and to the year 937 is attached the description, in alliterative verse, of the great battle of Brunanburh to which reference has already been made. The later English chroniclers—Florence of Worcester, Symeon of Durham, William of Malmesbury, and Henry of Huntingdon—accept these dates, and two of them slightly expand the bare entry of 934 in such a way that Athelstan's progress through Scotland takes on the aspect of a triumphal march.

According to Henry of Huntingdon: 'Since there was none to begin to oppose him or to persevere in opposing him he advanced everywhere through the country and raided at his will, and returned with the bays of triumph.' Symeon of Durham says that he 'subdued the enemy, and wasted Scotland with a land army as far as Dunnottar . . . and with a naval force harried it as far as Caithness'; and adds that he 'put to flight Owen, king of the Cumbrians, and Constantine, king of Scots.' But there is no mention of the battle in which he put them to flight, no word of any resistance to him on the long march to Dunnottar—which is not far from Aberdeen—or on the long return to the English border. Three years later, however, there is the urgent, poetic description of the fierce fight at Brunanburh in which Athelstan opposed the strong confederacy of Constantine II, king of Scots; Olaf Guthfrithson, whose father was king of Dublin, and his cousin Olaf Sigtryggson, sometime king of York; and the Welsh of Strathclyde under their king.

What seems probable is that the original chronicler, filling as best he could the empty record of neglected years, confused the course of events and put the victorious march before the successful battle. It is not likely that Athelstan would march deliberately through Scotland before having crushed its army—a march that would invite retaliation and summon the confederates to arms—

but if, having soundly beaten his enemies, he saw, a few years later, the signs of incipient revolt, he would have an excellent reason for undertaking a long progress 'to show the flag.'

The argument for reversing the recorded course of events is strengthened by the Icelandic saga of Egil Skallagrimson in which, almost certainly, the fight at Brunanburh is described, though it is given another name. The chronology of the sagas is often inaccurate, but the story of Egil is connected with events abroad to which it must have some relation in time, and according to the saga Egil fought in a battle, which seems to have been Brunanburh, soon after Athelstan's succession to the throne, and revisited him several years later. But if, as the Chronicle avers, the battle was fought in 937, Egil would probably have come too late to see him; for Athelstan died in 939. If, however, it was fought in some year between 927 and 934, there was ample time for Egil's second visit and for a march to show the flag in mutinous lands beyond the Tweed.

What may well have occurred—and what would be a logical sequence of events—was that Athelstan, when he marched to York in 927 to evict Olaf Sigtryggson and his Irish ally Guthfrith, took the opportunity to demand acknowledgment of his supremacy from Constantine of Scotland and the others who are recorded as having done homage with him. Then, a year or two later, resentful of the indignity to which he had been forced to submit, Constantine formed an alliance against England, and Athelstan defeated him at a place called Brunanburh, which was probably on the shore of the Solway Firth. If any reliance can be placed on the dating of events in Egil's saga, the battle was fought before 934, and it was within the next few years that a new wave of unrest persuaded Athelstan that it would be politic to march through Scotland and prevent revolt by a show of force. Brunanburh was the only major battle of his reign, and the earliest possible date for it will best suit the authority and great reputation he undoubtedly enjoyed, not only as a sovereign in Britain, but as a king who could treat on terms of equality with his fellow monarchs in Europe.

In 919 his sister Eadgifu had married Charles the Simple, king of France, who a few years before had ceded land in the province that became Normandy to the Norse invader Marching Rolf.

When Charles lost his throne Eadgifu took their son Louis to England, where he grew up under Athelstan's protection. Another sister, Eadhild, was married to Hugh the Great, count of Paris; and a third, Edith, to Otto, son of Henry the Fowler, king of the Germans, who after Edith's death became emperor of the Romans. In 936 Eadgifu's son Louis, known as Louis d'Outremer, was restored to the French throne with the help of his uncle Hugh. Another of Athelstan's wards was Alan, later called Alan 'of the twisted beard,' who was a grandson of Alan the Great, last ruler of all Brittany; and it was with Athelstan's help that he regained some part of his patrimony.

Early in his reign Athelstan had welcomed a mission of goodwill from Harald Fairhair of Norway, who had grounds of common interest with him in their hostility to vikings. In the early years of the tenth century England was fortunate in its relative freedom from viking depredation—though it was much exposed to Norse attack from Ireland—and that relief it owed to the vikings' preoccupation with northern France, where Charles the Simple's original grant to Rolf was expanded by the arrival of new adventurers who sought land on which to settle. Having unified his own kingdom, Harald Fairhair had good reason to respect a monarch who ruled much of Britain and dominated all, and there is no reason to doubt the Norwegian tradition that his son Hakon, known as Athelstan's fosterling, was brought up in the English court.

Rex totius Britanniae: so Athelstan styled himself, and the exaggeration is not unpardonable in a man whose regal power was so widely recognised, whose interests were scholarly and far-ranging, who was a great law-maker and in his laws made manifest his humanity. True to his West Saxon blood he spent most of his reign in his own country in the south, and there, to the great courts and assemblies that he convened, went the local rulers of his land, bishop and earl and thane, English magnates and Scandinavians from the obedient Danelaw, to hear what he commanded and do his will. But the imposing structure of his power rested on himself alone, and when he died in 939 his kingdom fell apart.

He was succeeded by his brother Edmund, a courageous and excellent young man; but before he could prove himself the

Norsemen of Ireland erupted and spilled in sudden conquest across the north of England. They were led by Olaf Guthfrithson, king of Dublin, whose father had been driven out of York when he went to the help of Olaf Sigtryggson, his cousin. York fell to him without a blow, and then his army ravaged widely through the midlands. He met resistance at Tamworth, but much of the country lay before him apparently apathetic and certainly impotent; for when Edmund mustered an army and met him at Leicester, the young king agreed to a treaty which ignominiously surrendered the shires of Leicester and Derby, Nottingham and Lincoln.

It is hardly possible to explain this sudden collapse except by the inference that Athelstan's power had been absolute, and bereft of his authority men had neither the knowledge of what should be done nor the will to act. But Olaf Guthfrithson had no inhibitions, and leaving the fat midlands behind him he marched northward over the Tees to conquer, or at least to plunder, beyond the Tweed. Death put an end to his ambition, and Olaf Sigtryggson, who succeeded him, inherited neither his vigour nor ability. King Edmund drove him out of the midlands, the Northumbrians expelled him from York. For a year or two he maintained a dispute with Ragnald, a brother of the older Olaf, whom the Northumbrians had made their king, but in 944 Edmund solved their difficulties by expelling both and re-taking York for England.

Edmund was rapidly increasing his strength, and his re-conquest of Mercia was welcomed not only by the English, but by its Danish inhabitants who had resented the brief imposition of Norse rule: to the settled Danes of the Five Boroughs the Norse of Ireland were foreigners and enemies. In 945, according to the Anglo-Saxon Chronicle, Edmund initiated what was probably intended to be a policy of mutual assistance with Scotland by ravaging 'all Cumberland'—or the southernmost part of Strathclyde—and granting it 'to Malcolm, king of the Scots, on condition that he should be his ally both on sea and on land.' Because of its situation Strathclyde must have been much influenced by the Irish Norse, and it seems likely that Edmund hoped for Malcolm's help in establishing a common defence against them. But before the alliance could be put to the test of action, Edmund

was killed at Pucklechurch in Gloucestershire, where he went to
the rescue of his seneschal, who had been attacked by a thief.
His sons were children, and the crown was given to his brother
Eadred, who for most of his reign was plagued by trouble in
Northumbria.

He was, to begin with, accepted as its king, and in 947, says
the Chronicle, 'Archbishop Wulfstan (of York) and all the councillors of the Northumbrians pledged themselves' to him; but
'within a short space they were false to it all, both pledge and
oaths as well.' Their reason for recusancy was the arrival of Eric
Bloodaxe, son of Harald Fairhair, who flattered the nobility—
some, it is probable, of Norse descent—with the prospect of
independence under a king of royal blood. There followed a
period of great confusion in which Eadred ravaged the land and
drove out Eric, only to make room for Olaf Sigtryggson from
Ireland; but he in turn was expelled by Eric Bloodaxe, who for
two years ruled in York in some splendour, until removed by
death in circumstances which are obscure but almost certainly
were violent.

Eadred died childless in 955, and his brother Edmund's sons
Edwy and Edgar were still boys: Edgar only twelve, and Edwy,
who became king, two or three years older. He was fortunate
in that he succeeded to a kingdom untroubled by foreign invasion,
and he had good advisers; but he appears to have had an unstable
temperament. In the year after his succession the Chronicle records that 'Abbot Dunstan was driven across the sea,' and the reason for the expulsion of so eminent a churchman—connected by
blood with the royal family—was apparently his officious behaviour when the young king stole away from the tedious ban-
quet that followed his coronation, and Dunstan found him, his
crown thrown aside, in the company of a young woman called
Algifu and her mother. It was probably the mother who secured
Dunstan's banishment, for Edwy married Algifu; and was punished for it. By his unforgiving clergy he was separated from
her on the grounds of too close a relationship.

There is no record of his subsequent behaviour, but apparently
he offended not only the clergy, but the leading men of Mercia
and Northumbria, who in 957 rejected him and took his brother
Edgar as their king. Edwy died in 959, and when the West Sax-

ons accepted Edgar the kingdom was re-united. Of him the
Chronicle speaks in a way that is strangely at odds with the
customary tale of violent triumph or dire disaster. 'In his days,'
it is said, 'things improved greatly, and God granted him that he
lived in peace as long as he lived; and, as was necessary for him,
he laboured zealously for this; he exalted God's praise far and
wide, and loved God's law.' One of his first decisions was to
recall Abbot Dunstan from exile, to make him archbishop of
Canterbury; and there is little exaggeration in saying that Dunstan
dictated the policy of the reign and Edgar transacted it. The
reform and enlargement of monasticism was Dunstan's guiding
purpose, and the goodwill of a zealous king was fortuitously
aided by the peace of his frontiers. It is significant that Edgar
deferred his coronation, which took place in Bath, until he was
thirty—the age at which a priest could be ordained—and that in
the ceremony the anointing was given a larger importance than
the assumption of the crown. By emphasising the peculiar relationship that a monarch thus accepted with God, Edgar established the precedent by which later kings claimed an authority
superior to that of popular consent.

It is possible that the fame of his piety brought about the most
distinguished occurrence, or reported occurrence, of his reign;
when, according to the chronicle of Florence of Worcester, he
sailed to Chester and there received eight under-kings of Britain,
who swore allegiance to him and on a certain day rowed him on
the river Dee, in a boat that he steered, from his palace to the
monastery of St. John the Baptist. This story, however, may be
only an embellishment of an occasion on which Edgar did in fact
receive the nominal submission of kings or princes in the northern
and western parts of Britain. The thirteenth century chronicler
Roger Wendover declares that Kenneth, king of Scots, did homage to Edgar in return for the cession to him of all the lands of
Lothian between the Tweed and the Forth; and in the age of
feudalism, in the next chapter of the history of western Europe,
there was not a feudal baron in Christendom who would not
have taken an oath of allegiance, to any king in Christendom, for
so great a reward. The only reason for doubting Roger Wendover's tale is some suspicion of Edgar's power to cede Lothian.

Edgar was a prudent king whose fortune it was to have a

temperament in tune with a period of peace. He acknowledged
the right of his Danish subjects to live under their own laws,
and the freedom he gave them advertised the manifest blessings
of English rule. His authority, and those to whom he delegated
authority, seem to have been unquestioned and unchallenged; and
it is pleasant to learn that he was small in stature but strongly
built, for it was, perhaps, a quiet, unobtrusive force of character
that helped to make his reign so uneventful.

He died in 975, and left two sons by different mothers. Ethelred, the younger, was only eight or ten, but Edward, his older
brother, was so handicapped by an unruly temper and ungov-
erned speech that many of the nobility would have preferred
Ethelred for their king. Edward was duly crowned, and in his
brief reign, troubled by divided opinion, some of the monasteries
which had been enriched and enlarged under his pious father and
Dunstan's influence were stripped of their recent endowment by
neighbouring landowners who may have distrusted the growing
influence of the church, and certainly resented the late diminish-
ment of their own importance.

Three years after his accession, Edward was murdered, at
Corfe in Dorset, where he had gone to visit his stepmother and
his half-brother Ethelred. It was the 18th March, and in the evening he rode back, after hunting, and outside the castle was surrounded by men of the household. A cry escapes that impenetrable scene—'What do ye, breaking my right arm?'—and the
young king, still upon his horse, was stabbed to death at the
instigation of unknown conspirators. Ethelred was too young to
have been involved, and there is no evidence that his mother was
implicated. But Edward was buried without royal honours, and
no one was punished for his death, though the Chronicle declares
that 'no worse deed than this for the English people was committed since first they came to Britain.' Edward, the unruly boy,
got a martyr's fame, and his tomb inspired a legend of the miracles wrought above it; while Ethelred was crowned king in an
air that was heavy with suspicion.

He lived to be called Ethelred the Unready—the redeless, the
man without counsel or decision—and he proved, indeed, the
worst of kings. He had no skill in war, no judgment in peace, he
was soft and indolent and could be witlessly cruel. Untrust-

worthy himself, he gave his trust to few except those who had
little claim to it, and unlike his father he was unlucky. If the peace
of Edgar's reign had been maintained, history might have treated
Ethelred more leniently, but within two or three years of his
accession England was again exposed to Danish piracy. Its new
assailants were, to begin with, no better and no more than pirates.
They harried the south coast from Thanet to Cornwall and withdrew to their ships, with what booty they might carry, before
anything more than local resistance could be mobilised. They
were a destructive nuisance, but for several years no worse than
that; and as, a hundred years before, Harald Fairhair's unification
of Norway had turned many of his indignant fellow-countrymen
into vikings, so now the cause, or a contributory cause, of this
new eruption was Harald Bluetooth's unification of Denmark
and partial conquest of Norway.

The vikings of this era had an advantage which their predecessors had lacked, for on the other side of the English Channel
there were now friendly ports where they could wait for a propitious wind and to which they could retire to dress their wounds,
repair their ships, and sell their plunder. Though Normandy had
acquired the Christian faith and the French language, its people
retained a lively sympathy for the men of their own breed who
were boldly pillaging the opposite shore, and so obvious, and of
such material benefit, was the assistance they got in Normandy
that Ethelred protested not only to duke Richard I—grandson
of Marching Rolf—but also, as it seems, to the pope. Papal intervention followed, and in 991 a treaty was agreed between Richard of Normandy, who had ruled his turbulent land for half a
century, and young Ethelred of England, by which each pledged
himself to give no help to the other's enemies, and to settle
peacefully disputes between them. This was England's earliest
recognition, in a political sense, of the new power which was to
play so large a part in its history.

The ill luck which attended Ethelred prevented any benefit
from the treaty, and before the year was out it became evident
that piracy had been a preliminary to war. A fleet of ninety-
three ships arrived off Folkestone, harried in Kent, and sailed
north to Essex. Near Maldon was fought the glorious and in-
sanely heroic battle in which Byrhtnoth of Essex, indignantly re-

fusing the invaders' demand for blackmail, stood aside while they marched across a causeway and waited, before attacking, until they had brought their full strength into line of battle. Byrhtnoth was killed, the most gallant of his thanes followed him to death, and Ethelred and his craven Witan agreed to the shameful transaction that he had rejected, and bought a transitory peace for a first payment of ten thousand pounds of gold and silver. The leader of the invasion appears to have been Olaf Tryggvison, the great warrior who, when he became king of Norway, baptised it under threat of the sword.

In 992, says the Chronicle, Oswald, archbishop of York, 'left this life and attained the heavenly life.' If the statement can be accepted as true, Oswald was fortunate indeed, for he left a scene of shame. In that year an English fleet was mustered in the Thames, and command given to two bishops, a Northumbrian earl, and Alfric of Hampshire. The intention was to find and trap the invaders' fleet, but Alfric, in whom king Ethelred chiefly trusted, sent a messenger to warn the Danes, and himself deserted. The Danes plundered far and wide on the east coast, and an English army, mobilised against them, was betrayed by its leaders —perhaps of Danish blood—who took to flight when battle seemed imminent. To revenge himself on the faithless Alfric, Ethelred had his son blinded.

A year or two later a temporary but formidable alliance between Olaf Tryggvison and Sweyn Forkbeard, son of Harald Bluetooth, brought to England another great fleet of nearly a hundred ships, but an attack launched against London was defeated by valiant resistance. Though London was saved, the vikings did enormous damage in Essex and Kent, in Sussex and Hampshire—they reverted to old tactics, seized horses, and rode deep into the country—and again the king and his council bought a parcel of peace for the price, says the Chronicle, of sixteen thousand pounds and a winter's keep and quarters in Southampton. Sweyn went home to Denmark, and Olaf Tryggvison, already baptised by the saintly hermit whom he had found in the Scillies, was confirmed at Andover, with Ethelred as his sponsor, and promised never again to make war in England. He kept his promise, for thereafter he was fully occupied in Norway.

In 997 the war was renewed, and until its collapse in 1014 England was systematically pillaged and despoiled. A Danish fleet sailed into the Severn, an army ravaged Devon and Cornwall and south Wales. Next year it was Dorset's turn, where the Danes rode inland as far as they pleased. Then their ships came into the Thames and up the Medway, and laggard measures for the defence of Kent failed miserably. In 1000 the Danes went to Normandy and remained there for the better part of a year, presumably with the approval of duke Richard II. For a reason that history has forgotten Ethelred took this opportunity to mount a brief war against Strathclyde, but in the following year he could do little to save the southern counties from widespread devastation—though Exeter was successfully defended—and the vikings, contemptuously at ease, wintered in the Isle of Wight. In 1002 a year of peace was bought for twenty-four thousand pounds in money, and an agreement to provision the fleet; and Ethelred married Emma, the sister of duke Richard of Normandy. That there were political reasons for the marriage can hardly be doubted, and foremost among them must have been the English hope that Richard would close his harbours against the marauders. The alliance was to have larger results than that.

In the same year Ethelred uttered his infamous order for the massacre of 'all the Danish men who were in England,' because he had been told that they were conspiring to kill him and his councillors. It was manifestly impossible to perpetrate so monstrous a crime, but on St. Brice's Day, the 13th November, many were murdered and there is a tradition that among them was Gunnhild, a sister of Sweyn Forkbeard, who may have come to England as a hostage. At the great funeral-feast for his father, Sweyn had pledged himself to slay the English king or drive him from his realm, and if it is true that Gunnhild was murdered by Ethelred's command, Sweyn was assuredly reminded of his reckless oath, and in 1003 he himself led the invading army. He had lately defeated the warlike Olaf Tryggvison, he was on friendly terms with Sweden; he ruled Scania and much of Norway as well as his own kingdom, but though his strength was considerable he was not yet prepared for a war of total conquest. He carved bitter wounds on England, but met fierce resistance.

Exeter suffered first. Through the negligence or treachery of a Norman count to whom queen Emma had given command of the city, the Danes were allowed to enter, and Exeter was sacked. Then Wessex was plundered as far as Salisbury. In 1004 the fleet came to East Anglia, and Norwich was burnt. Plans were afoot to raise ransom-money when the Danes marched suddenly to Thetford, some thirty miles away, and plundered there. But their greed betrayed them, for a local magnate called Ulfkell or Ulfketil had raised an army and gave them so fierce a battle that they themselves said they had 'never met worse fighting in England.' Ulfkell had issued orders for the destruction of their ships, but those who were given the task failed him, and Sweyn escaped what might have been a conclusive defeat. He remained in England only till the following summer, but even in his absence England suffered; for the harvest failed and there was famine in the land.

In 1006 the Danes came again and plundered the south-east. A large army was mustered from all Wessex and Mercia, but through inefficiency or lack of will it failed to bring the enemy to battle, and in the autumn the Danes settled themselves comfortably in the Isle of Wight. A little while before Christmas they moved again, to plunder in Hampshire and Berkshire. They marched as far as Reading, and kept Yule in a movable feast, lighting beacons as they went. From Reading they marched to Wallingford over the Chilterns, and from Wallingford, in sheer bravado, across the north Wiltshire downs to somewhere near Avebury, where with contemptuous ease they defeated an English army and marched again, now past Winchester, to the coast. Their great raid had taken them fifty miles inland, and such was the terror they inspired that Ethelred and his council had to plead for a truce and buy peace. Sufficient food for the Danish army and thirty-six thousand pounds was the price that England paid for two years' respite.

A very belated attempt was then made to create some defences for the ravaged kingdom. Mercia was given a unified administration under an earl called Edric Streona, who was to acquire an evil reputation; and orders were issued 'over all England,' says the Chronicle, for the building of warships. A large fleet came into being, and early in 1009 it lay off Sandwich in readiness for the anticipated attack. But a Sussex man called Wulfnoth spread disaffection and sailed away with twenty ships to plunder the south coast for his own benefit. He was followed by a punitive fleet of eighty ships, but a great storm blew up, the pursuers were all driven ashore, and Wulfnoth burnt the abandoned wrecks. News of this disaster so unnerved king Ethelred and his councillors that they forsook the remnants of their new navy, and betook themselves home, as the Chronicle declares. The surviving ships were sailed into the Thames, and England was again defenceless.

The Danish offensive in 1009 was formidable indeed. The fleet came in two divisions, the one led by Thorkell the Tall, a brother of Sigvaldi, the Jomsburg chief; the second by his brother Hemming. Canterbury and east Kent immediately paid three thousand pounds for immunity, and for some months Sussex, Hampshire, and Berkshire were pillaged without any effective interruption from the army which Ethelred had mustered. The Danish army wintered in the Thames, and lived on plunder taken from either shore. In the new year London resisted attack, but the invaders marched to Oxford and burnt it. They returned to Kent to repair their ships, and sailed to East Anglia. They took Ipswich, and marched to give battle to an army, mustered from Cambridgeshire and East Anglia, that was commanded by the stout-hearted Ulfkell. The East Anglians were soon discouraged, but the Cambridgeshire men fought valiantly and lost heavily. The victorious Danes took horses and rode deep into eastern Mercia; Cambridge was burnt, and Northampton. Then they moved into Wessex, and the English army was successful only in avoiding them.

There is evidence now of real collapse, of the admission of defeat, and so dispirited was the whole land that no shire, it was said, would offer help to its neighbour. The Danish fleet wintered in England, and in 1011 Ethelred sued for peace. All eastern England, much in the midlands and much in the south, had been over-run, and 'all those disasters befell us through bad policy,' says the Chronicle, 'in that they were never offered tribute in time nor fought against; but when they had done most to our injury peace and truce were made with them.' The overtures for peace were apparently ignored, for in the autumn of 1011 the Danes laid siege to Canterbury, which was betrayed to them. They captured Alfheah, the archbishop, and took him to their ships at Greenwich. In the spring of 1012 they accepted, as the price of peace, the sum of forty-eight thousand pounds, and demanded more for ransom of the archbishop. He refused to let a ransom be paid, and the Danes, in a drunken fury, murdered him.

This outrage had the curious and unexpected effect of winning for Ethelred a powerful ally. Thorkell the Tall had defended the archbishop and offered all that he owned—all but his ship— to buy Alfheah's safety; and his quarrel with the majority of his fellow-countrymen was not healed by time. The Danish army left England before the end of the year, but Thorkell and forty-five ships remained with Ethelred.

To Sweyn Forkbeard it must have been evident that England had lost not only the power to resist but the will to resist, and the time was now ripe for its conquest. But the Danish king had seen much warfare by land and sea, and knew the vagaries of fortune to which ships and men were subject. There was no safeguard against gales of wind, and morale was sometimes as changeable as the weather. But by skilful, patient, and orderly preparation—by looking long and seeing clearly what should be done, and what was possible—the hazards of war could be reduced and the prospect of success brought very near. Sweyn spent another eighteen months on the preparation of his final effort, and some recent excavation in Denmark has discovered what may be remarkable proof of the intensive training to which his troops were subjected.

At Trelleborg in west Zealand is the site of a viking camp or fortress that is said to have been built about 1000. It covers an area of some sixteen acres and is surrounded by a circular rampart nearly twenty feet high. It was divided by axial roads into four quarters, and forming a square in each quarter were four wooden houses about ninety-six feet long; a ring of other houses, of a similar design but slightly smaller, stood gable-end to the inner wall of the rampart. That this was a military establishment is incontestable, and that it was able to accommodate a large force is equally certain. The antiquarians give it a date consistent with its having been built by king Sweyn, and it is hardly possible to imagine any reason for such building other than the concentration of soldiers for drill and discipline. A viking crew was subject to the natural discipline implicit in their acceptance of a leader, but in the viking age the only force reputed to have been subject to a deliberate or formal discipline was the Jomsburgers, with whom Sweyn in his youth had been associated.

In northern Jutland the most important waterway, to-day as it was a thousand years ago, is the Limfjord, opening on the west to the North Sea, on the east to the Kattegat. At Aggersund on the fjord is the site of another camp built to the same plan and with as mathematical a precision as Trelleborg; but the Aggersund camp was three times the size of Trelleborg. For a viking fleet about to sail west over sea to England, Limfjord was the natural place from which to start, the ideal place in which to muster; and it is very difficult to see the camp at Aggersund as anything but a military establishment designed for war against England. The idea of a viking army submitting to drill and train-ing for the offensive may seem strange, and incompatible with the fine freedom of an heroic age, but these camps admit no other explanation. It is not known if the Jomsburgers still existed as an organised force, but that Sweyn was still on friendly terms with the men of Jomsburg is shown by his employment of Thorkell the Tall, and Hemming, his brother; and it is possible that they had been re-organised. With his Jomsburgers to help him, Sweyn may have spent much of the years 1012 and 1013 in teaching an army of invasion its battle discipline.

He sailed in August, with the manifest intention of making himself king of England, and a clearly defined plan of campaign. In the political chaos and moral bankruptcy of England the men of the Danelaw would, almost certainly, welcome a Danish king, and having made his landfall at Sandwich, Sweyn sailed north to the Humber and in Lindsey, at Gainsborough on the Trent, disembarked his army. As he had anticipated, so it happened. Lindsey and Northumbria, the Five Boroughs and all England east of Watling Street, accepted him as king. He took hostages to ensure the good faith of those who had submitted, he com-mandeered horses and provisions, and with a show of force over-awed English Mercia. He marched to Oxford, then to Winchester, and both surrendered without a fight. From Wessex he turned east and launched an attack on London, which was defended, not only by its own levies and Ethelred's household troops, but by Thorkell the Tall and the crews of his forty-five ships; and there Sweyn's attack was rebuffed. He wasted no time on siege-works, but swiftly marched west again, by Wallingford to Bath, and received the submission of western England. Then he went north to his ships at Gainsborough. By this time, says the Chronicle, 'all the nation regarded him as full king. And after that the citizens of London submitted and gave hostages, for they were afraid that he would destroy them.'

Thorkell lay with his own men at Greenwich, and Ethelred with the English fleet in the Thames. The king sent his queen across the Channel to her brother in Normandy, and with her, his sons, the athelings Edward and Alfred; he himself spent Christmas in the Isle of Wight, and then prudently decided to join Emma in Rouen. Sweyn was left in possession of England, and in Dublin and the north of Britain plans were being laid for a major campaign, of which it seems likely he was cognisant, that was intended to bring Ireland under Scandinavian rule. Sweyn Forkbeard's mind may well have been filled with thoughts of his coronation when at Candlemas in the new year, on the 3rd February, he died.

Chapter IX

THE AFFAIR AT CLONTARF

C LONTARF, now a northern suburb of Dublin, was in 1014 the scene of a battle which occupies a major place in Irish annals, and requires more explanation for the importance accorded to it than the fact that the high-king Brian Boru died in the hour of a great victory over an army of dissident Leinstermen and Norse foreigners. Warfare between invaders and the native Irish—or between new invaders and the settled Norse and their Irish allies—had been recurrent for some two hundred years, and even the sensitive inhabitants of the Celtic homeland must have become inured to disaster and sceptical of success. But the campaign that found its troubled conclusion at Clontarf has always been given a special significance by Irish historians, and the defeated invaders—a Norse host of indeterminate numbers—agreed with their victors that the occasion was of uncommon gravity. English historians have paid less attention to the battle, but it seems to deserve a place in the history of England as well as in the distracted tale of Ireland.

In the Annals of Innisfallen, the earliest Irish account of the battle, a list of outstanding men who were killed is followed by the impressive statement that a slaughter was made 'of the Foreigners of the Western World.' The *Chronicon Scottorum* declares that 'Foreigners of the world, from those of them who were in Scandinavia and to the west of it, collected against Brian . . . they had with them a thousand men-at-arms.' According to the Annals of Ulster, Brian, king of Ireland, and Maelsechlainn, king of Tara, led an expedition against the men of Leinster, the Foreigners of Dublin, and 'an equal number of the Foreigners of Scandinavia, namely a thousand men-at-arms.' A bloody battle was fought, 'the like of which has not been found,' and the defeated army lost, in all, six thousand men; the majority, presumably, being Leinstermen.

But the fame of Clontarf grew with the years, and there is a more spacious account of it in *The Wars of the Irish with the Foreigners;* part of which was probably composed in the twelfth century, though for most of it a manuscript of the fourteenth century is the earliest authority. There it is said that when the Foreigners of Dublin heard of Brian's preparation for war they sent out messengers to seek allies from all sides, and among those who came to their aid were two earls from York and the north of England, who commanded a fleet and two thousand mail-clad warriors; Sigurd, earl of Orkney, with 'a levy of fierce, barbarous men' from Orkney and Shetland and the Hebrides; two barons from Cornwall, and Britons from Wales; two sons of the French king, and 'Platt, a powerful knight of Scandinavia.' The great army gathered in Dublin was divided into three hosts: the Scandinavians, the men of Leinster under their king Maelmorda, and the Foreigners of the Islands under Sigurd of Orkney and 'Brodir, chief of the Danes.' The battle was fought on Good Friday, the 23rd April, after a supernatural declaration of its result which cannot have comforted those who heard and believed it.

Brodir the Dane had some reputation as a wizard, and tried by sorcery to discover which side would win. The chilling answer he got was that if they fought on Friday, Brian would fall but have the victory; and if they fought before Friday, all would fall who were against king Brian. Both before and after the battle there were supernatural occurrences—or, more accurately, widely believed stories of supernatural occurrence—that reflect a sense of impending doom, or doom accomplished, which cannot be reconciled with the supposition that the fighting had no greater end in view than the crushing of a revolt instigated by a king of Leinster and the small city-state of Dublin.

Before the battle Brian is said to have been warned of his death by a pagan goddess who emerged from her sanctuary at Killaloe; and Brodir and his men, in their anchored ships, had for several nights suffered the alarming experience of being attacked by their own weapons. In Caithness, in the north of Scotland, a man called Dorrad saw, on the morning of Good Friday, the Valkyries riding

to a house in which they sat down to weave at a loom which had
men's heads for weights, the bowels of men for warp and woof,
and an arrow for a shuttle. They sang a song which began:

> 'See! warp is stretched
> For warriors' fall,
> Lo! weft in loom
> 'Tis wet with blood.'

When they had finished they tore the woven cloth in pieces,
mounted their horses, and rode away, six to the north and six to
the south. The same vision was seen by a man called Brand in the
Faeroes. In Iceland, on the same day, blood fell on the stole of the
priest at Swinefell, and at Thvattriver the priest saw a great gulf of
the sea open beside the altar. In Orkney a man called Harek
thought he saw earl Sigurd and some of his men; mounting a horse,
he rode to meet them, and went with them behind a hill. Others
watched their meeting, but Harek was never seen again. In the
Hebrides earl Gilli, who was Sigurd's brother-in-law, dreamt of a
man who came from Ireland and told him of the disaster at Clontarf.

It is conceivable that in his own country Brian's death gave
some particular significance to the battle, though more probably
it was the battle that made Brian famous; but it is not to be believed
that a king of Munster, who had lately become high-king of Ireland, was sufficiently well known in Iceland and Caithness and the
Faeroes to provoke, by rumour of his death, the sense of fore-
boding or despair that gave birth to such stories as these. Sigurd of
Orkney was well known in the northern world as a man of power
and prowess, but he was not great enough, in character or achievements, to fill the air with supernatural pictures and the noise of
mourning for his loss. Nor can it be supposed—as sometimes it has
been—that the pagan north shuddered at the news of a Christian
victory, and saw in strange signs and portents the doom of their
heathen gods: the pagan north had never been over-reverent of its
gods, and now had largely discarded them; and it is impossible to
see Clontarf as a victory for the Christian church when king Brian
was opposed by Leinstermen who must be credited with as much
piety as the men of Munster, and by Sigurd and his islanders who
had been, at least nominally, Christian for nearly twenty years. In

Iceland, moreover, they were Christian priests who suffered or saw the portents of doom.

It matters little whether those portents were the product of some neurotic disturbance, prevalent about the time of the battle, or subsequently invented by saga-tellers to illustrate the gloom and awareness of disaster that followed the news of defeat. Either as fiction or as symptoms of neurosis they are evidence of the importance attached to the battle by men of Norse blood in the northern parts of Britain and as far away as Iceland; and it is quite improbable that the death of an Irish king, or the intervention of an Orkney earl in one of the many internecine wars of Ireland, could have given the battle an importance so widely recognised and so deeply felt. Clontarf was not the only battle, in that fierce age, in which the loss of life was heavy; but it is the only one to be so lavishly adorned with supernatural addition. Worth noting also is a plain, straightforward assertion in the saga of Thorstein, son of the Icelander Hall of the Side, that the battle of Clontarf 'has been the most famous in the west beyond the sea, both because of the numbers who fought in it, and because of the importance of the result.' To discover what the result was, and was meant to be, one must first consider the planning of the campaign.

In the saga of Burnt Njal—perhaps the greatest of the Icelandic sagas—there is an account of the preliminaries to war, on the northern side, that is worth re-telling because, in addition to its immediate interest, it presents a very striking picture of Norse manners in the heroic age that was now fast coming to an end.

Old Njal—whose name might as well be spelt Neil: there was, presumably, Celtic blood in his ancestry—was a man of great wisdom, a notable lawyer, and a man of peace, whose story reaches a culmination when, in consequence of a long and complicated feud, his house in the south of Iceland is surrounded by a great company of his enemies and set on fire. Njal and Bergthora, his wife, three of their sons, and a grandchild who would not leave the old people, were all killed or died in the flames, but Kari Solmundson, Njal's gallant son-in-law, made a daring escape through the blazing roof, and lived to take revenge on the burners: whose leader, a good man driven to evil courses by a sense of duty, was called Flosi. A prolonged legal dispute follows the burning, and the burners are banished from Iceland. Flosi takes ship, and in a great gale is wrecked on the Mainland of Orkney.

He and his followers go to the hall of earl Sigurd, who knows of their crime and does not welcome them; for one of Njal's sons, killed by Flosi, had served in his bodyguard. But Flosi has a friend at court, he and Sigurd are reconciled, and at the earl's Yule feast he is a fellow-guest with other distinguished visitors.

Sigurd, called Sigurd the Stout, was a man of wide authority who still maintained the old viking way of life. He ruled not only Orkney and Shetland, but all that northern part of Scotland which is now Caithness and Sutherland, and in his regular viking cruises he plundered as far south as the Isle of Man and Ireland. He was himself partly Irish, for his father, earl of Orkney before him, had married Edna, daughter of the Irish king Kjarval, of whom mention has been made. She was a dominating woman whose formidable character was reinforced by a reputed skill in magic. Sigurd was officially a Christian, for in 995 he had accepted baptism when taken at a disadvantage by Olaf Tryggvison, later king of Norway; and he was married, in a useful political alliance, to a daughter of Malcolm II, king of Scots.

At his Yule feast in 1013 Sigurd's guests, in addition to Flosi and the other Icelanders, were Sigtrygg Silkbeard, the Norse or Danish king of Dublin, and Gilli, earl of the Southern Isles and Sigurd's brother-in-law. Sigtrygg was the son of Olaf Cuaran, also in his time a king in Dublin, and his mother, like Sigurd's, was a dangerous woman who had the misfortune to be well favoured by nature except in the matter of judgment. She was good-looking but ill-advised. Called Gormflaith by the Irish and Kormlada by the Norse, she had, before marrying Olaf Cuaran, been the wife of Brian Boru, for whom she had acquired a violent and enduring hatred that may have been aggravated in the year 999 when Brian defeated the Danes, sacked Dublin, and drove out Sigtrygg. The Danes made their peace with Brian in the following year, but Gormflaith never forgave him, and in Njal's saga it is said that Sigtrygg's arrival in Orkney was in consequence of his mother's insistence: he was to seek an ally who would help him to kill Brian; though Brian was now so old that death was already his near neighbour.

Before political discussion could begin, however, there was entertainment, but their entertainment was very rudely interrupted. The visitors wanted to hear about the burning of old Njal, and Gunnar Lambison, one of the banished Icelanders who had taken part in the crime, began to tell the story. He told it unfairly—decorated the tale with malice—and when he said that the bravest of Njal's sons had wept before he died, the door of the hall was thrown open, a man with a drawn sword ran in, and with one tremendous stroke silenced the liar forever; his severed head fell bloodily on the table before Sigtrygg and the earls.

The intruder was Kari Solmundson, Njal's valiant son-in-law. He had spent some weeks in Fair Isle, between Orkney and Shetland, where he got news of what was going on, and from Fair Isle he had sailed in the winter gloom to Orkney, and walked to earl Sigurd's hall. He knew it well, for at one time—like Njal's son Helgi—he had served in the earl's bodyguard. He had listened by an open window to Gunnar's lying tale, and when he could bear no longer the slander of his friends, he broke into the crowded hall and struck that memorable blow.

The earl cried, 'Seize Kari and put him to death.' But no one moved. Kari said, 'Some may think, my lord, that I have served you well by taking revenge for the death of Helgi Njal's son.' And Flosi—Flosi who had been the leader of the burners, the chief of Kari's enemies—said, 'Kari has not done this without cause. We have made no atonement with him, and he did what he had a right to do.' Kari turned and walked out—still no one stirred—and going back to his ship, sailed south, on a fine Christmas day, to Caithness.

As an exhibition of heroic good manners, the story is remarkable. Kari's instant resolution and strength of arm are matched by the scrupulous cold beauty of Flosi's judgment: Flosi's sense of fair play had an edge as keen as Kari's sword, and that exquisite apprehension of fairness is typical of the Icelandic sagas in which, again and again, judgment appears to have an aesthetic rather than a moral basis. There are, admittedly, critics who dismiss the story as a northern fiction; but in several parts of it there is a curious ring of truth. In the assertion, for example, that no one moved when the earl cried, 'Seize Kari!' and in Sigurd's recorded comment, after Kari had left the hall, 'There is no one like him for courage,' there is the very tone of voice of a man quick to act but slow to think, who had the rather sluggish magnanimity—nodding his hard warrior's head as thought slowly percolated—to admit that his immediate impulse had been wrong. And when the saga condescends to detail, and reports that Gunnar's dead body was carried out and the blood-stained table scrubbed clean before story-telling was resumed, there is the echo of a tale told by those who had seen the act: a tale told and re-told long before it was set down in writing. It was Flosi himself who finished the story of the burning, and all he said was so manifestly fair that all believed him.

Later in the day king Sigtrygg spoke of his purpose in coming to Orkney, and asked Sigurd to join him in war against Brian Boru. Sigurd, at first, would have nothing to do with so reckless a proposal, and those about him—his chosen elders and men of rank in Orkney—were equally opposed to it. But then Sigurd named his price. If they defeated Brian, he said, he must become king of Ireland, and as a sort of passport to authority he would marry Gormflaith, Sigtrygg's redoubtable mother. Sigtrygg accepted his terms, and Sigurd pledged himself to be in Dublin, with his army, on Palm Sunday of the approaching year.

The fallacy in this report of their agreement is obvious. On his own authority Sigtrygg had no power to promise Sigurd the high-kingship of Ireland, and the suggestion that what he may have offered was his own city-state of Dublin is unrealistic for two reasons: it is absurd to suppose that Sigtrygg was willing to give away his own regality, and go to war without hope of profit, for no better purpose than revenge on the seventy-year-old Brian; and, on the other hand, Dublin was hardly a sufficient reward for the powerful earl of Orkney. Fifteen years before, Dublin had been sacked by Brian—it was vulnerable—and it may have been subject to the neighbouring kingdom of Leinster, or in uneasy alliance with it.

That Sigurd was promised reward of a substantial sort is not to be doubted, and if, as the saga states, it was the high-kingship of all Ireland, then Sigtrygg was speaking as the emissary of someone whose rank and power far exceeded his. In the saga there is no mention of such a person, but the sagas are not interested in politics. They are concerned with specific people and occasions distinguished by remarkable behaviour, and seldom condescend to explanation of either. The absence of background is often exasperating, but has to be accepted as part of the convention within which the saga-tellers told and the saga-writers wrote. Explanation must be sought elsewhere, and can sometimes be found in contemporary history.

In the Christmas season of 1013 the dominating figure in the sea-divided western world was Sweyn Forkbeard, whom all England now regarded as its king. Sweyn had won what he set out to win; but was the conquest of England the limit of his intention?

He was a warrior-king of vast experience, and to all appearances his pride and vigour were unabated by age, his ambition still unsatisfied. He was certainly a strategist, and to a strategic eye it must have been apparent that his possession of England would be made more secure by a firm control of Ireland; whose Norse or Danish residents had so often taken advantage of propinquity to seize York, ravage Northumbria, or pillage the shores of the Bristol Channel. His slowly matured plan of conquest may well have included a design for Ireland's subjugation—a design to safe-guard his western shore—and for such a project Sigurd of Orkney was the perfect instrument. He was virtually independent in his earldom, and the power of an earldom that reached from Shetland to the Dornoch Firth and the Hebrides was considerable, especially when it was supported by alliance with the king of Scots. He too had had long experience in war, and while his brother-in-law, earl Gilli, held the Hebrides for him, the sea-road to Ireland was secure. Nor would he be a stranger in Ireland: he had plundered its shores, and his mother was the daughter of an Irish king.

If Sigtrygg of Dublin was Sweyn's emissary, his promise to Sigurd of the high-kingship is explicable, and may even be thought realistic; while Sigurd, for his hazardous enterprise, had the prospect of such a reward as justified a bold decision. Given that explanation, moreover, the sense of doom that followed his defeat—the far-spread dismay that provoked visions of blood in Swinefell and Valkyries in Caithness—becomes almost comprehensible. For such a venture he would recruit his forces from all the warlike lands within his reach, and the rumour of his intention may have run through the northern parts of Scotland, from Shetland to the Isle of Man, and reached the ears of loose-footed, reckless men wherever they were wintering. The Irish chronicle that describes his army as the Foreigners of the Western World may have a core of truth within its loud exaggeration, and if he did indeed command an array so various, a force recruited with the promise of a kingdom for reward, then defeat could well have been followed by a gloom as deep as hope had been high.

The battle was fought on the 23rd April, so it is probable that Sigurd left Orkney in early March—and perhaps earlier—to gather reinforcement and muster his allies on the southward voyage. Nothing is told of the voyage, but in the saga there is the description of an episode at the Isle of Man which appears misplaced in time, and most of which is clearly fictitious. It is said that when Sigtrygg returned to Dublin and told his mother of Sigurd's agreement to join the alliance, she was well pleased but said they still needed greater strength. In the Isle of Man, she said, there were two vikings of formidable reputation, called Ospak and Brodir, who commanded a fleet of thirty ships; and Sigtrygg must go there and use all his persuasion to enlist their help.

According to the saga Sigtrygg obeys his mother, and offers Brodir the same inducement as had succeeded in Orkney: Brodir, that is, is promised the kingdom of Ireland and Gormflaith's hand in marriage, but to Sigurd he must say nothing of the bargain. This, of course, is a story-teller's invention, and confidence in the narrative fails again when it is said that Brodir and Ospak quarrel, and Ospak refuses to make war against Brian because 'he had no wish to fight against so good a king.' The reputed virtue of an opponent was unlikely to deter a viking from war, but valid cause for dispute can be found if the dispute is deferred for a few weeks: until, that is, Sigurd with his fleet arrives in Man to complete arrangements for the assault. The island was the natural *point d'appui* from which to mount the attack, and well known to Sigurd. It may be, indeed, that the Isle of Man was the appointed rendezvous for all the Foreigners of the West.

But between the time of Sigurd's Yule feast and his arrival off the coast of Ireland there had occurred a calamity which—if the hypothesis is accepted that Sweyn Forkbeard had inspired the operation—radically and disastrously changed the whole situation. For Sweyn was dead. And so it may be that when Sigurd came to Man he found there a deep division of opinion. Perhaps there were those who, having made ready for battle, were still prepared to fight; but others, more cautious, were disinclined for a war which could no longer be regarded as part of a great strategic plan, but had been reduced to mere adventure. Ospak was one of the cautious, and from their joint fleet withdrew his ten ships, leaving Brodir with twenty. Brodir is said to have been a Christian who had reverted to paganism.

On the Irish side there was, before the battle began, a more drastic reduction of king Brian's army. He had marched to Dublin with his own men from Munster, allies from south Connaught, and an army under Maelsechlainn, king of Tara. But Maelsechlainn's men were not committed to battle, though it is said in Irish annals that the two kings were on friendly terms. There may have been jealousy, however, for Maelsechlainn had previously been recognised as high-king. When, therefore, it became known to him that Ireland's danger had been diminished by Sweyn Forkbeard's death, he may have decided that honour did not compel him to join a battle which, if Brian won, would have little consequence other than to enhance the old king's reputation. Whatever his reason, Maelsechlainn stood aside as Ospak had done.

In the romantic history called *The Wars of the Irish with the Foreigners* it is said that the battle lasted from dawn till sunset, and there and elsewhere are vivid illustrations of savage fighting and fearful casualties. In one account there is a saying that the dead fell like a field of oats when the reapers go in; and in another, that before the end of the day the armies looked like a wood in which all the young trees had been cut down, and only the old ones left standing. Brian was killed, Brodir and Sigurd died, but Sigtrygg of Dublin, who prudently remained in town, survived. Fifteen Icelanders who had been banished with Flosi and come south with Sigurd were killed, but the Icelander Thorstein lived to call the battle the most famous of battles beyond the sea, 'both because of the numbers who fought in it, and the importance of the result.'

But what was the result? The defeat of rebellious Leinstermen, of the Foreigners of Dublin and their allies, can hardly be recognised as a result of major importance—after two hundred years of such warfare—unless the intention of the defeated side had generally been recognised as a threat to all Ireland. Unless, that is, the battle had originally been planned as part of Sweyn Forkbeard's grandiose strategy; and if that is so, then Clontarf may have been as important as the battle of Hastings—but a battle of Hastings which went the other way.

Chapter X

ENGLAND UNDER CNUT

THE sudden death of Sweyn Forkbeard postponed the coronation of a foreigner for three years. His son Cnut, who was with the Danish fleet on the Trent, was immediately chosen to succeed him, but Cnut was young and inexperienced, and when he was brought face to face with the necessity of fighting for a kingdom that, a few weeks before, appeared to have been won, he embarked his army and retired to Denmark. It seems strange that in so well trained a force there was no commander of sufficient authority to serve as the young king's lieutenant-general, but mutual jealousy may have disarmed its captains, or Sweyn may have ruled so absolutely that none had been given power above the rest.

The English magnates, both laity and churchmen, had taken heart and sent messengers to Ethelred in Normandy to invite his return 'if he would govern them more justly than he did before.' He gave a gracious reply, promising to reform 'all the things which they all hated,' and came home in the early spring. An army was quickly mustered, and he marched to Lindsey where he found the Danes unprepared for battle. The people of Lindsey had agreed to provide Cnut with horses and join him in raiding, but he put to sea and left them to suffer the cruel punishment which a revengeful English army promptly administered. Cnut sailed down the coast as far as Sandwich, where he put ashore the hostages his father had taken, and according to the Chronicle mutilated them before their release. At no other time is he accused of such revolting behaviour, but the possibility cannot be denied that in a rage of disappointment he did that shameful thing.

Ethelred left hatred behind him in Lindsey, and cannot have endeared himself in the south by levying the large sum of twenty-one thousand pounds to pay the army of Thorkell the Tall at Greenwich. Nor, with the going of the Danes, had the curse of unseemly misfortune gone from England; for when, early in 1015, a great assembly was convened at Oxford, Edric Streona of Mercia disgraced the occasion by treacherously murdering Sigeferth and Morcar, two leaders of the northern Danelaw. Ethelred himself appears to have connived at the murder, for he took possession of the dead men's estates and ordered the arrest of Sigeferth's widow. But his action roused rebellion in his own household, for Edmund, his oldest son, carried off the imprisoned widow, married her, and seized all the lands belonging to both Sigeferth and Morcar; whose people, remembering how Ethelred had ravaged their country, made him welcome.

Another heinous deed may have been covered by history's forgetfulness, for something happened to make Thorkell the Tall resign from Ethelred's service and sail to Denmark with nine ships of the forty-five he had originally commanded. Why he took that action is not known, but there is a story, preserved in the north, that Hemming, his brother, with a company under his command, had been treacherously killed after the death of Sweyn; and the massacre of St. Brice's Day is evidence that Ethelred was not averse from a policy of assassination.

Whatever the reason for his transferred loyalty, Thorkell brought valuable support to the young Cnut, who in Denmark had been made welcome by its new king, his elder brother Harald. It is said, though with dubious authority, that Cnut had asked Harald for a share of his kingdom, but Harald, without hurt to their friendship, had refused and advised him to try his fortune again in England. It is possible that Harald went with him, when he sailed west again, and almost certainly it was through Harald's influence that Cnut found a Norwegian ally of the utmost distinction. This was Eric Hakonson, earl of Lade, the greatest nobleman in Norway, and a warrior of old renown who had played a decisive part in the great sea-fight at Svold. With Eric of Lade to guide his judgment, Cnut was freed from the disabilities of youth, and Thorkell the Jomsburger, who knew England almost as well as the deck of his ship, was a most potent aid. Cnut grew quickly in experience and became a sagacious, successful, and welcome monarch in a stricken land that longed for the peace which only strength could give it; but the strength he brought to England was initially the wisdom of Eric and the robustness of tall Thorkell.

When, in 1015, Cnut sailed again, he avoided the Humber, where people remembered his betrayal of them, and steered to Poole and plunder, once more, in Wessex. Edric of Mercia, the persistent traitor, obliged him with a renewal of treachery. He and Edmund—Ethelred's rebellious son—raised armies and joined forces, but quickly broke apart when Edmund had cause to doubt Edric's good faith; and Edric crossed over to the Danes. He went with Cnut on a deep raid into Warwickshire, while Edmund, having seen his original army abandon him and go home, made an alliance with Uhtred of Northumbria and despoiled the property of Mercian landowners in Cheshire, Staffordshire, and Shropshire. Then Cnut invaded the Danelaw and threatened Northumbria. Earl Uhtred submitted, but gained nothing by prudence; for he was murdered, probably at Edric Streona's instigation. The earldom of Northumbria was given to the Norwegian, Eric Hakonson of Lade, and while Edmund joined his father in London, Cnut led his army back to the ships that lay in Poole harbour and made ready for an attack on London.

On the 23rd April, 1016, Ethelred died, and in London Edmund was promptly chosen as his successor; but in Southampton the magnates of Wessex swore allegiance to Cnut. When the Danes sailed to London, Edmund marched into Wessex and had the better of the exchange; for he left in London a sufficient force to defend the city against an unadventurous siege, and in Wessex the Danish party was unable to withstand him. Cnut made a foray to the west, fought two indeterminate battles, and returned to London where Edmund won a tactical victory but lost so heavily that he could not exploit it. He retired to Wessex and the siege of London continued.

It was war of the old pattern again—Wessex and London against Danish invaders—and under Edmund the English were showing their old spirit. Cnut launched another attack on London, by land and water, and was again rebuffed. He withdrew to his ships, and sailing to the river Orwell provisioned the fleet by deep raiding into East Anglia. He returned to the Medway, mounted his army, and rode into Kent. Edmund overtook him, defeated him at Otford, and drove him into Sheppey. That this was a major victory is proved by the fact that Edric of Mercia deserted Cnut and returned to what then appeared to be the winning side.

The Danes still had their ships, and they crossed the Thames to raid in Essex. Edmund, still on the offensive, followed with a great army—'all the English nation,' says the Chronicle—and met his enemy at Ashingdon south of the river Crouch. Battle was joined, but when Edric of Mercia fled there was a gap in the line, and others followed him; the English were defeated with heavy loss, and among their leaders who were killed was the valiant Ulfkell of East Anglia. Now in Snorri Sturluson's saga of the kings of Norway it is said that he who killed Ulfkell was none other than Eric Hakonson of Lade, and it is significant that he took part in the decisive battle of the war. In the period of inconclusive fighting in the south he, presumably, kept the north under control; and then, after the defeat at Otford, Cnut may have sent for help —or Eric decided that without his help the war might be lost— and at Ashingdon his presence ensured victory.

But even in defeat, even as a fugitive, Edmund was still dangerous and commanded respect. Cnut marched westward as far as the Severn, and it was decided that he and Edmund must come to terms. Edric of Mercia, who had served on both sides, was a useful go-between, and the two kings, having exchanged hostages, met and pledged themselves to peace and friendship. England was again divided—though only for a little while—and Edmund kept Wessex while all beyond the Thames went to Cnut. London had to buy its own peace, and the Danes, with their fleet in the Thames, wintered in the city. But before winter had darkened it, the spirit of England was darkened by Edmund's death. He died on St. Andrew's Day, having well earned the name of Edmund Ironside, and the West Saxons acknowledged an irreparable loss by accepting Cnut as their king. England was united under a Danish monarch who, with Scandinavian adaptability, took pains to acquire an English colouring.

His first administrative act was to divide the country into the four great earldoms of Northumbria under Eric Hakonson; all Mercia under Edric Streona; East Anglia under Thorkell the Tall; and Wessex in his own hands. But before the year was out the Chronicle recorded the death, apparently by summary execution, of four prominent Englishmen, one of whom, it is gratifying to learn, was Edric Streona; though the others may have suffered some injustice, there is every reason to suppose that Edric got his deserts. Cnut, or his advisers, had also time to look abroad and consider relations with Normandy; the consequence being that he sent for Ethelred's widow—Emma, sister of Richard of Normandy—and married her. Emma's sons by Ethelred had been brought up in the duchy, and Richard may be supposed to have had some interest in their welfare; the twelfth century chronicler William of Malmesbury suggested that the purpose of the marriage was to provide the duke with nephews who would divert his affection from the older pair, and it seems likely indeed that Cnut's purpose was to establish friendship with Normandy rather than to ingratiate himself with the English by taking pity on their late king's widow.

He did not discard a woman known as Algifu of Northampton who was his mistress, and so remained throughout his reign. She was a woman of remarkable character who is said by the Danish historian or fabulist Saxo Grammaticus to have been, a little earlier, the mistress of Olaf the Stout—sometime king of Norway and after his death called St. Olaf—from whose side Cnut seduced her. She bore him two sons, Harald and Sweyn, and later in Norway acted as regent for Sweyn, but made herself unpopular by her tyrannical government. That Emma, before her marriage, knew of Algifu's existence and position in the royal household is shown by the fact that she—or, more probably, duke Richard on her behalf—secured the exclusion of Algifu's children from any claim to the succession.

The initial severities of Cnut's military rule were soon relaxed, and in 1018 he showed remarkable confidence by sending the greater part of his fleet back to Denmark. In the spring he had won a notable victory over a viking horde that had apparently seen a prospect of gain in England's troubled waters, and put to the sword the crews of thirty ships. Of his own fleet he kept only forty, and before dismissing the others extracted from his new-won kingdom the large sum of seventy-two thousand pounds for their payment, and from the citizens of London an additional ten thousand pounds. A relaxation of military rule was shown by the release of Wessex from his personal government—it was divided between two appointed earls—and the fragmentation of Mercia after Edric Streona's death; but his assessment of England for tax—the Danegeld he took to pay his fleet—does not suggest that his rule became weak and languid.

He deliberately asserted his intention to retain the basic system of law by which England had been governed in the past—though indifferently, perhaps, in the immediate past—by the enactment of a legal code whose statutes were of native origin; and it seems probable that the framing of his code, which was promulgated from a council convened in Oxford, owed much to the benign advice of archbishop Wulfstan. At this time, too, Cnut's territorial ambitions were conservative rather than expansive; though later they were to alter. His father, the restless Sweyn Forkbeard, may have entertained the vision of a northern empire, but Cnut showed a cool, unexcited calculation of his strength and interests when Malcolm II, king of Scots, defeated the Northumbrians at the battle of Carham in 1018, or perhaps a year or two earlier.

That part of Northumbria which lay beyond the Tweed had been ceded to Kenneth of Scotland by the peace-loving king Edgar; and for more than thirty years the frontier had been quiet. But in 1006, Malcolm, son of Kenneth, invaded Northumbria and laid siege to Durham. Earl Waltheof was too old for war, but Uhtred, his son, was young and vigorous, and Uhtred beat Malcolm with so great a slaughter as to deserve savage celebration. The dead Scots were beheaded, and their heads—'ornamented as was the fashion at that time with braided hair,' says Symeon of Durham—were washed by four women, each of whom was paid a cow for her trouble, and set on stakes round the walls of Durham. But ten or a dozen years later Malcolm marched again, with Owen of Strathclyde in alliance, and took his revenge at Carham: a victory which underlined king Edgar's cession of Lothian, and firmly established Scotland's southern frontier on the Tweed. To a monarch whose judgment was ill balanced this strong assertion might have seemed a menace which demanded immediate reply; but Cnut in his prudence discounted so distant a threat and deferred his answer for many years. The Northumbrian earldom was ruled by the Norwegian, Eric Hakonson; and to him, perhaps, should credit also be paid for the realism exhibited by his king.

The uneventfulness of Cnut's reign is proof of its success, and proof, too, that England preferred peace under a foreign conqueror, who ruled fairly, to the wretchedness of warfare under native ineptitude. His rule was maintained, and peace was guarded, by the earls he created, and most of his earls were Danish. A new English nobility emerged, some from families not hitherto distinguished, but Cnut relied chiefly on his fellow-countrymen, and to support their dignity they required estates. In all parts of the country much land was transferred to new owners, but in many cases expropriation may have been made easy by the recent abeyance of order, the dissolution of an old society, the absence of natural heirs. Of the Englishmen advanced by his favour the most notable were Leofric, of a Mercian family, who became earl of Mercia; and Godwine, who was made earl of Wessex. Godwine's father was Wulfnoth, who may have been the thane of Sussex who, in 1009, when Ethelred the Unready had built a great fleet, seduced the crews of twenty ships and took to piracy. Godwine married Edith, the sister of Ulf of Denmark, who was Cnut's brother-in-law; and of their children the most notable were Edith, who in the course of time married Edward the Confessor, and Harold, who took the throne of England and lost it to William the Conqueror. In the two major earldoms thus re-created under English rulers, a traditional enmity woke again; and that was one of several reasons for Harold's defeat.

Nowhere did Cnut show his wisdom more clearly or more significantly than in his relations with the church; and it may be that his willing obeisance to its authority was, in the beginning, a natural response of his youth. In 1017, when he felt strong enough to dismiss the greater part of his fleet, he was only twenty-two or twenty-three, and such a figure as archbishop Wulfstan, who had dared declare that England's defeat was God's punishment for its wickedness, must have deeply impressed a young man who was intelligent enough to compare the spiritual poverty of his father's court with the riches of the English church, which exalted piety with scholarship, and had maintained, in a general decrepitude, the dignity of faith and some part, at least, of the splendour of its earthly endowment. Cnut had been baptised in Germany, and there is no reason to suppose that he had to make pretence of Christian belief. There is, however, every reason for thinking that his belief was enormously reinforced by the visible evidence of the church's authority in England, and his awakening knowledge

of the church universal, on the pathway of whose power and learning Europe was moving out of the Dark Ages into the brilliant
though narrow illumination of mediaevalism. By conquest Cnut
made himself an English king, and with the fervency of a great
discoverer became an English churchman. He accepted with enthusiasm the tradition that a king who held authority from God
must lend authority to God's instrument on earth.

But England and its reformation was not his only care. The
death of his brother Harald, who died childless in 1018 or 1019,
left him heir to Denmark, and to look after his interests he had to
spend the winter of 1019 in his native land. In 1020, according to
the Chronicle, he returned to England, and in the following year
he outlawed earl Thorkell. The Chronicle offers no explanation of
this momentous decision, but Thorkell the Tall, sometime a chief
of the Jomsburg vikings, had been foremost among Cnut's magnates in England, and in Cnut's absence may have exercised too
arbitrary an authority. Under the date 1022 the Chronicle records:
'In this year king Cnut went out with his ships to the Isle of
Wight, and archbishop Ethelnoth went to Rome.' Ethelnoth had
become archbishop of Canterbury after the death of Wulfstan,
and went to Rome to receive his pallium; but why Cnut mobilised
his fleet is less clear.

Had the old Jomsburger, weary of settled dignity and obedience
to a king—but still wedded to adventure—found in Scandinavia a
host of other restless men prepared to threaten an established realm
in the hope of booty that would keep them richly independent for
a northern winter? That, it seems, is the explanation, and equally
clear—though in a shrouded clarity—is the apparent fact that
Cnut, with great daring, sailed east to Denmark, and having confronted Thorkell, was persuaded to accept an agreement that
Thorkell must have proposed. For in 1023 the Chronicle reads: 'In
this year king Cnut came back to England, and Thorkell and he
were reconciled, and he entrusted Denmark and his son for Thorkell to maintain and the king took Thorkell's son with him to England.' They exchanged hostages, that is, and while Cnut prudently
accepted an uncertain alliance, the old viking enjoyed a last chapter
of splendour and triumph. He died within three years, and Cnut's
authority over Denmark was sufficient to impose in his place, as
regent, his brother-in-law Ulf, son of a nobleman called Thorgils

Sprakalegg, who had married Cnut's sister Estrith; and Ulf was made guardian of Harthacnut, Cnut's son by Emma of Normandy, Ethelred's widow.

It is necessary now to look away from an England quiescent under an established throne to a renewal of contest and confusion in Scandinavia; and the exposure of its unsettled state will do something to explain eruptions from Norway and Denmark in subsequent years. In 1025, says the Chronicle, 'King Cnut went with ships to Denmark to the Holme at the Holy River'—in Scania in southern Sweden—'and there came against him Ulf and Eilaf and a very great army, both a land force and a naval force, from Sweden. And there very many men on king Cnut's side were destroyed, both Danish and English men, and the Swedes had control of the field.'

The leader of the confederacy that defeated Cnut was the Norwegian king Olaf the Stout. A son of Harald the Grenlander and a descendant of Harald Fairhair, he had had a life of burly adventure, and according to the saga of the kings of Norway he played a very distinguished part, on the English side, in the fighting about London in Sweyn Forkbeard's last campaign. In the saga there is a detailed description of how he broke down London Bridge and stormed the Danish positions in Southwark, and though it is difficult to accommodate these stirring operations in the English narrative of events, it is highly probable that a core of truth exists within an envelope of exaggeration. Later he served in Normandy, under duke Richard, and returned to England at the restoration of Ethelred. When he saw an opportunity to make himself king of Norway—the great earl Eric of Lade was with Cnut in England—he sailed boldly into the Oslo fjord and defeated Eric's son Hakon in a battle that was the prelude to larger success, and realised his hope.

He entered an alliance with Onund, king of Sweden, the purpose of which was to make war on their Danish neighbours: for Denmark, with the wealth of England to reinforce it, had become too strong for Swedish approval. Quite inexplicably the alliance was joined by Ulf, Cnut's regent in Denmark, and his brother Eilaf to whom Cnut had given an English earldom. Presumably their viking instincts had broken the restraints incumbent on a settled authority, and with the prospect of looting the rich province of

Scania they dismissed, as a barren formality, their allegiance to their king. But Cnut acted with exemplary speed, and in the Kattegat his ships met and dispersed the Norwegian fleet; and sailed on to Scania and the mouth of the Holy River. There the Swedish fleet lay, and Cnut is said to have been defeated, not so much by force of arms, as by the curious device of damming the stream and then, at an opportune moment, breaking the dam to release an irresistible flood. Though Cnut was beaten he appears to have retained sufficient influence to repay Ulf's treason by having him assassinated.

The Norwegian saga makes it clear that Olaf the Stout governed his land as a Christian autocrat intolerant of opposition, and from his overbearing rule many fled across the sea, as in the days of Harald Fairhair. But now the refugees—who sought arms for rebellion rather than a refuge—had an obvious source of assistance in the court of king Cnut, who by lavish bribery had done much to encourage disaffection. His ambition found ready servants in all who resented Olaf's pious tyranny and relished an open-handed reward for their resentment, and when, in 1028, Cnut sailed again, with a fleet of fifty ships that was reinforced by another fleet from Jutland, Olaf's strength had so dwindled that he could not offer battle, but had to retreat into the Oslo fjord. Cnut sailed up the west coast, everywhere receiving submission, and at Nidaros was acknowledged as king.

In 1029 Cnut returned to England, leaving his son Harthacnut as king in Denmark, and earl Hakon, son of the great Eric of Lade —now dead—as his governor in Norway. Hakon, while in England, had received many of the dissidents who fled from Olaf's rule, and in Norway he was popular. He seems to have been a good, genial man, but he was unlucky. He sailed to England, to meet a promised bride, and on his homeward voyage was drowned in the Pentland Firth. In that year Olaf the Stout made a daring attempt to regain his lost kingdom, but near the Trondheim fjord met an indignant army mustered largely from the bonders, the land-owning farmers whom his harsh piety had offended, and was killed at the great battle of Stiklestad. His death opened the way for Sweyn, the son of Cnut and Algifu of Northampton, whom Cnut appointed to fill Hakon's place under the regency of his mother. Cnut's power in the north was now supreme. To his conquest of England in 1016 he had added Denmark in 1018, and now, in 1030, Norway; but Algifu soon undermined the power that he had won. Where Olaf had demanded obedience, she exacted heavy taxes; where he had imposed a Christian conformity, she punished criminals with a severity unprecedented in the north. Under the penalties of alien rule a popular revulsion of feeling restored dead Olaf to favour, and on his posthumous fame grafted sanctity. Within a few years Algifu and young Sweyn had to flee for safety into Denmark, and Olaf's son Magnus took his father's kingdom.

Concern for his northern dominions had not overshadowed Cnut's lively awareness of the dignity of his English throne, or of the opportunities it offered, the obligations it imposed. In 1027, after his defeat at the Holy River, he went to Rome to attend the coronation of the emperor Conrad II. He went as a monarch entitled to respect among the Christian princes of Europe; as a statesman he secured some valuable privileges for the people he ruled; and as an English king he made known in England what he had done for its benefit. The taxes and tolls levied on pilgrims and merchants travelling to Rome were reduced, and Cnut wrote proudly to record his success and a vow he had made to amend his life and to rule justly in all his kingdoms. He wanted, he said, to let his people be gladdened by his success 'because, as you yourselves know, I have never spared, nor will I spare in the future, to devote myself and my toil for the need and benefit of my people.' With the emperor he established a relationship that continued to be friendly, and in later years Conrad ceded Schleswig to Denmark and married his son Henry to Cnut's daughter Gunnhild.

Riding overland to Denmark, Cnut came back to England and immediately led an army into Scotland. His victory at Carham, in 1018, may have encouraged king Malcolm to make some show of aggression in the north, and Cnut found it necessary to assert his authority. Nothing is known of his expedition other than a brief statement in the Chronicle that the Scottish king and two minor kings submitted to him; but Scotland's frontier on the Tweed was not disputed. He who now governed Northumbria, in Cnut's interest, was the warrior Siward, a grandson of earl Ulf of Denmark, who had been appointed after the murder in 1016 of Uhtred, son of Waltheof of the old native ruling family. Waltheof's family had not been dispossessed of its lands and partial authority, and Siward, who married a grand-daughter of Uhtred and christened one of his sons Waltheof, was probably made welcome in the country whose local gentry had once received Eric Bloodaxe with acclamation; for the new earl came of a noble stock. Siward made no attempt to expand his rule into Scotland, but pushed his conquests westward to the Solway.

The increased power that Cnut had brought to England created friction between him and duke Robert of Normandy, the son of Richard II. Robert's jealousy was natural enough—it may, indeed, have been aggravated by some tincture of alarm—but a story, for whose truth there is little evidence other than popular belief in it, alleges that a domestic quarrel first precipitated ill-will. Cnut, it is said, gave his sister Estrith in marriage to Robert—Estrith who later married earl Ulf of Denmark—and Robert sent her home again. In Robert's court were the athelings Edward and Alfred, sons of his father's sister Emma, and on their behalf he may have resented Cnut's usurpation of the throne to which they had the claim of their blood. There was reason for Robert's growing enmity, and another story, which also lacks evidence, cannot lightly be disregarded. The Norman chronicler William of Jumièges declares that Robert prepared an invasion of England, for the restoration of the athelings, but the fleet which he had mustered met a gale in the Channel and was blown westwards to Brittany; where the troops aboard were employed to suppress a Breton revolt. More than once has England owed its safety to foul weather—and the story may be true.

During the last few years of his life the Chronicle makes no reference to Cnut: he had imposed peace upon the land, and no rude occurrence broke his peace. He was in his fortieth year when he died in Shaftesbury in 1035, and it is difficult to suppress speculation about the course that English history might have taken had he lived half as long again. He was a great king, and the fable that all know, of how he rebuked his courtiers' flattery by commanding the flood-tide to come no farther, is illustration of a humility that only greatness could assume or afford. He professed his humility before God and the established church, and taxed his people to pay for his benefactions to the church and for a policy maintained by lavish spending. His taxes were heavy, but they bought order and peace. His life was a little disfigured by a harsh and violent temper, but his viking ancestry was more amiably revealed by an addiction to poetry and his generosity to visiting poets. As an administrator he was second only to Alfred, and in the rough climate of his time he enjoyed the advantage of physical excellence: he was heavily built, strong, fair-haired, and keen of eye; of handsome appearance but for a nose hooked and thin and too high in the bridge.

His death was followed by five years of deplorable untidiness. He left one legitimate son by Emma, who was the ill-conditioned young man called Harthacnut; two, illegitimate, by Algifu, who were Harald Harefoot and Sweyn; and in Normandy, to complicate the picture, were Alfred and Edward, the sons of Emma and Ethelred the Unready. Harthacnut, already king in Denmark, was Cnut's intended heir to England, but could not take up his inheritance because St. Olaf's son Magnus, now ruling Norway, threatened Denmark with invasion. Godwine of Wessex and queen Emma, with all the chief men of Wessex to support them, were in favour of electing Harthacnut *in absentia;* but at an assembly in Oxford, attended by earl Leofric of Mercia, most of the thanes who lived north of the Thames, and representatives of London's seamen, preferred a regency under Harald Harefoot. Godwine and Emma gave way to the stronger party, but Emma was allowed to establish herself in Winchester, with a bodyguard of Harthacnut's housecarls, to secure his interest in Wessex. In Winchester, where Cnut lay buried, was the royal treasury, which Harald Harefoot plundered in spite of Emma's protests.

His mother, Algifu, whose calamitous regency in Norway had brought about the expulsion of her and her son Sweyn, had returned to England where she was able to enlist the support of a majority of English magnates to form a new king's party. Sweyn had died in Denmark, but Harald was alive in England, and by Algifu's craft and contrivance—cajolery and menace may both have been her weapons—Harald in 1037 was recognised as king; and queen Emma fled to the court of Baldwin, count of Flanders.

In the previous year her son Alfred had crossed the Channel to visit his mother, whom he had not seen since her marriage to Cnut. By this time it had become apparent that the king's party managed by Algifu was in the ascendant, and Godwine of Wessex abandoned

Emma's cause for the prospering side. He prevented Alfred from going to Winchester, killed some of his escorts, and let the atheling be taken aboard a ship and carried to Ely; where he was so cruelly blinded that he died of his injuries. There can be little doubt that Godwine was primarily culpable of that appalling deed.

Two or three years later Magnus of Norway and Harthacnut of Denmark made peace and came to an agreement by which either would succeed to the other's kingdom if it were left without an heir. Harthacnut sailed to Bruges, where the exiled queen Emma was living, but went no farther until he had heard of Harald's death. A shadowy, unsubstantial figure, Harald Harefoot probably lived under his mother's apron, but her influence seems to have united England in allegiance to him. When he died Harthacnut was summoned to succeed him, and came, as if doubtful of his reception, with a supporting fleet of sixty-two ships. He promptly alienated all affection by levying Danegeld to pay their crews, and sending his housecarls to collect the tax.

Succinctly the Chronicle declares: 'And all who had wanted him before were then ill-disposed towards him. And also he did nothing worthy of a king as long as he ruled. He had the dead Harald dug up and thrown into the fen.' This crude revenge appears to have been motivated by Harthacnut's genuine detestation of the late king and those who had been associated, under him, in the murder of the atheling Alfred; for Godwine and the bishop of Worcester were prosecuted for their part in the crime. The bishop was expelled from his see, and Godwine bought his peace with the gift of a splendid warship manned by eighty picked warriors, all well armed, and an oath that he had done nothing wrong except by order of Harald Harefoot.

To Harthacnut's credit stands the fact that he invited his half-brother Edward to England, made him a member of his household, and probably named him as his heir. To his discredit is the unexplained but treacherous murder of Eadwulf of Northumbria, a son of earl Uhtred, whom he had accepted into his peace. Harthacnut was a drunkard, and a genuine kindliness may have alternated with moods of barbarous ferocity. He was no older than twenty-five when at a wedding-feast in Lambeth, in the high summer of 1042, while 'standing at his drink, he suddenly fell to the ground with fearful convulsions, and those who were near caught him, and he spoke no word afterwards.'

Before he was buried, Edward, son of Ethelred the Unready and Emma of Normandy, was chosen king; and quickly after that Denmark was invaded by Magnus of Norway, who claimed the kingdom by right of his treaty with Harthacnut.

Chapter XI

THE COMMONWEALTH OF ICELAND

ICELAND offers something like a laboratory-in-history for a study of the nature and achievement of the Norse people; and the story of their development in isolation may throw some light on the effect of their settlements in contact with Anglo-Saxons. Though the Scandinavian establishment in England is usually called Danish—the words Danelaw and Danegeld have had that effect—the evidence of previous chapters has demonstrated a mixed infiltration: the Irish invasions into the north of England were largely of Norwegian origin, Eric Bloodaxe of Norway and Hakon of Lade in Norway were influential in Northumbria, Olaf Tryggvison of Norway and Sweyn Forkbeard of Denmark were associated in invasion, and in the professional viking hordes there is little doubt that recruitment was quite indifferent to national origins. The essentially Norse colonisation of Iceland is not beyond the range of interest of a study centred on the mixed colonisation of England, and Iceland is drawn nearer when it is acknowledged—as surely it must be—that although differences may be detected between the social or moral habits and temperament of Danes and Norwegians, the resemblances between them are of much greater significance.

When Iceland was discovered, in 870 or earlier, it was an almost empty land, and its aspect was forbidding. In boats of primitive construction, and by inconceivable navigation, a few Christian hermits of Irish origin had found their way there, but when strangers appeared they retreated, none knows whither, leaving as evidence of their sojourn some books and other religious relics. Its Norse discoverer gave the island the name that still distinguishes it, but failed to establish a settlement, for his cattle died in the winter cold. Then, in 874, the chieftain Ingolf Arnarson, sailing from Norway, made his landfall somewhere on the black and snow-topped south-east coast, sailed westward still, and north of the long peninsula of Reykjanes threw into the sea the posts of the high-seat that he had brought from his Norwegian drinking-hall, and the tide took them into a sheltered beach above which now stands the town of Reykjavik. Ingolf followed, and built a house.

Within sixty years all those parts of Iceland capable of supporting life had been occupied: its seaward fringes, that is, for the interior is a vast, forbidding desert some two or three thousand feet high, with mountains that rise to seven thousand feet, from whose slopes great fields of ice descend to the black lava-barrens thrown out by its two score volcanoes. So rapid a colonisation of so grim a country requires an explanation, and hunger for land was not the only cause; a hunger for freedom may have been keener. It is no longer possible to suppose that Harald Fairhair's conclusive victory at the battle of Hafrsfjord inaugurated the colonisation of Iceland, but it expedited and encouraged the flight of men who were refugees, not from fear, but from subservience: men who, rather than endure the blight of authority, packed their womenfolk, their weapons, and their cattle into ships, and accepted the danger of sailing more than six hundred miles across the North Atlantic to find new pastures.

A kind of directory, called *Landnámabók* and compiled early in the twelfth century, records the names of the original four hundred families who settled in Iceland, their ancestry, the countries they came from, the size of their new estates. It is, though less detailed and much smaller, comparable with Domesday Book, the great economic survey of England made for William the Conqueror. Though the large majority of names were Norwegian, a few—perhaps one in six or one in seven—were of mixed origin: the names of families that came from Ireland or the Hebrides where earlier Norse voyagers had married Celtic women and made their home; and with them came serfs of pure Celtic blood. All the settlers were either Scandinavians or Celts, or a blend of both, and in their isolation the native genius of those races must be given credit for the system of law they established and failed to honour; for the literature they created; and for a liveliness of mind— an agile and generous cast of mind—which let them appreciate the humanising influence of Christianity, the fertilising influence of Latin writing, and so acquire the ability to transform a traditional

stock of poetry, legend, and saga into that literature, which in
its own time had no compeer in Europe. It is this adaptability, this
eagerness and openness of mind, which shows so clearly their consanguinity with the invaders of Normandy who took advantage
of the country they had conquered to acquire its language and
those of its customs which seemed likely to promote a wider culture than that to which they had been born.

The earliest or senior achievement of the Icelanders—other than
material achievement—was their preservation of the heroic and
mythological tales that survive, in written form, in the thirteenth
century manuscript known as the *Elder Edda*. They include the
Lay of Atli, in which the defeat of the Burgundians by the Huns in
the year 437 is seen as a domestic quarrel in which Atli, or Attila,
kills his brother-in-law; and the story of the Volsungs which in
Austria became the *Nibelungenlied*. The memory they disclose
of folk-wandering in the darkest of the Dark Ages has already
undergone a strongly civilising influence; tales of far-off things, of
murder long ago and improbable adventure with dragons, have
been transformed by literary good manners into serious entertainment for minds acquainted with men and history, and accustomed
to the refinements of poetry.

Outstanding in the *Edda* is the *Voluspa*, or 'Sibyl's Prophecy.'
This is the noblest and most terrible preservation of heathen belief,
and moves rapidly from a picture of Chaos to the benign arrival of
the Gods and the creation of a brief period of happiness that came
with the invention of tools. But happiness does not survive the
malignant influence of Giantland. War wrecks the age of gold,
and the terrible calamity is foreseen of the death of Baldur, son of
Odin, who will be killed by a mistletoe shaft. The whole scene
darkens as a witch in Ironwood breeds the wolf Fenris, whose kin
will cast the moon out of heaven and feed on mortal men. Under
the earth a bright red cock with soot-red comb is crowing for
doom, and Garm the hell-hound bays. Fenris the wolf is still
chained, but the chain will snap, and brother shall fight against
brother. Swords and wolves will rule the world, the Giants break
loose. A good man might stand with his Gods and share their
doom, but could hope for no more happiness than that.

Side by side with the 'Sibyl's Prophecy,' however, is an ethical
poem called *The Guest's Wisdom* that begins very cheerfully with

the plain statement that 'he who comes to a meal needs water, a towel, a welcome, good fellowship, and a hearing and kind answer if he could get it.' It proceeds to other assertions, equally sound, such as:

'Let the cup go round, yet drink thy share of mead; speak fair or not at all. No one can blame thee for ill-breeding though thou go early to sleep.

'No man can bear a better baggage on his way than wisdom.

'He that is never silent talks much folly.

'Middling wise should a man be, never too wise. For a wise man's heart is seldom glad, if its owner be a true sage.

'No man should trust a maiden's talk, nor any woman's word.

'The slumbering wolf seldom gets a joint, nor the sleeping man victory.

'Go on, be not a guest for ever in the same house. *Welcome* becomes *Wearisome* if he sit too long at another's table.'[1]

The mind of the travelled Icelander was not too blackly darkened by the 'Sibyl's Prophecy' and the baying of Garm the hellhound. He had, in combination with heroic temper, an acceptable, self-mocking, worldly wisdom. The aristocracy that established a commonwealth and created out of anarchy a system of law without government was within the harsh conditions of its time a sophisticated, not a barbaric, society; and with the example of Iceland thus exposed, it is impossible to believe that the invaders of France and England—who were of the same or a nearby race—were mindless savages. They were men whose merciless demeanour on the field of battle did not exclude a code of manners, and whose valiant pessimism never inhibited the hope implicit in offensive action. When inflamed by war they could be cruel, but for circumstances of peace they had the elements of social order.

The Icelanders' regard for family and the legends transmitted by word of mouth begot in the course of time a copious and admirable literature; but more remarkable was the conjoint impulse that united the thirty-nine dominating families of the island in a common desire to initiate, in that place of natural anarchy, the rule of law. In 930, less than sixty years after the arrival of Ingolf Arnarson, the Althing was established: a general assembly of local au-

---

[1] Vigfusson and Powell, *Corpus Poeticum Boreale*.

thorities, a parliament in essence though it lacked executive power. There had previously been local assemblies, vested with judicial power, but now, with a population of perhaps forty thousand, many of whom were serfs, Iceland became a recognisable state, a republic without a president, that asserted its identity by an annual meeting of representatives from the whole country whose functions were both judicial and legislative—and, perhaps one should add, matrimonial; for a good deal of marriage-broking was done at the Althing.

The meeting-place was Thingvellir, some thirty miles east of modern Reykjavik, and no parliament in the world has ever deliberated within more spacious, awe-provoking architecture. No building housed debate, but geology and volcanic action had raised a lava-black rampart of cliffs three miles long, over which the river Axewater fell in white thunder, and some profound convulsion had pulled the land apart, leaving great rifts and narrow chasms to split and divide the green water-meadows that lay below the cliff. A lake reflected sunshine, great hills to the north gathered clouds. And there, in that enormous setting, the notabilities of Iceland, with their wives and daughters and their warlike servants, gathered every year to spend two weeks on judgment and debate, in gossip and the disposal of their daughters, and sometimes in the promotion of new feuds to take the place of feuds that had been settled. They lived in booths built of stone and turf, and decorated them richly with the spoils of distant warfare. Once a year, from all the coastal parts of Iceland, they came to Thingvellir and there combined with the solemn deliberation of their supreme court and hereditary legislature the social opportunities of the Dublin Horse Show, a mediaeval tournament, and a marriage-mart.

Their most notable parliament was that of the year 1000, when the island was divided between heathen and Christian: between, as it were, the Old Conservatives and the New Liberals. Five years before that, the fighting king of Norway, Olaf Tryggvison, had set about converting the north by the apostolic power of his sword, and in 997 he sent to Iceland a Saxon priest called Thangbrand, a man, it is reputed, of great learning but of murderous temper: a man who killed two poetasters who concocted some libellous verses on him, and three others during his Icelandic mission. He was accompanied by an assistant called Gudlief, said to have been immensely strong and notorious for manslaughter, and was coldly received. But Hall of the Side, a great chieftain in the south of the island, made them welcome, and he and all his household were baptised.—In a previous chapter that discusses the battle of Clontarf there is mention of Thorstein, who fought there, and his recorded opinion of its unique importance: Hall of the Side was his father.—Thereafter Hall went with Thangbrand on his mission, and was with him when he concluded an argument with a very aggressive heathen, called Thorkell, by killing him.

Thangbrand made several converts, and persuaded others that what he was talking about deserved their most earnest thought: one of these was Flosi of Swinefell, who led the burners of old Njal's house and in earl Sigurd's hall in Orkney saw the killing of Gunnar Lambison by Kari Solmundson. Thangbrand's companion Gudlief killed a wizard called Hedinn, and Weatherlid, a poet strongly opposed to Christianity, was also killed. But at Njal's great house of Bergthorsknoll—the house that was burnt —Njal and all his family were baptised. Thangbrand was allowed to speak at the Althing, but without consequence, and he and his little party dared face two hundred angry heathen, in whose presence they killed a maniacal berserk. They converted a man called Gest—he and all his household were baptised—and Gest gave Thangbrand good advice. He could do no more, said Gest, and glossed unwelcome judgment with the philosophic reminder that 'no tree falls at the first stroke.' Thangbrand admitted defeat, and old Njal and Hall of the Side took care of him until a ship could be found that would carry him back to Norway.

King Olaf was undeterred by Thangbrand's failure. He had at his court two Christian Icelanders, who offered to take over the mission, and quickly made preparation for their voyage. In Iceland they found horses and rode, in a company of thirty, to Thingvellir where the Althing was in session. On their way they were joined by many others who had accepted Christianity, and at Thingvellir they found the heathen gathered and prepared for battle. Under the long rampart of the black cliff there was such an uproar that none could make himself heard, and fighting seemed inevitable. But battle was avoided by a very curious exhibition of the power of law.

The Christian party chose, as their advocate, Hall of the Side; but Hall, with singular audacity, went to the old Speaker of the Law, who was the heathen priest Thorgeir, and paid him three marks of silver—his proper fee—to declare by what laws the land should, in future, be governed. For a whole day, it is said, Thorgeir lay with a cloak over his head, and none dared speak to him. And then, from the Hill of Laws, he gave his verdict.

He said first: 'It seems to me as though our matters were come to a deadlock, if we are not all to have one and the same law; for if there be a sundering of the laws, then there will be a sundering of the peace, and we shall never be able to live in the land. Now I will ask both Christian men and heathen, whether they will hold to these laws which I utter?'

There was general agreement, and from both sides Thorgeir took pledges of obedience.

Then he said: 'This is the beginning of our laws, that all men shall be Christians here in the land, and believe in one God, the Father, the Son, and the Holy Ghost, but leave off all idol-worship, not expose children to perish, and not eat horseflesh. It shall be outlawry if such things are proved openly against any man; but if these things are done by stealth, then it shall be blameless.'[2]

It was a remarkable verdict. When the two faiths were in open conflict and threatened to disrupt the state, judgment was left to a heathen priest, an Old Conservative, who pronounced in favour of the New Liberalism, but suggested that Old Conservatives should be allowed to subscribe to their own beliefs if they did it unobtrusively. In comparison with that decision the judgment of Solomon was a schoolboy's joke, and the acceptance of Thorgeir's verdict by the whole assembly reflects the greatest credit on the political maturity and social good sense of Iceland in the year 1000; though it must be added that neither political maturity nor social good sense put an end to the extreme violence of family dissension, and the introduction of Christianity failed to instil any discernible respect for human life. But when the unity of Iceland was threatened, good sense prevailed.

Christianity was an historical necessity. That, despite his heathen prejudice, Thorgeir recognised. It was a decision made with great

[2] *The Story of Burnt Njal,* trans. Dasent.

bravery and wisdom, and with the happiest results. The introduction of Christianity brought to Iceland not only the invigoration of a faith that was not conceived in terms of inevitable defeat, but an expansion of the means by which it was possible to preserve and enlarge the old poetry and traditions of the past. As in the first strophes of the 'Sybil's Prophecy' the golden age was brought into being by men who knew the use of tools, so within the next three hundred years would Iceland, alone in Europe, create a spacious literature by the use of academic tools that the church brought in, with the knowledge and inspiration of Latin writing to encourage their manipulation.

As in Iceland, so in Normandy. The successors of Marching Rolf put on the garments of a new culture with the politic adaptability of the Icelanders who accepted Christianity without, as it appears, ever becoming aware of the basic importance of compassion in Christ's teaching. Under a European veneer—under their willing acceptance of churchly dogma and a new language—the Normans retained the hardihood, the practical brutality and propulsive temper of their predecessors. The Icelanders discarded their pagan gods, but with great respect preserved their memory with the aid of Christian teachers; the Normans became farmers and burnt their boats, but when they saw the prospect of new profit beyond the sea, their old instinct revived and they built another fleet.

The major Icelandic sagas are those that deal with Burnt Njal, Egil Skallagrimson, the people of Laxdale, and Grettir the Strong; and there are many smaller sagas. With the poetry of the *Elder Edda* and the elaborate court poetry of the heroic age they created Icelandic literature; and no part of it, as literature, has any relation to English writing or the development of English literature. But in the matter of the sagas there is a recurrent idea, or the revelation of an implicitly accepted habit of thought, that seems not unconnected with the development of administrative law in England, and with the English ethos.

In the British constitution there is no more important principle than the supremacy of law—subject only to the control of parliament—and embodied in that principle is the belief that all are equal before the law, and that justice must be done without fear or favour, affection or ill-will. That may be regarded as a formal and public dedication to the spirit of 'fair play' which has for long, if only intermittently, held a high place in English thought, although in English practice it has not always been evident. In theory, however, and in the practice of the courts, fair play in England has probably had a longer run of life than in other countries, and in the absence of any nearer or more probable origin it may well be that the principle or practice of it was first brought ashore from a viking longship. In their Icelandic laboratory the Norsemen created a literature that preserved both their history and their conception of good behaviour, and apart from the literary quality of the sagas—their gift of concise and nervous narrative, their faculty of exposing character through action and reported speech—their most astonishing feature is a capacity for absolute and relentless impartiality.

It is habitual in the sagas to write of men and their actions 'without fear or favour, affection or ill-will.' The faults of their heroes are exposed without rancour, and their villains, their malignants, are not deprived of dignity. Where there is judgment, it seems balanced, not on the broad blade of utilitarianism, but on the knife-edge of propriety. An example is the comment of Flosi of Swine-fell when the peace of earl Sigurd's Yule feast in Orkney was so rudely interrupted by Kari Solmundson who ran down the hall and struck off the lying head of Gunnar Lambison—Gunnar who was Flosi's companion in the burning of old Njal—and all that Flosi said was, 'Kari has not done this without good cause. We had made no atonement with him, and what he did he had a right to do.'

In that long saga there is an abominable character called Killing Hrapp. All that he does is malignant, he creates nothing but ill-will and destruction. But he dies well, and his death is recorded with a proper recognition of the only good quality that distinguished him: his fortitude. In Dasent's translation this is how it goes:

'Both Grim and Helgi see where Hrapp is, and they turned on him at once. Hrapp hews at Grim there and then with his axe; Helgi sees this and cuts at Hrapp's arm, and cuts it off, and down fell the axe.

'"In this," says Hrapp, "thou hast done a most needful work, for this hand hath wrought harm and death to many a man."

'"And so here an end shall be put to it," says Grim; and with that he ran him through with a spear, and then Hrapp fell down dead.'

There is no sentimentality—Hrapp gets what he deserves, and admits it—but justice is done to his bravery in defeat and there is no moralising about his ill deeds. This habit of cold, objective statement had a curious development—a literary development—for by the elimination of sentiment it made possible an epigrammatic brevity in the reporting of deeds that had been done, and in comment on them it often produced masterly examples of understatement of a sort that is still characteristic of English speech; and so, presumably, of English thought.

In the first half of Njal's saga a young woman called Hallgerda plays a mischievous and active part. She is beautiful, insufferably proud, pitiless, and passionate. She marries several times, and one of her husbands, infuriated by her extravagance, strikes her on the face. He goes off in a boat to an island where his men have been fishing, and Hallgerda's foster-father, a ruthless creature called Thiostolf, follows him. In a little while Thiostolf returns, carrying a blood-stained axe. 'What have you done?' asks Hallgerda. 'What will give you cause to get married again,' answers Thiostolf. Later in the story, when Hallgerda has re-married, she maintains a bitter feud with the household of old Njal, in which seven men die. When news is brought of the killing of another of their servants, Njal's redoubtable son Skarphedinn says thoughtfully—and almost with an English accent— 'Hallgerda doesn't let our housecarls die of old age.'

Fair dealing of a very striking sort—grudgingly given and strangely earned—is seen in the great saga of Egil Skallagrimson. Of all the saga heroes Egil is the most distinguished, for he is a true poet as well as a fierce and able soldier; his poet's voice, indeed, is as nimble and imaginative as the hard investigation of his sword. Beside king Athelstan of England he went to war against the Scots, and in later years shipwreck cast him into the hands of Eric Bloodaxe—when briefly he was a king in York—with whom, and his queen Gunnhild, Egil had been at bitter enmity. At Eric's court, however, Egil had a friend called Arinbiorn, who pleaded his cause with the king: Eric was roused to anger at the sight of his old enemy, and the fierce Gunnhild demanded that he be put to death immediately. But Arinbiorn won his reprieve for a night, and advised Egil to try for pardon by composing a poem in praise of the king. That he did—it was a long and elaborate poem—and the next day, in Eric's hall, in the presence of a great throng of men, he recited his *drapa*. Eric listened, sitting upright with glaring eyes, and when the *drapa* came to an end said in effect, 'That was very well done,' and gave Egil his freedom.

No one has ever pretended that Eric Bloodaxe was an amiable character, and his old quarrel with Egil was the consequence of an insult, deliberately devised by Egil, that even the mildest of men would have resented; but when Egil was in his power he was capable of recognising in Egil's poetry such virtuosity as compelled a kingly license to let the poet go unharmed. In a bad man wedded to a worse queen it was a remarkable example of the power of instinctive, not-to-be-denied fair play over a mind encumbered by hatred.

It cannot be said that an over-riding respect for fair play characterised the years of conquest after William of Normandy's victory at Hastings, though his insistence on law was absolute, and his respect for the old laws of England shrewd and statesmanlike. But in mediaeval England there was legislation to ensure honest manufacture, a just price for made goods, a fair wage for labourers, and a reasonable profit for the contractor: a demonstration of fair thinking—if not always of fair dealing—that cannot wholly be ascribed to Christian teaching. The mediaeval church was more interested in faith than ethics, and social practice had its ancestry in a sense of freedom, or will for freedom—often repressed but ever reviving—that may have been most durably imbedded in the Danelaw.

> 'The Law is the true embodiment
> Of everything that's excellent'—

so wrote W. S. Gilbert, perhaps with something less than full seriousness—though William of Normandy might have agreed with his words—and the most frequent corollary of respect for law is a delight in litigation. English social history is full of it, and the greatest of the Icelandic sagas reveals a passion for legal argument that is never deterred by the blood-letting that ensues from failure to find legal agreement, but is constantly renewed

FROM THE BAYEUX TAPESTRY

1. The building of the fleet.

FROM THE BAYEUX TAPESTRY

2. Led by William's flagship, the fleet crosses the channel.

FROM THE BAYEUX TAPESTRY

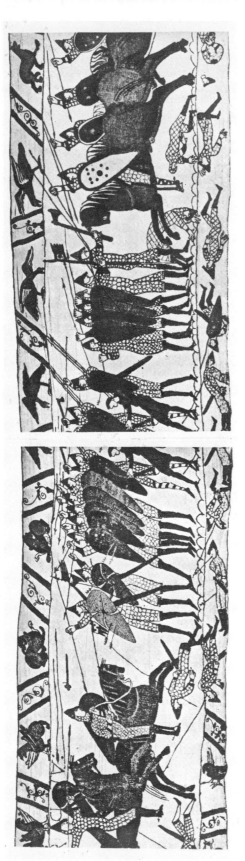

3. Norman cavalry against the shieldwall.

FROM THE BAYEUX TAPESTRY

4. "Here is William." At a crisis in the battle he raises his helmet.

by an appetite for intricate debate founded on dubious precedent and contested practice. For the very large incomes earned at the English bar, queen's counsel may in part be indebted to an old habit that began under the Hill of Laws at Thingvellir.

Chapter XII

THE REIGN OF EDWARD THE CONFESSOR

IMMEDIATELY after the death of Harthacnut, says the Chronicle, 'all the people then received Edward as king, as was his natural right.' He represented the old royal house of the West Saxons, he fetched his descent from Alfred the Great, and through him from Cerdic, the founder of their line in the sixth century. But only his father's blood saved him from being almost as much a foreigner as Cerdic had been when he first landed. For twenty-five years he had lived in Normandy, he had lately come to England as a stranger to the country, and as a king he was but poorly suited to fill a throne. But by name and birth he was English, and therefore more welcome than any of his possible rivals in Scandinavia.

There was Harold, son of Thorkell the Tall and a niece of king Cnut; but he was eliminated by murder. There was Sweyn, son of earl Ulf and Cnut's sister Estrith; but his claim was overlaid by Magnus of Norway who, asserting his right to both Denmark and England by virtue of his compact with Harthacnut, invaded Denmark and threatened preparation for a descent on England. His ambition was thwarted, or held at a distance, by Sweyn Estrithson's continuing war for Danish independence; and Edward on his ancestral throne was, in fact, troubled only by earl Godwine's ambition and his own temperament.

No single act, or series of acts, can quite explain the reputation of sanctity which gave him his byname, 'the Confessor,' and the natural piety that none denies him does not erase from his memory a curiously enigmatic quality. The nineteenth century historian E. A. Freeman, who wrote with magisterial amplitude and Victorian magniloquence of England's defeat and the Norman conquest, condemned his ineptitude with the devastating judgment that 'so far as a really good man can reproduce the character of a thoroughly bad one, Edward reproduced the character of his father, Ethelred.' He cites authority for charging him with sloth, with incapacity for steady attention to his duty, and with fits of energy that were often ill-timed and devoid of judgment. 'His virtues were those of a monk,' says Freeman; 'all the real man came out in his zeal for collecting relics, in his visions, in his religious exercises, in his gifts to churches and monasteries, in his desire to mark his reign, as its chief result, by the foundation of his great abbey of Saint Peter at Westminster.' How strange then—how painfully incongruous is Freeman's criticism—to find that this monkish man was as passionately devoted to falconry and stag-hunting as the brutal Normans who succeeded him.

In appearance he was handsome, with a plump and rosy face, his hair and beard prematurely white, his hands notably long and pallid. 'When not stirred up by passion, he was gentle and affable to all his men; he was liberal both to the poor and to his friends; but he had also the special art of giving a graceful refusal, so that the rejection of a suit by him was almost as pleasing as its acceptance by another.' Freeman gives his Latin authority for this delightful comment: *'Cunctis poscentibus ut benigne daret aut benigne negaret, ita et ut benigna negatio plurima videretur largitio'*—but he does not seem aware that he is crediting Edward with a remarkable cleverness quite inconsistent with the ineptitude and feeble temper that otherwise, in his description, so mark the king. He was, says Freeman, ever subject to the dominion of his favourites; his heart was French, his affections were lavished on his Norman priests and followers; and by the subjection of his realm to foreign influence he persuaded William the Bastard that England was already half won over to Norman rule. But the truth may be less simple, and Edward a more complex character than the pious, rosy weakling, with a passion for the chase, whom Freeman imagined.

He was crowned at Winchester in early April 1043—nearly ten months after his popular election—and in November, with the three earls, Leofric of Mercia, Godwine of Wessex, and Siward of Northumbria, he rode from Gloucester to Winchester again, where his mother was living, and took possession of all that she owned, both land and the great treasure she had in gold and silver. She had, apparently, treated him with conspicuous neglect and refused to share her wealth; but she was also accused of a worse error than parsimony or the failure of natural affection. She is said to have been in correspondence with Magnus of Norway and to have incited him, with a promise of her wealth, to invade England. It is, on the surface, a curious charge, for queen Emma had no obvious reason for favouring Magnus unless she remembered with pleasure that he had driven Algifu and her son Sweyn out of Norway—Algifu who had been Cnut's mistress and her rival—or truly respected the compact he had made with her own son Harthacnut; which did, in fact, give him a nominal claim to England.

It is more likely that her treasonable encouragement of Magnus was prompted by an old hatred of Godwine who, after the death of Cnut, had first supported Harthacnut's candidacy for the throne, but abandoned him for the more favoured Harald Harefoot, in whose brief reign she had been driven out of England. To that dire insult must be added Godwine's connivance in the murder of her son Alfred; and now Godwine enjoyed great authority in the land. To Emma her son Edward may have seemed a recreant who basely accepted, as his close counsellor, his brother's murderer; though Edward had little choice in the matter. It is possible, indeed, that England itself had excited her hatred. She was a Norman by birth, she had been the consort of a Danish king, and after his death she had watched England bow to the domination of Algifu of Northampton and Godwine of Wessex. Did she see a Norse invasion as its proper punishment? It is a great pity that no gifted Icelander was then domiciled in England who might have bequeathed a saga animated by the living speech of Algifu and Emma; for it seems probable that both deserved a place in the sagas' great portrait-gallery of hard, contentious, gifted women.

Emma was allowed to remain in Winchester, but her chaplain, Stigand, suspected of advising her, was deprived of his bishopric. Godwine's authority was confirmed by the marriage of his daughter Edith to the king, and demonstrated by the friendship shown to Sweyn Estrithson, who with changing fortune was struggling to keep Denmark independent. Sweyn, the nephew of Cnut, was also the nephew of Godwine's wife—Godwine had married a sister of earl Ulf—and two of his brothers came to live in England, Beorn, the elder, with an earl's dignity.

Norway was a menace that demanded a fleet in readiness against attack, and in 1045 Edward lay off Sandwich with thirty-five ships at his command. By the following year the fleet had grown—'No one,' says the Chronicle, 'had ever seen a larger naval force in this country'—but still Magnus did not come. Sweyn Estrithson, fighting stubbornly, was England's unacknowledged ally, but when he had to admit the loss of Denmark, and asked for fifty ships with which to renew the war, he was refused because, in English eyes, the Norwegian strength at sea was too formidable to challenge. Sweyn fled, and Denmark, submitting to compulsion, acknowledged Magnus as its king. Then, in the autumn of 1047, England was in grave danger, which was averted only by the accident of death. Magnus, in his own country called Magnus the Good, died before he could lay claim to England by force of arms.

Sweyn Estrithson returned to Denmark, and Norway readily welcomed to its throne the heroic Harald Hardrada, a half-brother of St. Olaf. He at once made peace with England, but did not forget the frail title to its throne that he had inherited from Magnus. For a long time he continued a profitless and inconclusive war with Denmark—Sweyn again asked for help and was again refused—and when, nineteen years after his accession, Harald Hardrada sailed at last and led his fleet into the Humber, another Harold quickly marched to meet him.

There were still viking ships on the narrow seas—the old profession was slow in dying—and in 1048, when parts of England suffered an earthquake, the crews of a fleet of twenty-five sail fought and plundered in the Isle of Wight and Sandwich, were beaten off in Thanet, but ravaged parts of Essex. They took many captives and an immense booty, and crossing the Channel sold their spoil in Flanders. Baldwin, count of Flanders, had joined a confederacy, led by Godfrey of Lorraine, which was waging an ineffectual war against the emperor Henry III, who had married Cnut's daughter Gunnhild; there was friction also between Flanders and England because Baldwin had given refuge to exiles and let pirates find a market for their stolen goods in his open ports. So, when the emperor sought the help of Denmark and England—the two countries which could command the narrow seas—to prevent the escape by sea of the Flemings he was about to defeat on land, Sweyn Estrithson gladly accepted so powerful an ally, and Edward, following his lead, mobilised a fleet to blockade the coast of Flanders.

So far as is known the fleet saw no action, but curiously it became something like a court of law for the condemnation of Godwine's eldest son, another Sweyn. He, sharing his father's advancement, had been made an earl, and in 1046, after an expedition into north Wales, seduced or kidnapped the abbess of Leominster, whom he let go when he had tired of her. He left England, presumably under compulsion, and for some time found refuge with his cousin Sweyn in Denmark; and then, for some dark but unknown reason, was again expelled. While Edward lay off Sandwich, Sweyn with eight ships sailed into Chichester harbour and tried to make his peace with the king. But Edward was obdurate, and Sweyn sought help from his cousin earl Beorn —brother of Sweyn Estrithson—who commanded a ship lying near Pevensey. Beorn was persuaded to return with Sweyn to Chichester, and there, for an unknown reason—drunken quarrel or his refusal to help—he was killed. The sequel was Edward's public denunciation of Sweyn, before a solemn assembly of English seamen, as a *nithing:* a dastard, a man devoid of honour. It was a condemnation known to the viking world, but it struck an unfamiliar note when pronounced by an English king before the sailors of his fleet. Was English law momentarily in abeyance to make room for an old Norse code? The sentence, moreover— if such it can be called—was effective: Sweyn's crews deserted him, and he fled for safety to that undiscriminating asylum, the court of Baldwin of Flanders.

Though England was no longer in danger of Norwegian invasion, there was no assurance that the sea had been swept clear of hostile shipping, and Edward's decision to disband his fleet and abolish the tax which paid his own retainers, though welcomed by the majority of his people, can only be explained as an early instance of the persistently recurring, the native and ineradicable English habit of economising, when economies are advisable, by first reducing expenditure on the armed services. The record of Edward's activities, from his accession till 1051, when the army tax was discontinued, does not on the whole substantiate Freeman's contempt for a king who had no virtues but those of the monkish sort. He had been energetic in defence of the realm, he showed clemency but decision in dealing with his treasonable mother, and for denunciation of the abominable Sweyn Godwineson he found an expression of devastating scorn. But, on the other hand, he had married Godwine's daughter Edith, and it is impossible to believe that such a marriage, or any marriage, was for him a willing transaction; Godwine was allowed to recall Sweyn from exile; and Edward's dismissal of his navy—his ignorance of England's constant need for ships of war—was indeed the exposure of his kingly insufficiency.

The common assertion that from the beginning of his reign he filled his court with Norman favourites is unjustified. There were Normans in his household, for he, a foreigner in a strange land, could hardly have lived without the comfort of some familiar voices; and naturally he preferred Norman priests. But the court was still largely Danish, as it had been in the time of Cnut, and it is idle to pretend that Norman influence could seriously affect a land dominated by the great earls of Wessex and Mercia and Northumbria. What is truly surprising is the continuing power of the authority established by Cnut. Of the three earls, Leofric of Mercia was English of the old stock—his father Leofwine had held Mercia under Ethelred—and Godwine, an Englishman of less certain origin, owed his position entirely to Cnut's favour. Godwine had married a sister of earl Ulf of Denmark, whose grandson Siward was earl of Northumbria. All three were Cnut's men.

In many ways the Anglo-Saxon Chronicle is an exasperating document, or confusion of documents. It records, with gloomy pertinacity, the death of eminent churchmen—'This year Alfric, archbishop of York, died, a man who was very venerable and wise'—and the recurrence of hard winters when sheep and cattle perished of starvation and hunger afflicted the land; then casually, in some intermission of such vital news, it lets slip the information that in 1051 'earl Godwine and all his sons were driven out of England. He went to Bruges with his wife and with his three sons, Sweyn, Tostig, and Gyrth. And Harold and

Leofwine went to Ireland.' No explanation is offered, and explanation must be garnered fitfully from other chronicles.

A family visit provoked the crisis. Eustace, count of Boulogne, was married to Goda, Edward's sister. They came to England to see the king, and when they were about to return to France a fight broke out between the Boulonnais and the men of Dover, in which many were wounded and twenty killed. Eustace rode indignantly to Gloucester, where the king was living, and the monkish man, enraged by the insult to his guests, ordered Godwine to harry the offending town. It was, according to the fashion of the time, an appropriate punishment, but Godwine refused to obey the royal command. Dover lay within his own earldom, and it is not impossible that French arrogance was to blame for the mishap; Godwine may have had good reason for his refusal, but such disobedience was tantamount to rebellion; and he seems to have contemplated rebellion.

His earldom of Wessex reached from Kent to the Bristol Channel; his reprobate son Sweyn was earl of a great territory that included the shires of Oxford, Gloucester, and Hereford; Harold, his younger son, had the earldom of East Anglia. On the 1st September, at Tetbury in the Cotswolds, not far from Gloucester, Godwine stood with an army drawn from his large resources and demanded from the king the surrender of count Eustace and his men, and a castle that a Norman lord had built in Herefordshire. Godwine had moved quickly, for the king had summoned a council to deal with the disaffection of his most powerful subject, and Godwine had arrived with an army a week before the council was due to meet. But Godwine's excessive strength in the land was also his weakness, for it made enemies; and his enemies came to the king's assistance.

Siward from the north and Leofric from the midlands came to Gloucester, and summoned reinforcements of their meagre companies when they saw the magnitude of Godwine's threat. The king's nephew Ralf—a son of his sister Goda by a marriage earlier than her alliance with Eustace of Boulogne—had fortunately been given an English earldom, and he too brought his contingent of loyalists. Godwine, who initially had moved with speed, apparently lacked the audacity to advance in open war against his king, and while he hesitated, the defensive force grew to a size equalling his own. But both sides, when they stood opposed in comparable strength, were sensible enough to avoid the inevitable disasters of a civil war, and it was agreed that the dispute should be referred to a national assembly of the Witan in London on the 24th September. By that agreement Godwine consented to defeat, for before the Witan he would be accused, he would have to answer charges of rebellion, and the army he had mobilised would lose confidence in a leader who had failed to fight when opportunity offered success.

The king ensured his defeat by calling out the whole militia of the realm, and the majority of Godwine's men were faced with a summons they dared not disobey. Godwine and his sons retained a considerable army with which to face the Witan, but the king's men outnumbered the rebels, who deserted a hopeless cause. Godwine tried to make terms, and the king returned a peremptory reply that he had five days of safety in which to leave England. Was it Edward's own voice that took revenge on the intolerable overseer under whom he had suffered—on the man who had murdered his brother and forced him into repugnant marriage—or was it an ultimatum devised by Leofric and Siward? The rosy-cheeked, monkish man may have recognised his opportunity, and used a strength that lay hidden beneath the gentleness of his customary mood, for after Godwine and his sons admitted defeat and fled, he celebrated freedom by dismissing from his court his unwanted wife. Her father found refuge in Flanders: his son Tostig had married a cousin of count Baldwin, whose ever-open court received Godwine, his wife, and three of his sons; while Ireland took the others.

Now it is true that Edward, rid of the domineering earl, brought Norman knights and clergy into England in such numbers as to provoke resentment. The vast estates of Godwine and his sons lay forfeit to the king, and a conservative people, both landowners and peasantry, may well have disliked new masters, whether French or English. It may be that popular feeling had been outraged by Godwine's expulsion; it appears certain that popular feeling was enlisted on his side during his twelve months' absence from the country. The king's authority, established by a show of force, ebbed away, but he took advantage of his year of freedom to nominate his heir and decide the history of England.

In one version of the Chronicle it is asserted that 'Count William came from overseas with a great force of Frenchmen,' and was received by the king; and if this statement is true there can be no doubt that the purpose of his visit was to receive assurance of his succession to the English throne, which at that time appeared to be within the king's gift. The story is suspect, however, because the duchy was then in some danger, and it is unlikely that William would have ventured to leave it. Far more probable is the story that Edward sent Robert of Jumièges, the newly appointed archbishop of Canterbury, to inform William of his intention. At one time abbot of Jumièges, Robert had been made bishop of London in 1044, and seven years later was translated to Canterbury. In the summer of 1051 he went to Rome to receive his pallium, and so auspicious a journey may well have been broken in Rouen to tell duke William of his promised heritage. It is significant that when Godwine returned to England, archbishop Robert was driven out and replaced by Stigand, bishop of Winchester, who himself had suffered exile when queen Emma was suspected of treason.

Emma died in 1052, and in that year, while the Welsh king Griffith ap Llewelyn was ravaging Herefordshire, Harold Godwineson came out of Ireland with a fleet that harried in Somerset and Devon. His father had already made a reconnaissance from Bruges and discovered that the Kentish coast was poorly guarded, and the men of Kent were ready to support him. The king had mustered a small fleet which was badly served and ineffectually commanded. It failed to prevent Godwine's return to Bruges, and later, when withdrawn into the Thames, its crews deserted and all the south coast was left defenceless. Godwine wasted no time but sailed immediately to the Isle of Wight, provisioned his ships, and continued his westward voyage to a rendezvous with Harold. They were politic in their dealing with the coastal parts of southern England, made only moderate demands, and sailing in company came into the estuary of the Thames with a considerable strength of men and ships drawn from Hastings, Romney, Folkestone, Dover, and Sandwich.

Now the king had to pay for parsimony and the dismissal of

his navy. He had some fifty ships, but from the fact that they lay moored on the north bank of the river, above London Bridge, it is obvious that they were unprepared for battle or their crews were unwilling to fight. Godwine went ashore on the south bank, and having made prudent investigation from Southwark, discovered that the citizens of London favoured him in preference to the king's Frenchmen. He moved up river on the tide, and his ships formed a screen round the royal fleet. The king had a large force on land, but again, as at Tetbury, men were reluctant to fight against their own neighbours. Edward was loth to admit defeat, and Godwine's sailors grew impatient. Then, with the help of bishop Stigand and other intermediaries, a truce was arranged and safeguarded by the exchange of hostages.

Before the Witan, assembled outside London, Godwine denied all the offences with which he was charged, and was formally acquitted. Failure to acquit him would have provoked the battle that no one on the king's side wanted, and Edward was publicly humiliated for the sake of peace. To Godwine and his sons their earldoms were unconditionally restored, and Frenchmen who had made themselves objectionable were dismissed from such offices as they had acquired. The king's discomfiture was complete, and Godwine's authority in England established beyond the reach of challenge. For the king in his sorrow there was no lenitive but news of the timely death of Godwine's iniquitous son Sweyn: he, submitting to a spiritual compulsion common in that age, had gone as a pilgrim to Jerusalem, and died in Constantinople on his way home. The *nithing* was removed from the scene, but his father's unpardonable conduct had revealed to northern Europe—where Harald Hardrada had a watchful interest in the affairs of England—that the kingdom had no defence on the sea, and was so deeply divided in its loyalties that in a renewed crisis it might fall apart. For William of Normandy there was no longer the prospect of a peaceful succession, for the ancient power of Wessex had enveloped the king, and Wessex, after expelling the king's unpopular Frenchmen, was unlikely to welcome a Norman duke.

Godwine lived only a few months to enjoy his triumph. He died in April 1053, having suffered a stroke while dining with the king at Winchester, and his son Harold succeeded to an earldom enlarged by a great part of the territory that his brother Sweyn had ruled. Harold's former earldom of East Anglia went to a son of Leofric of Mercia, and the king's nephew Ralf extended his dominion. But the most significant change in local authority occurred when Siward of Northumbria died in 1055. Duncan, king of Scots, had married Siward's sister, and after Duncan was defeated and killed by Macbeth, Siward protected Duncan's son Malcolm, and on his behalf made war against the usurper. In that war his older son was killed, and when Siward died in the following year his surviving son, Waltheof, was only a boy. So Harold's brother Tostig was given the earldom—Tostig who was Siward's cousin—and secured the northern frontier by establishing a warm friendship with Malcolm of Scotland: so warm a friendship, indeed, that they were said to have sworn brotherhood. For ten years Tostig ruled his northern earldom in peace; or in such comparative peace as to leave no record of war.

There was more trouble on the Welsh border, where the ambition of Griffith ap Llewelyn, king of Gwynedd and Powys, found an ally in Alfgar, the son of Leofric of Mercia. Griffith made himself king of all Wales, and success fed hostility to England. In 1055 Alfgar, who had been made earl of East Anglia, was outlawed, for an unspecified act of treason, in circumstances which suggest that his real offence was to have fallen foul of Harold Godwineson and so re-awakened the old enmity between Wessex and Mercia. In exile he went to Ireland, where he found free-minded vikings in sufficient number to man eighteen ships, and with them joined Griffith in an invasion of England. They defeated the militia of Herefordshire, burnt Hereford, and pillaged the cathedral. Harold mustered an army and marched against them, but in the confined country of Welsh hill-and-valley appears to have given his opponents a tactical advantage of which they took masterly opportunity; for, without fighting, a peace was concluded that re-established Alfgar in his earldom.

The Welsh war continued until Griffith was able to demand a grant of land west of the river Dee in return for his oath of allegiance to Edward; and for a year he respected his oath. In 1057 the natural heir to the throne, who was Edward, son of the king's half-brother Edmund Ironside, was brought home from the distant refuge in Hungary to which, as a child, he had been taken to avoid Cnut's destructive hands. For forty years he had lived in exile—honoured in the court of Stephen of Hungary and married to a lady of the royal family—and soon after his return to England he died without having seen his uncle the king. It was so 'brought about,' says the Chronicle, that he was not allowed to see him, 'but we do not know for what reason'; nor is the manner of his death explained, though his 'miserable fate' is deplored. In the same year Ralf of Hereford, the king's nephew, and Leofric of Mercia died. Alfgar resigned the earldom of East Anglia to succeed his father, and East Anglia was divided to form new earldoms for Harold's younger brothers, Gyrth and Leofwine; while Harold took Ralf's earldom of Hereford. With this formidable increase of power the house of Godwine presented an obvious threat to Alfgar of Mercia, and Alfgar replied with a violence that the Chronicle does not condescend to explain or describe.

The Chronicle is careful to record the consecration by bishop Aldred of the monastic church at Gloucester; the death of pope Stephen IX and his succession by Benedict X 'who sent the pallium into this country for archbishop Stigand'; and the death of Heca, bishop of Sussex. But of a major threat to England all it has to say is: 'In this year (1058) earl Alfgar was banished but he came back forthwith by violence through Griffith's help. And a naval force came from Norway. It is tedious to relate fully how things went.' Tedious it may have been for that dull-witted, idle monk, but the Irish Annals of Tigernach and the Annales Cambriae offer a glimpse of an alliance that gathered to launch an organised and dangerous attack on England. According to the latter, Griffith of Wales joined Magnus, son of Harald Hardrada, in a devastating raid, while the former declares that 'a fleet (was led) by the son of the king of the Scandinavians, along with the Foreigners of the Orkneys, and of the Hebrides, and of Dublin, in order to take the kingdom of England. But God permitted it not.'

The Irish statement that the purpose of the expedition was 'to take England' is an exaggeration, for there is no mention of any such major enterprise in Snorri Sturluson's saga of the kings of Norway or in the Orkney saga; but what appears certain is that Alfgar's resentment of the growing power of Harold Godwineson, and Griffith's hostility to England, gave Harald Hardrada a chance to make a reconnaissance in force of the land he was to invade a few years later. It is proper, moreover, to infer that the raid was successful, for Alfgar was again restored to his earldom, his alliance with Griffith continued, and when he died in 1062 he was succeeded by his young son Edwin.

It seems evident, indeed, that for four years the alliance of Alfgar and Griffith was strong enough to hold Harold in check and maintain a balanced peace; for when Alfgar died Harold immediately took advantage of Griffith's isolation to lead a winter invasion of north Wales, and in the following summer he and his brother Tostig—Harold from the south and Tostig from the north—waged a war that splintered the brief unity of Griffith's kingdom and so discredited him that he was killed by his own people. It is recorded that 'his head was brought to earl Harold, and Harold brought it to the king.' Wales, also dismembered, was entrusted to Griffith's half-brothers, who pledged allegiance to Edward.

Now Harold was supreme in England. There was none to challenge his authority. Edwin of Mercia was too young to mould the strength of Mercia into opposition, and though Edward the exile, who had come home from Hungary to die so quickly, had left a son, called Edgar the Atheling, he was a child whose pretention to the throne would not be supported and could not be regarded as a practical answer to an ever-enlarging question. The king had reigned for more than twenty years, he was not an old man, but he was not a robust man; he was childless, and would die childless. Who, then, would succeed him? That was the question looming larger in men's minds, and it cannot be doubted that Harold saw himself as the destined heir. That Edward had promised the throne to William of Normandy was a difficulty which could not be ignored—that Harald Hardrada would forcibly assert his claim was highly probable—but when the throne should fall vacant, Harold Godwineson would have the tactical advantage of living within easy reach of it, and the natural advantage of his English blood. Once before, when Harold and his father were in exile, and Edward filled his court with Frenchmen, the English had turned against the foreigners and shown clearly their preference for one of their own sort.

It was, then, by a stroke of bitter irony that Harold, while on some continental mission for the king, fell into William's power and, on the vivid testimony of the Bayeux Tapestry, was compelled to take an oath of allegiance to him. It is very clear, however—and in centuries so haunted by religious dread it may seem strange—that even the holiest of relics could not guarantee an oath against perjury, and he who swore the oath rarely esteemed it so highly as he who exacted it. Harold's brief captivity in Normandy was an embarrassing misadventure, but less embarrassing than a grave disturbance of the peace in Northumbria.

Tostig had ruled his earldom for ten years before the harshness of his government provoked rebellion, and presumably a decade of power had corrupted his temper and impaired his judgment. The rebels were serious, their mood was murderous. Tostig's bodyguards were killed, his treasury and his armoury looted; all his earldom 'unanimously deserted him and outlawed him,' because 'first he robbed God, and all those who were less powerful than himself he deprived of life and land.' It is a formidable indictment, though lacking detail, and Tostig's expulsion made room for the popular election of earl Morcar, brother of Edwin of Mercia. The two young earls, with a Welsh contingent to reinforce the large army they mustered in Northumbria and the midlands, marched to Northampton where they confronted Harold in such strength that he was compelled to acquiesce in their demands. The king confirmed the election of Morcar, Tostig and his family retired as usual to the court of Baldwin of Flanders, and the rebel earls celebrated their triumph by harrying Northamptonshire. On the eve of the year of crisis Harold's authority had been materially weakened.

Except for his approval of Morcar's election—and an earlier statement that Harold had presented him with the severed head of Griffith ap Llewelyn—there is, in the Chronicle, scarcely a mention of the king for more than a dozen years before his death; and the probable explanation is that when Godwine returned in triumph from his year of exile, and had all his lands and power restored to him, Edward's humiliation was so profound that he withdrew from public life to console himself with prayer and meditation, and his plans for a new church and palace at Westminster. Though demolished by Henry III, to make room for greater splendour, the Confessor's church in its own time was larger and more magnificent than any other in England.

From the apse at the east end and the choir under its central tower, to the twin towers at its west end, its length was enormous; there were twelve bays in the nave, and Norman columns in alternating pairs of cylindrical and large compound patterns that its builder had seen at Jumièges. For fourteen years Edward spent a tenth of his income on that noble memorial to St. Peter and himself. His income was derived from a great number of royal manors, some of which included, as well as farms and villages, men of rank, free peasants and slaves, and a growing number of traders and craftsmen who had been attracted to them by the security they offered; their inhabitants paid a substantial rent, either in produce or money, and the king's income was certainly not small.

His church and his piety combined to create a legend of his sanctity that was accepted while he was still alive, and before he died he had the happiness of seeing his abbey completed, though he was too ill to be present at its consecration. It was consecrated on the 28th December, 1065, and he died a few days later.

Chapter XIII

NOVITIATE OF A KING

WHEN Richard I of Normandy, grandson of Marching Rolf, died in 996, he was succeeded by his son Richard II, in whose time a significant relationship was established with England.

Soon after his accession the peace of the duchy was torn apart by a peasants' revolt which appears to have been organised with a formality and skill beyond the power of a simple *jacquerie*. The peasants of the rebellious districts are said to have been represented by delegates in a general assembly, where they asserted some sort of democratic principles and demanded new forest-laws; the explanation may be that there was a continuing influx into Normandy of unsettled men, and the pressure of an increasing population so threatened the security of those of its native inhabitants who had survived the coming of the Norsemen that they united with descendants of the earliest colonists to resist the newcomers and oppose their encroachment on diminished properties and common land. Whatever may have been its nature and the wrongs that existed, the rebellion was brutally suppressed by Rodolf, count of Ivry, a half brother of Richard I.

It was, perhaps, a punitive English raid on the Cotentin peninsula that created a situation in which, for the first time, the need became clearly apparent for some treaty or agreement—or, at least, for the establishment of a relationship that would permit discussion—between England and Normandy. In the last years of the tenth century England had suffered severely from the depredation of vikings who found winter quarters across the Channel; and on the authority of William of Jumièges, Ethelred retaliated by ravaging the Cotentin. In 1002 he married Emma of Normandy, sister of Richard II, and the purpose of a political marriage may well have been to create an association by means of which the viking traffic could be controlled, and the enmity it fomented, mitigated.

The marriage treaty did not permanently close the Norman ports against pirates, and there is a measure of truth in the assertion, in Snorri Sturluson's saga of the kings, that 'the earls of Rouen, who claimed kinship with lords in Norway and for long set store by it, were always friends of the Norsemen and all Norsemen had sanctuary in Normandy if they cared to use it.' In 1014 duke Richard welcomed in Rouen a viking host that had been plundering in Brittany, and employed some part of it—under Olaf the Stout, later king and patron saint of Norway—in a campaign against Odo, count of Chartres. Olaf accepted Christianity, was baptised in Rouen by the archbishop, and then went to England with king Ethelred.

Under Richard II the duchy was strong, his own authority undisputed. According to the nineteenth century historian Freeman, 'he had imbibed to the full all the new-born aristocratic feelings of feudal and chivalrous France. He would have none but gentlemen about him.' It is a curious statement—it has a smack of the nineteenth century rather than the eleventh—but there may be some foundation for it in the fact that territorial titles first came into use in Richard's time. For various kinsmen he created the counties of Arques, Eu, the Hiésmois, Evreux, Brionne, and Mortain; and Rodolf, his father's half-brother, became count of Ivry. The *vicomtes* had made an earlier appearance, as officers in the central administration, when the only count in Normandy was its ruler; but from now on both counts and *vicomtes* became more numerous, and their responsibilities more definite.

Richard, who had married Judith of Brittany, died in 925 and was succeeded by his eldest son, Richard III, who lived thereafter for barely a year. He died young, but his younger brother, Robert, who was little more than a boy, was precocious enough to be suspected of having had him poisoned; though that suspicion may date from a later age. Sudden death was often ascribed to poison—eight years later, when Robert died, poison was said to have killed him—and there may be no more justification for the story than the fact that Robert succeeded his brother as count or duke of Normandy though Richard had left a legitimate son, a child called Nicholas; who was removed to a monastery.

At the beginning of Robert's short reign the duchy fell into disorder complicated by war with his cousin Alan of Brittany, and the turbulence of those early years must have been partly responsible for his later acquisition of a notorious nickname. There is no contemporary evidence that he was called Robert the Devil, and perhaps a French romance of that name should take a share of the blame for his cognomen: he may have been confused with a quite fictitious hero whose temper was not unlike his own. It was, presumably, a division of loyalties between him and his dead brother that provoked a civil war—that and a newly rich nobility's discerning eye for the profit to be found in troubled waters—and the conflict with Brittany was a cousinly dispute about the succession. It is probable, however, that Robert was reckless and harsh of judgment, for in the course of the war he laid siege to Evreux and his uncle Robert, who, as well as being count of Evreux, was archbishop of Rouen; it was he who had baptised Olaf of Norway.

Archbishop Robert appears to have been a man who added the capacity of a statesman to the great power of his lands and ecclesiastical office, and combined magnanimity with both. He was forced into exile, but when Robert was compelled to recall him—for none other could repair the broken fabric of the duchy —he and his headstrong nephew were reconciled, he brought the war with Brittany to an end, and re-established peace and prosperity in Normandy. No confirmation can be found of the story, mentioned elsewhere, that Robert married and promptly repudiated Cnut's sister Estrith—or of its rumoured sequel that he mobilised a fleet for the invasion of England—but the athelings Alfred and Edward were certainly living in the duchy, and on their behalf he may have undertaken some impetuous action and permitted himself the luxury of a distant insult to Cnut.

Of larger interest is his association with the tanner's daughter Herlève—more commonly known as Arlette—and the consequent birth of William the Bastard, who in the course of time acquired a more honourable title. There is a well-known tale that in the streets of Falaise Robert saw a young girl dancing— or, alternatively, washing her linen—and having promptly fallen in love with her, made her his mistress and the mother of an illegitimate son. Shorn of some possible decoration, that is the accepted story, and it is neither improbable nor especially remarkable. The girl's father is said to have been called Fulbert, and the tradition that he was a tanner may be substantiated by the fact that the commerce of Falaise depended on tanneries and woollen mills.

What is remarkable, and perplexing, is the subsequent fortune of both the bastard and his mother; but the brief story of duke Robert must be finished before that is considered. In 1031 a fortunate decision was made, either by duke Robert or archbishop Robert, when Henry I, king of France, fled from the hostile coalition of his mother and a count of Chartres, and sought refuge in Normandy: duke Robert fulfilled his feudal obligation, succoured the king, enabled him to regain his throne, and instilled in the monarch a feeling of friendship for Normandy that was later to prove very useful. But Robert was not committed to utilitarian policies, and three years later shocked his nobility— those of his nobility who were nearest and most loyal to him— by declaring his intention of making a pilgrimage to Jerusalem, though his prolonged absence from the duchy would certainly create difficulties and might prove disastrous.

The rulers of western Europe were, in that era, almost as compulsively drawn to Rome and Jerusalem as pious Moslems to Mecca. That men possessed of a passionate Christian faith should wish to kneel in reverence at the seat of Christian authority or in the city of Christ's redeeming death is no matter for surprise, but what cannot fail to astonish is the fascination that the holy places could exercise on men whose lives had been dominated by secular ambition, and on men who were downright wicked. The abominable Sweyn Godwineson lost his life on pilgrimage, and Edward the Confessor is said to have built his great abbey of Westminster in expiation of his failure to undergo the penance of a hard and dangerous journey. Cnut the Great was a pilgrim, and so were earl Thorfinn of Orkney, Macbeth of Scotland, and warfaring Norsemen of high lineage. Desire of the Holy Land could show the strength of obsession, and a man obsessed has no respect for the common demands of duty. Despite all opposition Robert was determined to go where inclination beckoned, and before embarking on the journey, which gave him great honour and from which he never returned, he summoned the leaders of his nobility and induced them to accept the boy William as his heir and swear obedience to him.

That their agreement to do this was largely exacted by the authority of archbishop Robert can hardly be doubted, and it was probably by his forethought that Henry I of France—who had lately been succoured in Normandy—was persuaded, as the boy's feudal superior, to admit his claim and recognise his title. But why did the archbishop approve the adoption, as heir to the duchy, of a bastard who, so far as is known, had nothing to recommend him to favour but his father's preference? There were others who could show as good or better a title to the succession. There was Nicholas, son of Richard III, who had been relegated to a monastery, and, indeed, appeared to be contented with his lot. There were two half-brothers of Richard III, of doubtful legitimacy, and his nephew, Guy of Burgundy, a son of his sister Alice. But William the Bastard was the archbishop's choice, though 'the recognition of duke Robert's illegitimate son as heir to his father's lordship would have been impossible in any country where the church, and the theory of the state for which it stood, had their accustomed influence.'[1]

Before Robert's departure for the Holy Land the boy's mother, Herlève, was married to Herluin, *vicomte* of Conteville, and so handsome a disposal of his discarded mistress must again cause surprise. That Robert should wish to make decent provision for her might be expected, but surely a more natural reward, for the daughter of a tanner who had briefly pleased him, would be marriage to some respectable tradesman of Falaise, or the mediaeval equivalent of a groom of the chambers or clerk of the kitchen. Herlève, however, married the *vicomte* of Conteville and lived out her life in such dignity, in such association with the nobility, that Odo and Robert, her sons by Herluin, became two of the greatest magnates in William's English kingdom: Odo, bishop of Bayeux, was created earl of Kent, and Robert, count of Mortain, acquired properties that made him one of the richest landowners in the country.

A story was confected in England that Herlève was a grand-

[1] Sir Frank Stenton, *Anglo-Saxon England*.

daughter of Edmund Ironside, the gallant son of Ethelred the Unready. Her mother, according to the fable, had disgraced herself by intrigue with her father's tanner, to whom she bore three daughters, and with whom she fled to Normandy, where they were given kindness and help by duke Richard II. The story is told by Freeman, who is careful to make clear his rejection of it; and it is, indeed, too obviously fabricated to command belief. But it does awaken curiosity about the identity of Herlève's mother.

It has been observed that Robert, before leaving on his pilgrimage, was very careful to ensure William's recognition and acceptance as his heir. He did not, however, take the most obvious measure to ensure the child's acceptance. The easiest way in which to make the boy eligible would have been to marry his mother and legitimate him; and Herlève, by her union with the *vicomte* of Conteville, was apparently not ill-suited to the dignity of a lordly marriage. There may, however, have been some obstacle to her marriage with Robert, and it is an interesting coincidence that the wife of archbishop Robert was also called Herlève.—He married her, presumably, in his capacity as count of Evreux rather than in his role as archbishop.—Now it is tempting to suppose that the child Herlève was so christened to win the favour or protection of the countess, and that strongly suggests a family connexion which may supply the reason for duke Robert's inability to marry his mistress. He and the young Herlève—a bastard like the son she bore—may have been within the prohibited degrees of relationship.

There lies a possible explanation of the archbishop's sturdy interest in the boy William, and also of the extraordinary favour shown to Herlève. Respect of ancestry—a deep regard for the virtue of noble blood—was certainly a dominating influence in the Scandinavian countries, and Normandy, where titles of nobility had lately been adopted and already were proliferating, was not so remote from its northern antecedents as to have lost all sense of the past. If Herlève was related to the ruling family by a mother who had been as indiscreet as Herlève herself, then much that appears bewildering is made comprehensible.

For a couple of years after duke Robert's departure from Normandy, the archbishop maintained peace in the land and the authority of his government; but in 1037 his death precipitated a collapse of order in which many of the nobility reverted to that primitive concept of society as a state of life in which a man must defend his own property, and a strong man may extend it. It cannot be said that Normandy fell into total anarchy, for the dynasty was maintained, and though the structure of government was dislocated and its functions crippled, the image of a continuing government was not erased. In comparison with the peace of Richard II's reign, however, the disorder was fearful, and complicated by a merciless struggle for possession and control of the boy William. Within the ducal castle there was fear on the stairs and murder in the courtyard. Osbern the steward, who had been one of those who swore allegiance to the boy before his father left, was killed in William's bedroom, and Herlève's brother Walter is said to have taken him, night after night, to the safety of refuge in some humble cottage.

It seems, however, that William was recognised as the true heir of the dynasty and its power—or perhaps as a symbol of its power—for those members of the family who might have contended for his heritage now united to preserve and buttress it. The half-brothers of duke Robert, Mauger and William—sons of Richard II by a woman called Papia—acquired new authority when Mauger, to keep the see of Rouen in the family, was appointed its archbishop; and William became count of Arques. Guy of Burgundy, a grandson of duke Richard, and Ralph of Gacé, a son of archbishop Robert, also received advancement. But the dynasty was preserved amid the confusion of increasing violence, and as if to re-awaken memories of a northern ancestry old feuds were revived that might have been copied from Icelandic sagas; though the revenge exacted was sometimes too sophisticated for Iceland.

Though the duchy was torn by civil war, it was not a war clearly defined by opposing causes. It was, rather, a war in which the ducal house strove for order against anarchy, and with the assistance of the church, whose bishops remained loyal, an organised ducal force maintained a semblance of administration and from parts of the duchy still collected revenue. In these chaotic conditions many simple castles were built, and that was a military innovation of major interest. The idea of the castle came from

Carolingian France, and the motte, as it was called, was a built-up mound, surrounded by a moat, and crowned by a palisade that enclosed a wooden tower. If the mound was large enough to accommodate a walled courtyard, the construction was known as a motte and bailey. To a noble family at war with its neighbours or liable to sudden attack, such a castle was of manifest value, and its subsequent development, later in the century, was of considerable importance in establishing Norman rule over England.

The spirit which roused the peasants to rebellion in the early years of Richard II was still strong enough to unite their sons in organised resistance, here and there, against the lawless nobility, but such rural protest had no appreciable effect. It was the intervention of Henry of France that checked the extravagance of the lordly anarchists, and on at least two occasions restored a measure of order by force of arms. He was William's feudal superior to whom the boy had been sent to do homage, and from whom, at some uncertain date, he received knighthood. Henry had the right to intervene in the troubled affairs of a vassal's territory when they affected his own security, and the responsibility for protection of a vassal who could be regarded as his ward. That he remembered with gratitude the help given him by William's father in 1031 need not be doubted, but gratitude was not his only motive.

In 1046 the confused and long-continued dissension in the duchy found a uniting purpose and a leader in Guy of Burgundy, who headed an organised revolt against the young duke and found massive support in middle, western, and lower Normandy. Now both William and his duchy were in danger of extinction, and so immediate was the danger, that William escaped from the midst of his enemies only by riding hard through the darkness of a long night. He reached the safety of Falaise, and from there hastened to the French king at Poissy, and as a vassal claimed the help of his lord. Gratitude for an old benefit may have lingered in the king's memory, but it was policy that determined his decision; for rebellion against the duke of Normandy was perilously near rejection of his sovereignty.

A French army advanced on Caen, and in 1047 at Val-ès-Dunes, between the Orne and the Dives, met the rebels in a fierce, unordered cavalry engagement in which both Henry of France and young William of Normandy fought in the front of battle. Henry was unhorsed, but his assailant was killed while the king lay helpless, and William gave proof of that handiness in war—his physical supremacy and dextrous hardihood—which laid the foundation for his eventual hardihood in council chamber and on the throne. In hand-to-hand conflict he killed a notable warrior on the insurgent side, and after severe fighting the rebels broke and lost in flight so many, slaughtered or drowned in the Orne, that a mill on the river-bank was stopped by dead bodies.

The result of the battle was the proclamation, in a solemn assembly near Caen, of the Truce of God. This curiously naïve assertion of ecclesiastical authority, which had been introduced into France in the tenth century, forbade private warfare—as if it were flesh on Friday—from Wednesday night till Monday morning and throughout the holy seasons of the church. That its maintenance might sometimes depend on the goodwill of secular authority as well as on the church's sanction is fairly obvious, but the assembly at Caen did what it could to ensure the efficacy of the Truce by excluding the king and the duke from the prohibition it laid on others; and Norman chroniclers of a later date regarded the victory at Val-ès-Dunes, and the proclamation which followed it, as the conclusion of William's minority and the beginning of his power in the duchy. But in 1047 there was no evidence of a dominating or established power.

The leader of the revolt, Guy of Burgundy, occupied the fortress of Brionne, some twenty-five miles south-west of Rouen, where his strength was such that he was able to withstand a pertinacious siege and elaborate siege-works for nearly three years; and it is impossible to believe that William had much freedom of movement—he may even have been excluded from Rouen—until 1050, when Guy surrendered and was banished. It was at Caen that the Truce of God had been proclaimed, and Caen may have been the seat of his restricted government; it was about this time that the town began to grow towards the importance which was later made manifest by its great churches and William's decision to be buried there.

No sooner had Guy of Burgundy yielded than a new enemy began to move towards the duchy. This was Geoffrey Martel, count of Anjou. South of Normandy, and divided from it by Maine, lay Anjou and Touraine; and from 1044 Touraine had been subject to Anjou. By his possession of Tours Geoffrey controlled the valley of the Loire, and when disorder afflicted Maine he saw his opportunity to extend his power northward; his by-name, Martel, means the Hammer. At the time of the battle of Val-ès-Dunes he was fighting in the south of Maine, and a year later, at the invitation of its citizens, he occupied Le Mans, its capital. Between Maine and Normandy lay the debatable lands of Bellême, dominated by the fortresses of Domfront and Alençon, and when both fell to Geoffrey, the king's peace was threatened as well as Normandy. William was serving Henry's interest when he went to war against Anjou.

He conducted a short, brilliant, and merciless campaign in which a threat to Domfront drew Geoffrey Martel into battle, where he was worsted. Geoffrey withdrew, and William laid siege to Domfront. While the siege continued he marched eastward to Alençon, and moving swiftly, took it by surprise. Fearful punishment was inflicted on its defenders, and report of their treatment unnerved the garrison in Domfront, which appealed for mercy and surrendered. William's frontier in Bellême, thus tolerably secure, was further strengthened by the marriage of his friend and supporter, Roger of Montgomery, to an heiress of Bellême. He needed all the strength that friends and success in war could give him, for now occurred a radical change in his relations with Henry of France. For no clear reason—though presumably he judged the friendship of Anjou to be worth more than that of Normandy—the king made overtures of peace to Geoffrey, and presently concluded an alliance with him that brought to a rude end his favouring interest in William. Then the young duke, weakened by loss of the king's protection, was confronted by the disaffection and revolt of one of the greatest magnates in Normandy, his uncle William, count of Arques, whose brother Mauger was archbishop of Rouen.

It must have been evident that there was some connexion between the rupture of relations with the French king and this massive revolt, but William was not deterred from action by dread of the great coalition that might have been formed against him. He was in the Cotentin when he heard of the rebellion, and with only a small company rode swiftly towards the very strong fortress which his uncle had lately built above the little river Arques, that runs into the sea at Dieppe. It was too strong to be taken by assault, but he had gathered a sufficient force to invest it and leave him with strength enough to watch, with a mobile army, for the arrival of the count's allies. The king of France disclosed his association with William of Arques by marching to join him, and found duke William astride his route. The king's purpose was to relieve the invested garrison, and William's to prevent its relief. His men were the more alert, or better led, and part of Henry's army marched into an ambush where it suffered such heavy losses that the invaders had to withdraw. Starvation reduced the castle, and William of Arques, his jealous hope destroyed, was banished from Normandy.

The rebuff to the king, however, had not been decisive, and Geoffrey of Anjou was meditating an attack in the west. The king mustered a large and powerful army which advanced in two divisions. That which he led concentrated at Mantes and ravaged the country of Evreux, while the other, under his brother Odo, entered eastern Normandy between the head-waters of the Bresle and the Epte and dispersed to plunder in the district about Mortemer. Now William's recent victory at Arques proved of decisive value, for out of the northern corner of the duchy came the men whose allegiance he had won to meet the French. Their leaders had names which later gathered fame—Robert, count of Eu, and Roger of Mortemer, Walter Giffard, and William of Warenne—and the French under Odo, the king's brother, caught unprepared, were utterly defeated in a prolonged, untidy, savage battle. So great was their loss that when news of it reached the king, west of the Seine, he lost heart and withdrew without further fighting. Geoffrey of Anjou, his enterprise barely begun, also retreated, and Mauger, archbishop of Rouen and brother of the banished William of Arques, was deposed by an ecclesiastical council sitting at Lisieux.

The battle of Mortemer was fought in 1054 when William— the date of his birth is uncertain—was probably about twenty-six. In the seven years since the battle of Val-ès-Dunes he had shown an aptitude for war and warlike policy. He knew the value of rapid movement, and he had elaborated a successful technique for laying siege to defended castles by erecting against them counter-works which formed a *point d'appui* for attack and gave some protection to the besiegers. He had discovered that a policy of deliberate ferocity could produce elsewhere a situation in which he could afford to be unexpectedly lenient. He had survived personal danger in circumstances which required instant decision and burly action, and he had revealed a natural habit of command—an inspiring instinct for command—which had drawn to him many of the younger men on whose service he would increasingly rely and increasingly reward. In 1054 he crossed the watershed that divided the anarchy of his boyhood and the perils of his youth from the political growth of his young manhood and the success—that was never free from danger—of his maturity. In the year before the battle of Mortemer Harold Godwineson had succeeded his father in the earldom of Wessex; he too was advancing towards a fateful maturity.

Some sort of reconciliation was effected with the king, and a renewal of war with Anjou, in the debatable land between Normandy and Maine, resulted in a local success for Normandy that did nothing to dislodge Geoffrey from his dominating power in Maine. When the king resumed hostilities against the duchy, he was in alliance with Geoffrey, and together they advanced from the south towards Bayeux and Caen, while William, commanding an army at Falaise, permitted the pillaging of his land for the sake of a tactical advantage. It was not until the invaders turned east to cross the river Dives by a ford near Varaville that he struck. Then, while the king's army, laden with plunder, was divided by the flowing tide, he attacked, and is said to have annihilated its rearward part. The king retreated without further action, and in the following months there were perceptible signs of the weakening of Angevin authority in Maine.

Now it was William's turn to take the offensive, and he moved across his south-western border into the Vexin; where, nearly thirty years later, he was to fight his last war. It was a divided land, part Norman, part French. Between the Andelle and the Epte lay the Norman Vexin; between the Epte and the Oise was French, where the principal town was Mantes. William captured the French fortress of Thimert, not far from Dreux, and in the summer of 1058 the king laid siege to it. The fortress held out, and the siege continued. It continued into the following year, and the year after that. Thimert was still untaken when Henry died, early in 1060; and in November of that year, as if to complete its beneficence, Geoffrey Martel died too.

Henry I of France was succeeded by his son Philip, a child whose guardian was Baldwin V, count of Flanders. Baldwin had married Adela, the dead king's sister, and their daughter Matilda was married to William of Normandy. He had married her in 1051 or 1052 despite the injunction of pope Leo IX, who forbade their union for an unknown reason. It has been conjectured that they were distantly related by common descent from Marching Rolf, and other shadowy obstacles have been imagined but never confirmed. In spite of the opposition it aroused, the marriage was patently of benefit to William when he was fighting against heavy odds to maintain his inheritance—while Baldwin, in the context of his own political problems, must have seen some profit in allying himself with a vassal of the French king—and when his father-in-law accepted tutelage of the boy Philip its advantage to William was clearly enlarged. In the near future he need no longer fear the hostility of France. In view, however, of William's later relations with the church it is necessary to observe that while still repudiating all objection to the marriage, he instigated friendly advances to the papacy which eventually brought about reconciliation and the removal of pope Leo's prohibition. It was in return—or so it is said—for their promise to build two monastic churches in Caen that pope Nicholas II at last recognised the validity of the marriage of William of Normandy and Matilda of Flanders.

There remained six years for preparation of his major enterprise, and some degree of conscious preparation there must have been if the story is true that in 1051 or 1052 William received from Edward the Confessor the promise of succession to the English throne. The story is generally accepted, and there is no reason to doubt it. It is, however, extremely interesting to look back to that momentous year. With victory at Val-ès-Dunes behind him, and the fortress of Brionne again in his hands, William probably appeared, to foreign observers, to be assured of success, and therefore, in the Confessor's eyes, a proper heir to his kingdom, and in Baldwin's view a respectable son-in-law. The prom-

ise of succession must have come at or about the time when
William was a suitor for Matilda's hand; and if Baldwin knew
of it, the young duke's splendid prospect may well have advanced
his suit. But was Baldwin told? That was the year when earl
Godwine and most of his family, exiled from England, were refugees at his court. It requires little imagination to frame a picture
of intrigue in which, on the one side, Baldwin gives his cautious
help to Godwine, planning revenge on the Confessor, and, on the
other, takes advantage of the Confessor's promise to marry his
daughter to the Confessor's heir. Baldwin may have regarded
diplomacy as a game devised for entertainment as well as profit.

And now, in 1060, Baldwin had a new guest at court—a new
game to play—and William had acquired the authority of success.
In an age when physical strength was still of value to a ruler,
he had shown strength above the common mean; he had proved
his faculty of command; and he had out-lived his rivals. In order
to undertake the conquest of England he had to create, by means
of the authority he had won, a coherent force within his duchy
that would be able to endure the labour of conquest and willing
to accept his direction. He could not impose the discipline inherent in a fully developed feudal society, because in Normandy
feudalism was still in its infancy; or, at the most, adolescence. He
had to exact an obedience that was largely voluntary, and maintain his rule as one who, though more than *primus inter pares*,
the first among his equals, was not so far removed from that
aristocratic distinction as to make the comparison unrealistic.

In Dudo of St. Quentin's record of the interrogation of Norse
seamen they had replied, when asked what title their commander
used, 'None. We're all equal here.' And though their answer was
not true, and could not be true, it indicated a sturdy dislike of
absolute law and positive order. As recently, moreover, as the
reign of William's father, duke Robert, many of his nobility, or
the younger sons of noble families, had left the duchy to pursue
a life of profitable adventure in Italy. No monarch, possessed of
the full power of monarchy, would have let them go when he
himself required their service; but duke Robert had no authority
to prevent their exercise of free will. Since his death there had
grown—out of a seed-bed of anarchy, as it appears—a new
territorial aristocracy of remarkable vigour, and these were the

families on which William would chiefly depend for the prosecution of a daring intention. He was the Confessor's nominated
heir—and he may have compelled Harold Godwineson to swear
allegiance—but he can hardly have contemplated his translation
to the English throne without having to fight for it.

His aristocracy, in a semi-feudal society whose obligations had
not yet been clarified, consisted of 'new men' in so far as the
estates which they had acquired or been granted were their new,
or relatively new, possessions. There is no known family whose
tenure of land can be traced to a grant by Marching Rolf or
William Longsword, and this lack of deeply rooted family-trees is
almost certainly due to the fluency of early Norman society;
till the beginning of the eleventh century the population of
Normandy, growing by occasional overflow from wandering
viking fleets, may not have entertained that respect for property
which emerges from a conception of permanent possession. But
in the thirty years before the year 1066 the nobility that rooted
in fields ploughed up by civil war grew strong and multiplied.
The *vicomtes* on whom the ruling house had depended for the
maintenance of its bruised and dislocated administration were rewarded, or rewarded themselves, by their establishment on an
hereditary basis. Those who had aided William got the wages of
loyalty in the shape of lands confiscated from others who had
been less than loyal. And William, powerful with the prestige of
success, shaped and moulded his energetic young aristocracy to
his own purpose and an acceptance of their common interest
without discouraging its energy by too close a definition of the
service it owed. The magnates of the church, and some of the
nobility, acknowledged a definite obligation, but the time was
not yet ripe for the imposition of feudal bonds on all.

In the present century it is not without difficulty that one can
imagine a young and vigorous landed nobility as the ardent
supporters of religious revival and, in particular, of monasticism.
But the eleventh century was one of the great seasons of religious
enthusiasm, and under its spell the warlike, viking province of
Normandy won renown throughout Europe for the liberality of
its churchly endowments. The old Christian foundations had
almost disappeared beneath the first waves of Norse attack and
the heathen back-wash that followed the murder of William

Longsword; but revival had begun in the time of duke Richard I, and in William's broken heritage there remained a tradition of dynastic patronage which he cultivated till it flowered in a splendid hybrid bloom of ducal power and episcopal dignity.

The revival had acquired new strength, about the time of his accession, from the pervasive influence of the Benedictine abbey established at Cluny, in Burgundy, in 910. At Cluny devotion wore a solemn and liturgical habit which impressed all who came into contact with it, and Cluniac teachers enjoyed a vast influence which, in Normandy, was modified by the strong idiosyncracy of that redoubtable land. The Cluniacs, on the whole, preferred an elaborate ritual of worship to exercise of the intellect; but in their Norman monasteries study was pursued and the necessity of teaching was respected. It seems also that the original practice of St. Benedict was restored, who very sensibly had decreed that his monasteries must live on their own produce—that prayer and devotion must not exclude labour with the hands—for the monasteries so lavishly endowed in Normandy had usually an economic as well as a spiritual function. From the teaching of St. Benedict the monks had learnt, better than the laity, how to cultivate their lands, how to produce wine and wool and wheat, and many of the Norman monasteries, enriched with fields previously uncultivated or of marginal worth, paid a substantial rent from the growth of the acres that they worked; they were not only a gift to the church and an assertion of Christian faith, but a sound investment.

It must not be thought, however, that economic calculation determined all churchly endowments. The essence of a motive so prevalent that between 1035 and 1066 nearly a score of new religious foundations were established by an *arriviste* aristocracy, was primarily spiritual—a simple devotion to the Christian faith that passes the comprehension of more sophisticated times—and secondarily social; for a nobleman who wanted to fortify the precedence of his rank by popular estimation of his piety had to improve his title by maintaining either monks or clergy on his estate.

There was a marked difference between these servitors of God. The monasteries reflected the spiritual temper of their time, and in the peculiar circumstances of Normandy the monastic rule could build, on a bank of the Risle, its famous church and convent of Le Bec where Lanfranc studied and taught, among others, the great Anselm, who also would become archbishop of Canterbury. But the prelacy, the high dignitaries of the church, were the nominees, and usually relations, of the ducal family, who served their purpose by a generous patronage and efficient administration that may have excused the absence, in some cases, of any marked vocation for their office.

In William's infancy the see of Rouen was held by Robert, brother of duke Richard II, who was followed by archbishop Mauger, a half-brother of William's father, duke Robert. Odo, the valiant bishop of Bayeux, who lavished his wealth on good craftsmen and fought doughtily in battle, was the son of Herlève, by Herluin, *vicomte* of Conteville; and there were other members of the family who fortified episcopal dignity with dynastic authority. Over them all, in the power of his latter years, stood William himself, who regularly attended the councils of the church—they met at his command—and by his influence so fashioned the ecclesiastical revival that it served all Normandy as well as God. As he had persuaded his aristocrats that their interests were identical with his own, so by benefaction and, it must be presumed, by skill in argument, he induced his bishops and his abbots to equate the expansion of their church with Normandy's expansion. With ability in battle he matched ability in ratiocination, and though in the secular society of his time he could never have said *L'état, c'est moi,* he who swore by the splendour of God might have been within visible distance of the truth had he boasted, within his own duchy, *L'église, c'est moi.* When he invaded England, the blessing of Rome went with him to direct the Channel winds; and he had won its blessing by a policy indistinguishable from faith.

Chapter XIV

THE NORTHERN BATTLES

T HE old church had stood on what was once a reedy island in the Thames. It was dedicated to St. Peter, whom Edward the Confessor especially venerated, and when, after obscure negotiation with the papacy, the king resolved and was encouraged to erect a new minster and a larger monastery on the old foundations, he showed his devotion by planning structures so grandiose as to exceed in size all other English houses of worship. The building of the new West Minster was his major interest in the latter half of his reign, and it would be ungracious to grudge him the pleasure with which he saw the completion of his work. The new church was ready for consecration by Christmas 1065.

By then, however, Edward was a dying man. The revolt in Northumbria and the expulsion of Tostig may have so harassed a mind unfit for the cares of state that his feeble constitution failed beneath a new burden of anxiety; or death may have followed some simple but unrecorded infection. He died in the darkness of early January, and on the day after his death his body was carried from his new palace of Westminster to his new abbey, and buried before St. Peter's altar. A few hours after the funeral the abbey resounded to the hurried tread of a new king's courtiers, and the friends of Harold Godwineson watched his coronation by Aldred, archbishop of York. Stigand, the archbishop of Canterbury, had been excommunicated by several popes, and though he continued to enjoy his office and its revenues, he was manifestly unfitted—even to the tolerant eyes of Englishmen—to consecrate a bishop or ordain a king. Edgar the Atheling, a surviving member of the royal house and heir by birth to the throne, was also set aside. He was still a child, and January 1066, was no time to put a child on the throne. Harold had made that clear by a promptitude which gave the Atheling's supporters no time to count their strength and concert a policy.

Harold, as king, retained his own earldom of Wessex, with which Somerset and Berkshire had been re-united, and Hereford added after the death of its earl, Ralf, the old king's nephew. To keep the solid south of England, and its western extension, in his own hands was a sound decision. It was on the south that he could most certainly depend for loyalty, and that the south must face the hostility of Normandy was emphasised by duke William's immediate protest against the coronation. Nor, indeed, was there any clearly sufficient candidate for the great earldom, had Harold chosen to delegate authority. Since 1057 his brother Leofwine had ruled a confected earldom consisting of Kent, Surrey, and the shires about London; his brother Gyrth was earl of East Anglia.

There is no evidence that the earls Edwin of Mercia and Morcar of Northumbria opposed Harold's election, but in Northumbria there was popular opposition, a brief refusal to accept him as king which, though it did not amount to armed rebellion, was serious enough to require his own presence and a visible demonstration of his authority to quell it. He went north with Wulfstan, bishop of Worcester, in attendance, and a peaceful approach secured from the dissidents a peaceful acknowledgment of his title. Credit for the gentle resolution of an urgent problem has been given to the sanctity of bishop Wulfstan, but one may prefer to think that king Harold himself, by a display of firmness and his good sense, won the goodwill of his doubtful subjects. It was many years since a king of England had been seen in Northumbria, and the spectacle of royalty in their midst may well have impressed even the hard-headed men of the north. He could, moreover, have told them, with the strong simplicity of unpainted truth, of their danger from attack by Tostig or Harald of Norway, or both of them together. Very few were likely to face that prospect with anything but hatred of the invaders. The two earls, Edwin and Morcar, were soundly opposed to Tostig, and Harold could rely on them to defend his northern shore with vigour and emotion; but to fortify their association he married their sister Edith, lately widowed by the death of the Welsh prince Griffith.

He marched south again with a diplomatic victory to encourage him in his bold and comprehensive plan for defence of the kingdom. He was in London by Easter, and in London, his head-quarters and the chosen capital of his realm, he prepared for mobilisation and maintained under threatening skies—a sky that Halley's comet lit so balefully—such administrative services as existed. He took steps to expand the economy by a large addition to the quantity of money in circulation. Coins were minted in forty-four different places, from York and Chester in the north to Exeter and Romney in the south; on the obverse the new coinage bore an image of Harold wearing an arched crown decorated with pearls, and on the reverse the splendidly urbane promise of *Pax*.

Potentially the military strength of England was great, both at sea and ashore, but mobilisation was difficult because the country was not organised for war on a large scale or for national defence. There was no fleet in being, no standing army; the housecarls of the king and his magnates could be regarded only as the nucleus of an army. The housecarls were professional soldiers, but of themselves not numerous enough to constitute an army; and though some may have been liable for garrison service, the majority, in peacetime, lived at home. The king could call upon his housecarls for immediate service, and summon his thanes to the military duty they owed him. The peasantry, too, had obliga-tions of service, and in theory the king could muster all able-bodied men throughout the country. But total mobilisation was clearly impossible, and the effectiveness of partial mobilisation, which might be slow to begin with, was ultimately limited by the means available to maintain those mobilised. To muster and maintain a fleet was, perhaps, even more difficult. Some of the southern ports had lately agreed to furnish, at need, a certain number of ships, and the king's right to press crews and requisi-tion vessels was generally recognised, if ill-defined. But though a fleet might gradually be acquired, there was no administrative machinery for re-victualling it. Despite all these difficulties—despite every handicap—Harold made his bold plans and prepared to mobilise both ships and men on an unprecedented scale. He intended, moreover, to maintain them, at sea or under arms, for as long as might be necessary.

As serious a disability as lack of organisation was the ob-

solescence of English military practice. England could depend
upon its infantry, but had nothing else. Its marching soldiers were
so good that even in Harald Hardrada's battle-proud country it
was permissible to suggest that an English housecarl was worth
two Norwegians. But though infantry is indispensable, and good
infantry invaluable, infantry alone, in a changing world, is not
always capable of winning battles; and Harold had neither archers
nor cavalry to supplement his Saxon spears and axes. A few
archers there may have been—the Norse account of the battle of
Stamford Bridge suggests that—but there were no archer-com-
panies, no tactical employment of bowmen. Throughout the
kingdom horses were in everyday use, but Harold had no cavalry,
no knowledge of the tactical shock of a charge of horse. And on
the continent a military commander could economise in defence
with a well-sited castle from which a small garrison could dominate a necessary road or river-crossing; but England was not yet
a castled land. England had for its defence only an untrained,
half-victualled fleet manned by pressed men, and its stubborn
infantry.

Early in May, before the fleet had been mobilised, Tostig
appeared off the Isle of Wight with ships that may have been
given to him by his brother-in-law, Baldwin of Flanders, to
whom he had fled for refuge after his expulsion from England.
Baldwin's policy defied scrutiny, and Baldwin was the father-in-
law of duke William. It may have seemed to Harold that Tostig's
movements, and his aggressive intention, were known to William,
and, even, perhaps, supported by him. He may have regarded
Tostig's attack as a preliminary to the early offensive of duke
William and his Normans. But Tostig had found an ally elsewhere.

His immediate purpose was probably a reconnaissance in force,
and on that reconnaissance he was joined by a Northumbrian
called Copsi, who came with seventeen ships from Orkney. Copsi
had been in exile since the previous year; and Orkney, after many
years of virtual independence, was again subject to Norway's
haphazard authority. The two young men who ruled the islands
—sons of earl Thorfinn—were mild, unwarlike creatures, and
obviously dominated by Harald Hardrada. Except by his will it
is quite improbable that Copsi could have recruited for Tostig a

reinforcement that may have been of considerable strength. If the seventeen ships were all longships of twenty benches—and it seems unlikely that smaller vessels would have been sent on so long a voyage—their total complement may have numbered thirteen or fourteen hundred men.

It seems necessary, at this point, to pay much more attention to Tostig than is commonly done. Revolt in Northumbria, his flight to Bruges, his hostile re-appearance off the Isle of Wight: that is all one usually hears about Tostig, his misfortune and activities, in those pregnant months between the autumn of 1065 and the early summer of 1066. But in Snorri Sturluson's saga of the kings of Norway there is a fairly long and fairly detailed account of his movements and evolving policy that deserves attention and may seem worthy of belief. Admittedly the sagas are not to be trusted as historical documents. The saga-writers had little reverence for time or the order of events, and no interest at all in politics. But they were interested in people, and about people they were often very good.

In the saga of the kings Tostig is treated with great respect. He is said to have been a very wise man who left England, not because of Northumbrian revolt, but because he was indignant at the injustice done to him when Harold, his younger brother, seized the English throne. According to Snorri Sturluson he went first to Flanders, then to Denmark, whose king, Sweyn, was his cousin; for Tostig's mother, Gyda, was the sister of Sweyn's father, Ulf. Of Sweyn he asked help and men to let him regain his heritage in England; and if Sweyn was not prepared to come to his assistance, then, said Tostig, 'I will give you all I have in England if you, like Cnut, your mother's brother, will take a Danish army to win the realm of England.'

But Sweyn prudently replied, 'I am so much less a man than king Cnut that I can scarcely hold my own country against the Norwegians.'

Tostig was disappointed, and said he must look elsewhere for friendship, even where friendship might seem improbable. And he went to the court of Sweyn's old enemy in Norway.

From Harald Hardrada he first asked help to regain 'his kingdom in England.' The Norwegian answered that his people would not be too eager to fight there for the benefit of an

English lord; for 'men say that Englishmen are not wholly to be trusted.'

Tostig answered, 'Is it not true that king Magnus, your kinsman, told king Edward of England that he owned England no less than Denmark, by reason of his agreement with Harthacnut?'

'Why, then,' said the Norwegian, 'did he not take it, if he owned it?'

'Why,' said Tostig, 'have you not taken Denmark, as Magnus did?'

'The Danes cannot boast too much about what they have done. We have burnt a lot of your cousins there out of house and home.'

'If you will not answer my question,' said Tostig, 'I shall answer it myself. King Magnus took Denmark because the great men there were on his side. You failed to take it because everyone was against you. Magnus did not fight for England because he knew that all its people were for Edward, their king. But if you have a mind to make England yours, I can help you by seeing to it that most of the great men there will join you; for I am as good as my brother Harold, except for the fact that I am not a king. Everyone knows that no such a fighting-man as you has ever been born in the north, and I think it extraordinary that you, after fighting for Denmark for fifteen years, will not bother to take England when it lies wide open before you.'

That conversation is a paraphrase of the saga—a paraphrase that reproduces both the tone and content of the original—and one cannot easily reject it as Snorri's invention because it has the tune of probability if not the ring of absolute truth; because it is congruous with what happened; and because it reveals Tostig as the sturdy, plausible adventurer he must have been. He may, indeed, have been an adventurer with a real sense of injustice to inspire him.

The saga then says that Hardrada and Tostig talked long and often about Tostig's suggestion, and finally it was concluded that 'in the summer they should fare to England and win the land.' And in the spring Tostig sailed west to Flanders again, where he found Flemish sympathisers and others who had fled from England to join him.

In view of what happened—that Tostig and Hardrada were

associated in invasion, and that Tostig in May was joined by the Northumbrian Copsi with a considerable fleet from Orkney— the Norwegian account may be substantially true, and Tostig's naval manoeuvres closely resemble a reconnaissance in force that failed to achieve the bridgehead he had hoped to win.

From the Isle of Wight he sailed eastward, harried the coast of Sussex, and having rounded the South Foreland, occupied Sandwich. It was there he was joined by the ships from Orkney. King Harold in London moved promptly as soon as he heard news of the Kentish invasion, but before he reached the coast Tostig had put to sea again with all the shipping he had found in Sandwich harbour to increase his fleet, and a large addition of pressed men. His whole fleet now numbered about sixty vessels, but some may have been small.

He sailed north, and on the north shore of Norfolk, where the river Burnham finds its way through salt-marsh to the sea, he landed to harry again. Then, somewhere on the south shore of the Humber, he brought his men ashore and reconnoitered fairly far inland; for he roused strong opposition and was heavily defeated by Edwin, earl of Mercia, and a local militia. An attempted landing in Yorkshire was driven off by earl Morcar and his Northumbrians, and Tostig, twice rebuffed, retired to a friendly Scotland with a fleet now reduced to twelve small ships. The pressed men from Sandwich had deserted, and the Orkney ships had presumably returned to the islands. For the rest of the summer Tostig stayed with Malcolm III, king of Scots, with whom his friendship was long-standing.

The defeat of Tostig's reconnaissance was proof of England's ability to defend herself against assault by light forces, and king Harold now gave orders for mobilisation, on the very large scale he had prepared, to meet the major attack anticipated in the south. A fleet lay off the Isle of Wight, commanded by the king himself, and the militia of the southern counties was called up to man defensive positions on the coast. There is no recorded action by the fleet, but some small engagements may have taken place. It would be strange indeed if, throughout the summer, the Channel was wholly peaceful, for surely, from time to time, duke William sent out his fighting ships to probe and test the English defences. But on shore nothing happened. Nothing broke the long monotony of watch and ward, but for week after week, and month after month, the bored and bewildered men of the militia stared glumly at the vacant sea and thought resentfully of their neglected fields. Hay-time came and went, and in many villages there may have been few men to bring in the hay. August came, and corn was ripe, but who would cut and bind?

Now service of that sort—a prolonged, inactive service—was quite unprecedented. By custom the militia-men were called up for a specific task, and discharged as soon as they had done their job, or failed to do it. What Harold required of them, however, was something like the tedious duty that, for many, fills so large a place in modern war, and it is remarkable that he was able to exact obedience for so long, from so many men who were un-accustomed to boredom under arms, and could see no purpose in it. His authority must have been absolute, and his authority, though disseminated through chosen leaders, had no source but in his anointed royalty, his own strength of mind, and a remark-able personality. No record remains of the measures he took to feed his troops, but his quartermasters must have improvised and maintained a system of supply with at least a moderate success; Harold was on good terms with his clergy, and they, it may be, were persuaded to help in this essential task. Nor is it known if the militia-men were paid, though the new-minted coinage may have supplemented their rations.

Did the king, during that long summer, receive information from the other side of the Channel? Had he some primitive kind of intelligence service? It is probable that occasional news of duke William's preparations reached him. The duke was working hard and cleverly, methodically and successfully, to create an army of invasion and the fleet to carry it, and news of his success, of the imminence of danger, would not only have justified Harold's policy, but fortified him against the mounting difficulties of keeping his army in being.

By early August William's concentration may have been com-plete, but contrary winds kept his fleet—his fighting ships and his hastily built great flock of transports—in or near the mouth of the Dives: south of Havre, that is, between Arromanches and Trou-ville. And while the wind blew from the north, the English fleet was ready for action in the weather berth. But on the 12th September the wind changed, it blew from the west, and William ordered his fleet to sail from the Dives to St. Valéry in the mouth of the Somme, a harbour nearer England.

This useful movement brought him within easy reach of the English shore, and the English shore was now undefended. The strain on Harold's quartermasters, on the seamen and the militia—if not on Harold himself—had at last become too great to be borne. Supplies could not be maintained, and the men's temper was worsening; they may have been hungry, they may have been wearied and perplexed beyond endurance by three months or more of purposeless inactivity. It was admitted their watch-and-ward could no longer be sustained, and by the 6th September the militia was dismissed, the fleet ordered to London. But the changing wind must have brought uncertain weather, for somewhere on the voyage many ships were lost. The Channel was open to William and his gathered army. Nothing remained to hinder him but the inconstant wind, which now blew again from the north.

While his militia-men were going home, and his ships were being driven ashore—from Thanet to Sheppey if a northerly gale had found them—Harold was surprised, and a lesser man would have been dismayed, by news that the king of Norway with a fleet of three hundred sail had invaded northern England. Tostig had joined him in the Tyne, they had sailed down to the Humber, then far up the Ouse, and landed at Riccall within ten miles of York. Turning his back on the naked south, Harold set off immediately, by forced march, to meet his other enemy. It is said that he was suffering from an attack of gout, but pain did not deter him when speed was necessary. He was in desperate straits, but if luck marched with him he might still have time to rebuff Norway and come back to deal with Normandy. He had his housecarls, and London volunteers may have joined him. It may be assumed that his brothers Gyrth and Leofwine, from their neighbouring earldoms, reinforced his increasing army with their housecarls and retainers. On his way he summoned local thanes and mustered available militia-men, as many as he could, and gathered a numerous army which marched with unrelenting speed.

The old roads which the Romans had built may have been serviceable still, though their watch-towers had fallen and their wide verges were overgrown. But they ran straight, they had been made for the swift traffic of the legions, not for country commerce, and for the victory that awaited him at Stamford Bridge Harold may have had to thank the Romans who had made it possible for him to move so fast. From London, through forest for much of the way, the road led north to Lincoln—over the Nene west of Peterborough, over the Welland west of the fens—and beyond Lincoln, and Edwin's earldom, over the rivers that pour their silt into the yellow Humber, to Tadcaster on the Wharfe—where a fleet of little English ships, running from the Norwegian navy, had found shelter—and thence, by the Roman High Street, to York itself.

In York he had news of defeat and surrender. The Norwegians had already been in action, and the brother earls Edwin and Morcar had lost a great battle in which both sides had suffered heavily. York had capitulated, and Harald Hardrada had been merciful. He had taken hostages to secure the good behaviour of the citizens, and retired to a position on the river Derwent, some seven miles away.

Neither of that preliminary battle, at Fulford, nor of the engagement which followed, and reversed the earlier decision, is there any full or detailed report in English annals. But in the saga of Harald Hardrada—in Snorri Sturluson's long saga of the kings—there is a spirited and romantic account of both, and though the Norwegian tale is inaccurate in many particulars, it is right and proper to give it consideration. The weakness of the sagas as historical documents has already been admitted, but specific weaknesses do not necessarily preclude all merit, and again and again the sagas offer little glimpses of men in action that have the lineaments of reality. In Harald's saga, for example, the narrative of events before the battle at Stamford Bridge stops suddenly to make room for a quick portrait of the English king. He was mounted, and Harald Hardrada paused to watch him. 'A little man,' he said, 'but stands stiffly in his stirrups.' The Norwegian was a man of heroic stature, and through his condescending eyes one can see Harold Godwineson as something less than that—a man of medium height—whose carriage was taut, his posture erect, alert, and commanding. 'Stiff in his stirrups': no giant, but a kingly figure.

From the battle of Stiklestad, in which he fought at the age of fifteen, Harald Hardrada's restless career had taken him to Constantinople, where he served in the Varangian Guard of the empress Zoe—to warfare in Sicily and north Africa and adventure on the Black Sea—before he returned to almost interminable war with Denmark. That war he may have intended as a preliminary to assault on England—an assault launched with the combined strength of both Norway and Denmark—and though intention had succumbed to war-weariness, he may have let an old ambition be revived by Tostig's argument. The saga may well be correct in its statement that it was Tostig who persuaded him to his last adventure, and there is no reason for disputing its account of his movements after he had made his fatal decision.

Under the Solund islands, which lie just north of the entrance to the long Sogne fjord, he mustered a fleet of nearly two hundred ships—not counting storeships and smaller vessels—and embarked a very large army. With a favouring wind he set sail for the west, and made his landfall in Shetland. From there he went south to Orkney, where he acquired a considerable reinforcement for his army, and put ashore his queen, Ellisif—the daughter of a king in Novgorod—and their daughters, Maria and Ingigerd. He took with him Paul and Erlend, the ruling earls of Orkney—sons of the great Thorfinn—and sailed southward by the east coast of Scotland before the north wind that kept duke William and his unwieldy fleet in the estuary of the Somme.

In the Tyne Harald made his rendezvous with Tostig and such ships as he had persuaded Malcolm of Scotland to give him—there were rovers who joined them too, one of whom was the Icelander Godfrey Crovan, later king of Man—and still taking advantage of the north wind, they cruised southward, pausing where it seemed of advantage, to harry the nearby shore. They harried Cleveland south of the Tees, and landing at Scarborough, set fire to the town with blazing logs that they threw down from the peninsular cliff onto the houses huddled below. They plundered the ruins and moved on to Holderness where there was some resistance; but not enough to hinder them.

They sailed into the Humber, and up the river Ouse as far as the village of Riccall on its left bank, a mile or two below the confluence of the Wharfe. There Harald Hardrada disembarked his army, and advanced on York in line, one wing on the river-bank and the other towards a watery fen. His army was confined to the firm ground between river and fen, and towards the fen his line was thin and straggling.

Edwin and Morcar had by then mustered a considerable army —that consisted, presumably, of housecarls, the thanes of Mercia and Northumbria and their retainers, and the local militia—and moved a little way south from York to the village of Gate Fulford. Here, too, the front was limited by marsh and river, and when battle was joined the English quickly made inroads on the right of the Norwegian line next to the fen. Harald Hardrada was on the left, under his banner called Landwaster, and as his right wing fell back he pressed forward with insistent strength, and his men by main force hewed their way through the English ranks. It was hand to hand, face to face, close fighting—no tactical finery, but savage cut and thrust—and seemingly the impetus of the Norwegian attack was such that the whole line wheeled round towards the fen and drove the English, now in general retreat, into a quaking marsh. So great was the slaughter, and so close lay the dead, that the Norwegians could walk dry-shod across the fen; or so says Snorri.

The English survivors retreated into York, where apparently they stood to fight again; for the slaughter was renewed. No harm was done to York itself, but negotiation began for its formal submission, and Harald took hostages and withdrew to his ships.

The battle of Fulford is certainly more important than is usually supposed. Though Snorri tells of the terrible losses suffered by the English, he says nothing of the Norwegian dead. But the Northumbrians were a warlike people, they were fighting in defence of their own land, and it is probable that the army of Harald Hardrada and Tostig also lost heavily, and was materially weakened. It is perhaps significant that the battle was fought on Wednesday, the 20th September, but York did not finally capitulate till the 24th, when its people pledged obedience to the Norwegian king. That delay, and Harald's failure to occupy York, may have been due to the wounds his army had received. He withdrew to his ships—the great armada crowding the narrow waters of the Ouse —and presumably his purpose was to replenish and re-group his forces. The saga says that Tostig's promise of English recruits was justified, and many of his friends came to join them; but there is no indication of the size of the English reinforcement, and if—as is fairly certain—the Norwegians had been substantially weakened, then Harold Godwineson's task on the 25th was made the easier.

On Monday Harald Hardrada again put an army ashore. One third of his whole force remained with the fleet, among whom were Olaf, the king's son, the two Orkney earls—who were no warriors—and a favourite of Harald's called Eystein Heathcock. The remainder marched to Stamford Bridge on the river Derwent, seven miles east of York, where, it had been arranged, more hostages from landward parts were to be delivered. The day was fine, the sun shone hotly, and the men, who were in high spirits and had no immediate expectation of another battle, marched without their byrnies, or coats of mail.

At Stamford Bridge several roads converged, and flat lands on either side of the sluggish stream sloped gradually towards it. It is quite clear that the Norwegians had no tactical reason for their new movement, and were indeed taken by surprise while some were on one bank, some on the other. Harold Godwineson had reached Tadcaster on the night before, and pressed on to York in the early morning. There he had been told of the lost battle at Fulford, and something of the Norwegians' present intentions, or something about the casualties they had suffered, which persuaded him to take no rest but march out at once and force an immediate engagement. Nine miles from Tadcaster to York, another seven to Stamford Bridge: an approach-march of sixteen miles, and a battle on top of it, are unusual. The English king must have seen some advantage to be gained from haste before he decided on committing his sweating army to a long afternoon of savage fighting.

Snorri has a splendid picture of the English army when first it came into view. There was a cloud above it, of dust and the rising steam of lathered horses, and as it drew nearer the gleam of bright weapons, glittering in brilliant sunshine, was like a mass of crumbling ice against the array of painted shields and steel-white byrnies. Then, says Snorri, there was some argument between Tostig and the Norwegian king. Tostig advised retreat to Riccall, to reinforce their army from the ships and put on the armour they had left behind; but the king was determined to stay and fight

where they were, having sent three mounted messengers with orders to Eystein Heathcock to come at speed with his reserves.

The saga tells nothing of what happened next—before battle
was joined, that is—but English chroniclers record an action like
that of Horatius on the bridge to Rome. The Norwegians on the
right bank of the river withdrew in some haste apparently, but one
man stood valiantly on the wooden bridge across the Derwent to
withstand the English advance, and took his toll before some
shrewd opponent saw gaps in the planking and stabbed him from
below. The Norwegians made no other attempt to contest the
crossing, but invited a formal battle by dressing their ranks in a
shield-ring: a defensive formation that preceded, by several centuries, the hollow square that later wars made famous. Harald
Hardrada and Tostig, however, with their own picked men, are
said to have remained outside the ring; and such a disposition was
convenient for the preliminaries to battle which Snorri records.

From the English side—or so he says—a score of mounted men
rode towards the Norwegians, and one of them asked, 'Is earl
Tostig in your army?' Tostig himself replied, and the English
spokesman said, 'Your brother Harold gives you greeting, and this
offer. You can have peace, and all Northumbria for your own. A
third of the kingdom rather than no agreement.'

'It is a better choice than you gave me last winter,' said Tostig,
'but what does king Harald of Norway get for his trouble?'

'Seven feet of English ground. Or, because he's taller than most,
as much again if he needs it.'

'Go back and tell Harold to make ready for battle,' said Tostig.
'It will never be said in Norway that I brought Harald Sigurdson
to England, and then left him to join his enemies.'

The English rode away, and Harald of Norway asked, 'Who
was that man who spoke so smoothly?'

'Harold Godwineson,' said Tostig.

'That I should have been told before. They came so near that
Harold should never have gone back to tell of what he saw.'

'True enough,' said Tostig. 'It was a reckless thing he did, and
we could have taken advantage from it. I saw he was going to offer me peace, and that I might be the death of him if I told you
who he was. But I would rather let him be the death of me.'

That is the conversation reported by Snorri—or a paraphrase of it—and that some such interchange took place is likely enough. To break an alliance by fair words is always cheaper than breaking it in battle, and Harold Godwineson, who was not incapable of impetuous action, may have decided to make his own appeal to Tostig. Nor can his offer to the Norwegian of seven feet of English ground be dismissed because it may have lacked originality; an answer out of stock can be just as apposite as a phrase newly coined. What is most remarkable in the conversation is Snorri's manifest desire to show Tostig in a good light. It is Tostig who emerges as the noble spirit, the faithful ally, and it is difficult to think of any reason for such a portrayal other than fidelity to fact. The Norse chroniclers had a marvellous respect for fair play—they would report a good deed by a bad man as willingly as misbehaviour by a hero—and it may well be that Tostig left a noble memory in the north. A sense of patriotism developed in England much earlier than in Scandinavia, and it is possible that Tostig's reputation in his own country has suffered unduly from the indignant patriotism of English writers.

The description of the battle is unfortunately marred by a major blunder. It was Snorri's belief that the English launched a series of cavalry charges against the Norwegian shield-ring, but in the absence of English cavalry that was clearly impossible. It is true that the English had horses, and it may be taken for granted that horses were used on the line of march. But they fought on foot. With this difference Snorri's account may be fairly accurate, and it is not unreasonable to suppose that the shield-ring withstood the first and repeated onslaughts. Some archers the English may have had, but throwing-spears and axes were their chief weapons against Norwegian sword and spear. Then, when the attack weakened, the Norwegians broke out of their ordered ring and tried to drive the English before them; and that was their great error. For the English—seemingly better disciplined—now confronted them with an ordered valour against which individual prowess failed. Where the battle was hardest the Norwegian king was himself foremost in the fight, and few could withstand his strength and mighty rage. But Harald Hardrada fell with an arrow or throwing-spear in his throat, and all those nearest to him were overwhelmed.

But the battle was not yet over. The dead king's banner, Landwaster, was retrieved, and under it earl Tostig rallied his men and

stood to fight again. Again the English king offered him peace—
peace to him and all who remained of the Norwegian army—
but loudly his offer was rejected, and with a roar of anger the
battle was renewed. In this, its second stage, Tostig was killed,
but England had not yet won its victory. For now from the
great fleet moored in the Ouse came Eystein Heathcock with
his reserve—they had come so fast that they were breathless and
blind with sweat—but recklessly they flung themselves into the
fight, and Landwaster was raised again. This part of the battle
was called Heathcock's Blow, and the desperate fury of tired
men made it more fierce than what had gone before. The fight
continued till the sky was darkening, but the battle was lost when
Harald Hardrada died, and before nightfall Harold of England
stood victor on the dreadful field.

It was the last battle won by the old Anglo-Saxon kingdom,
and never had Englishmen better earned their victory. In his hour
of triumph, moreover, Harold Godwineson showed himself mag-
nanimous. Against those of his enemies who were left alive he
might well have been bitter, for they had taken him in the rear
when he was facing the larger danger of Normandy; but he was
lenient. He could have taken revenge, but he gave them peace.
Young Olaf, Harald Hardrada's son, and the gentle Orkney earls
were treated most mercifully. They gave hostages for their good
behaviour, and were allowed to go home. Of the many ships,
now empty, moored in the Ouse, only a few were needed to
carry out of England the survivors of that wild invasion. From
the Norwegian fleet, it is said, no more than twenty-four went
down into the Humber and out to the North Sea.

There is a tradition that when the English king was at dinner,
two or three days later, there arrived a breathless messenger to
tell him that duke William of Normandy had landed in Sussex.
It is a pleasant story, because it brings the drama of that over-
wrought year to the homely setting of a dinner-table, and so
appears to domesticate it. But almost certainly the story is untrue.
The time-table of events will be looked at more closely in the
next chapter; here it is enough to say that Harold had no time
to dally in York when, as he knew, his Norman enemy, ready to
invade, was waiting for his opportunity.

It is infinitely more probable that Harold Godwineson was on his way south—perhaps two days' march south of York—when the messenger met him. And with the king were probably no larger a company than his brothers, the earls Gyrth and Leofwine, with a few hundred horsemen: housecarls who, being better armoured, had had the better chance of survival. The earls Edwin and Morcar were not with him, nor did they follow to join him at Hastings, and Freeman, the Victorian scholar, blames them bitterly for their abstention. But Freeman had not fought at Gate Fulford. Edwin and Morcar had served their turn and done their duty. Their absence from the later field is easily explained by the simple supposition that they and their followers— the remnants of an army broken in battle—were in no state to face the rigours of a forced march to the south.

Chapter XV

THE BATTLE OF HASTINGS

ACCORDING to the contemporary chronicler William of Jumièges, William of Normandy issued his protest against Harold's coronation as soon as he heard of it. He cannot have thought that words alone would unseat the newly crowned king, so the inference is that his decision to assert his right by force in the affairs of England was immediate. He wasted no time searching his mind for intention, but found it at once, and thereafter made his plans for invasion with energy, precision, and a comprehensive grasp of all he needed—from the church's blessing to popular support and a sufficient fleet—that ultimately brought him success. But his decision was a gamble which, for its success, owed as much to his adversary's several difficulties as to his own thoroughness and daring.

His nobility had first to be persuaded that the venture was feasible, and there is contemporary evidence—or the evidence of chroniclers who wrote not long after the events which they describe—that William was assiduous in the propagation of his purpose and his faith in the outcome. Even were there no evidence of this, it would still be obvious that he had expounded his cause with fervour and conviction, for the loyalty of his own subjects and the apparent unanimity with which they supported him were very remarkable; the more so when one remembers the troubled state of his duchy some years before. He may have had to argue more closely, with a greater respect for facts and probabilities, than Harald Hardrada had found it necessary to do when he was mobilising, but it seems indisputable that the spirit of viking enterprise lay only lightly buried in William's Norman and Breton subjects; and their response to an heroic appeal and magnetic leadership must, in essence, have been very like the willingness with which his Norwegian subjects followed Harald.

William's son Robert, a boy of fourteen, was named his heir, and apparently accepted as such by the nobles. The duchess Matilda was invested with responsibility for the maintenance of government in something like a council of regency that included Roger of Beaumont and Roger of Montgomery. His own people having been converted, William showed both prudence and imagination in soliciting for his adventure that spiritual authority which might give it at least the complexion of a crusade. Under Gilbert, archdeacon of Lisieux, a mission was sent to Rome to ask from pope Alexander II a judgment in support of William's claim to the English throne. He had been named as his heir by Edward the Confessor, and Harold Godwineson, having taken an oath of allegiance to him, had violated his oath: that must have been the substance of the case which Gilbert presented, and in the circumstances of the time there were good reasons why the pope should listen to him with a favouring ear. The papacy was intent on reform of the members and manners of the church, and on establishing its freedom from the secular authority which, until a few years before, had largely controlled it. Now, in southern Italy, there was a new force which the pope might use, or hope to use, against the German emperor or the Roman aristocracy: the Norman adventurers in Capua and Apulia had had their conquests recognised as fiefs of the Holy See. William of Normandy, of the same race, had reformed and re-invigorated his duchy and nurtured its clergy. Of great influence at the papal court was Hildebrand, later pope as Gregory VII, who had the reputation of combining in his own character both saint and revolutionary; and when he, with habitual vigour, supported William and his enterprise, Alexander gave them his blessing and a papal banner to flaunt against the English breeze.

In Normandy William made grants to the church and gave charters to its clergy. His duchess's foundation of Holy Trinity in Caen was ratified with its rich endowment, and to the abbey church at Fécamp a grant of land in Sussex was promised if God's favour should bring Sussex within his gift. The see of Avranches was enriched, as was Holy Trinity in Rouen when Roger of Montgomery took example from the duke; and other nobles also saw the advantage of generosity.

Diplomatic approaches were made to neighbouring states, and

met with success. Both Philip I of France and the emperor Henry IV were young, and under tutelage. During the minority of Philip, whose mother was a daughter of Jarisleif, prince of Novgorod—whose daughter, Ellisif, Harald Hardrada had married—France accepted the regency of Baldwin of Flanders, and it is unlikely that William found any difficulty in conversation with him. The emperor was dominated by a council of churchmen and nobles, and from them William got a promise of help if he should need it. Such agreement, made easier by papal approval, gave him wide freedom of enlistment when volunteers were invited from beyond the frontiers of the duchy.

Through feudatories and allies William had effective control of the whole coast and its harbours from the Scheldt to Finisterre; but the harbours were almost empty. His most pressing material need was for a navy, and in particular for a large fleet of transports. It must have been early in the year when he set about building them. In the Bayeux Tapestry there is vivid evidence of this vast activity, and the sequence of pictures that show William's response to the news of Harold's coronation has marvellously captured the sense of haste and urgency that animated the year.

In the first of them the great comet flares across the sky while frightened men point wondering hands aloft, and the enthroned Harold listens to one who tells him of the ominous star. The season is Easter. Then an English ship crosses the Channel and William is told of Harold's treachery. Beside him sits a tonsured priest, his half-brother bishop Odo, and the inscription reads '*Hic Wilhelm Dux ju(ssit) naves edifica(re)*.'—'Here William bade them build ships.' One cannot believe, however, that vital news travelled so slowly that William did not hear until after Easter of what had happened in England; and the explanation is that the artist of the Tapestry changed the order of events to increase the dramatic tension of his story. Immediately there follows a picture that shows foresters at work, felling trees with great axes and laying up planks of wood; and another in which shipwrights are at work on two nearly completed hulls, with the finished hulls of larger ships lying nearby. Then there are men naked to the waist, who with the help of pulleys drag ships down to the sea—'*Hic trahunt naves ad mare*'—and carry aboard victuals and various armament: helmets, swords and spears and shirts of mail, and barrels of wine. The knights ride their horses to the beach, and horses are taken aboard. The fleet puts to sea, and duke William leads it in a ship that flies the papal banner.

The pictorial précis of what occurred is both admirable and exciting, but it leaves unsatisfied the questioner who asks, how large was William's army? It is difficult to find a convincing reply, but the size and nature of the invasion fleet—if they can be established —should return a tentative answer. The great nobles of the land were seemingly required to furnish an agreed quota of ships, and lists are extant of those who accepted such a duty and of the numbers they built. William fitz Osbern built, or promised to build, no fewer than sixty; as did Roger of Montgomery, Roger of Beaumont, and Hugh of Avranches who became earl of Chester. Fifty ships and sixty knights were contributed by Hugh of Montfort, forty by Fulk the Lame and Gerald the Seneschal. Walter Giffard offered thirty ships and a hundred knights. The duke's half-brothers, Roger, count of Mortain, and bishop Odo—the sons of Herlève—gave between them two hundred and twenty ships. So the catalogue continues, but it was not compiled till after the year of conquest, and while the catalogue itself presents the ideal figure of 1000 as the sum of the quotas, more recent authorities give other totals. The magisterial Victorian, E. A. Freeman, says the lowest reckoning shows the exact number to be 696, and that scholarly historian David Douglas seems to prefer 777. William of Jumièges, who had the advantage of living in the eleventh century, says the fleet numbered 3000; but that figure is intended for the greater glory of the duke rather than to satisfy enquiry.

Estimates of the number of soldiers carried in this uncertain fleet also vary widely. William of Poitiers is another contemporary whose *Gesta Guillelmi ducis Normannorum* is quite unlike James Boswell's *Life of Samuel Johnson*. 'I profess to write, not his panegyrick, but his life,' says Boswell; but panegyric was the purpose of William of Poitiers, and the figures given by him—at one time 50,000, at another 60,000—can only be interpreted as expressions of awe. To meet and illustrate the greatness of the duke, his army must number such-and-such: that is the basis of William of Poitiers' calculation. Orderic Vitalis, who wrote an ecclesiastical history of England and Normandy, and probably died about 1140, says the duke commanded '*quinquaginta millia militum cum copia peditum*,' which means 50,000 knights with plenty of infantry, and only makes one marvel at the credulity of a man who, in his own field, was a writer of outstanding merit. Freeman mentions an author, Maxentius, who gives a figure as low as 14,000; but even that is probably too high.

The invasion fleet was apparently ready for sea by early August. The shipwrights, it is clear, had no time to build great vessels of the sort that the Jomsburg vikings used, or that put to sea under king Cnut; there was nothing to compare with St. Olaf's *Bison*, or Olaf Tryggvison's *Long Serpent*, or earl Eric Hakonson's *Iron-beak*. There was no tradition of shipbuilding of that sort on the coasts of Flanders and Normandy, and no shipwright, one imagines, with the necessary skill and experience to lay the keel of another *Long Serpent*; but all the village carpenters were conscribed and put to work. Obvious, too, is the fact that there was no seasoned timber available; all was felled, split into planks, and nailed while still green. Now it is clear, from the Tapestry, that there were three main sorts of vessels in the fleet, and one sort was very small: mere cock-boats. There is a picture in which shipwrights are seen at work on a boat whose sides are no higher than a man's knee, and other boats, crossing the Channel, appear to be manned by four or five men only: these pictures do not, of course, pretend to show their true complement, but illustrate the difference between them and the larger vessels. In some of these the men aboard seem to be crowded together, and in the starboard side of one there are sixteen oar-locks. That may be an accurate representation, designed to show the size of the largest transports, as the shields displayed on others distinguish the fighting-ships. The fleet must have included an appreciable number of fighting-ships, for until the 8th September the English fleet was in being, and before then the Channel crossing would not have been uncontested. No horses, it may be noted, are shown aboard the fighting-ships.

It is probably safe to assume that the fleet which put to sea numbered fewer vessels than are shown on any of the lists that were later compiled; they, it seems likely, indicate the intention rather than the accomplishment of the named donors. That the great majority of the ships were very small—cock-boats rather than ships—is also likely, and that for two reasons: for country carpenters pressed into service as shipwrights they would be much the easiest sort to build, and while the better timber of the forests that were felled would necessarily be used in the large transports, the cock-boats could be built from the very large supply of short, inferior planks. It may then be realistic to allow for some fifty fighting-ships, each with a complement of perhaps forty men; about two hundred large transports, with room for thirty men apiece, provender, and other cargo, and as many as ten horses; and perhaps three hundred cock-boats carrying a dozen or fifteen men. The whole force may have numbered about 12,000, of whom perhaps 1500 were mounted, and several hundred were non-combatant shipmen; for the ships, when they discharged upon the English beach, can hardly have been left unattended.

Obviously, of course, this calculation is speculative, but the estimated total of 12,000, though modest in comparison with earlier calculation, still seems large when one considers the difficulty, in a country whose economy was seasonal and simple, of feeding and paying so many men. Mobilisation was complete, or almost complete, in early August, and to fill twelve thousand bellies for six or seven weeks was a prodigious task, and it is possible that William received help from a source undisclosed by history. It was he who brought the Jews into England, from a Jewish quarter in Rouen. His motive, it is thought, was to increase the flow of coinage and so facilitate the payment of feudal debts in cash. But he may also have had to reward those who helped him to pay and feed his waiting army.

Men liable for military service in ducal lands and the lands of William's vassals may have formed half his army, or more than that. Volunteers from near and far, from Maine and Brittany and Flanders, from central France and southern Italy, were attracted; and wandering mercenaries brought the army to its required strength. Discipline had to be inculcated, and because the soldiers were paid, it was easier to maintain discipline. The enlisted soldiers were forbidden to pillage—so says William of Poitiers—and the peasantry's flocks and herds suffered no hurt. There was no trespass on ripened harvest-fields, and the feeble and the harmless could move freely and without fear. This idyllic picture may be too brightly painted, but there is no disputing the fact that William scored his first victory over Harold on the 8th September, when

Harold had to dismiss the militia of the southern counties while the army of invasion still drew its rations.

Throughout August it lay near the mouth of the Dives, north-east of Caen, and when the weather broke on the 12th September and the wind blew from the west it embarked and sailed eastward to St. Valéry. It is unlikely that the coastwise voyage, of more than a hundred miles, was made without loss or damage, but when the wind veered to the north the fleet was again storm-bound and there was time for repair and recovery. For a fortnight the ships lay in the mouth of the Somme, and now the duke grew impatient, and chroniclers describe both his prayers for a southerly slant and his angry inspection of the weather-vane on the church tower. At last the change came, and hurriedly the army was embarked to sail before evening on the 27th: two days, that is, after Harold's victory at Stamford Bridge.

When darkness fell a lantern was hoisted to the mast-head of the duke's ship, and leading the fleet she ran before the following wind. She was a vessel called *Mora*, larger than the rest, which the duchess Matilda had given to her lord. She sailed faster than the others, and somewhere in mid-Channel it was discovered that she sailed alone. The fleet had been left far behind, and aboard the *Mora* there was consternation. But the sail was lowered, the duke re-assured his men, and by ordering breakfast to be served, and sensibly sitting down as comfortably as if he were in his own house —so says William of Poitiers—he restored confidence. The sky was lightening and gradually the approaching fleet came in sight. The voyage was resumed, and on the morning of the 28th the invading army landed, unopposed, on the flat shore of Pevensey bay, north-east of Beachy Head.

What was left of the English fleet still lay in the Thames. William had found an undefended shore, and audacity had won its first reward from luck. He cannot have known what to expect in England. It would be unrealistic to suppose that he had heard nothing of Harald Hardrada's preparation—he may have been well informed of the Norwegian's progress—but he had not heard of his defeat at Stamford Bridge, and he may have contemplated the possible necessity of fighting first against Harold Godwineson, then against Harald Hardrada and Tostig.

On the Sussex shore he balanced audacity with caution. At Pevensey he threw up a rampart within the walls of the old Roman fort, and as soon as it became apparent that no immediate attack need be expected he ordered an eastward movement, by both ships and men, to Hastings ten miles away. At Hastings, as the coast then lay, there was a sufficient harbour for his ships, and on either side was the protection of shallow estuaries which have since dried. Hastings commanded the London road and coastal roads. To the north was the high ground of Telham Hill, beyond that the weald and its woods. The defences of Hastings were strengthened by a ditch, and on the evidence of the Bayeux Tapestry a wooden castle was built.

Vividly, too, the Tapestry shows the Norman invaders enjoying their first meal snatched from the rich fields of England: *'Hic milites festinaverunt Hestinga ut cibum raperentur. Hic est Wadard. Hic coquitur caro. Et hic ministraverunt ministri. Hic fecerunt prandium. Et hic episcopus cibum at potum benedicit.'* ('Here the soldiers hurried to Hastings to seize food. Here is Wadard. Here the meat is cooked. And here the servants serve it. Here they made a feast. And here the bishop blesses the food and drink.') In front of his little house an English peasant is made to kill an ox, others bring a sheep, a pig, and what looks like an enormous round sausage. Wadard was evidently a cook whom everyone knew, and under his supervision a great pot is being boiled and joints of meat are already spitted for roasting. A baker is pulling loaves from an oven, servants carry meat on spits, one of them blows a horn to announce dinner is ready, and the duke and his chief nobles sit down to a well-furnished semi-circular table, which bishop Odo blesses. It is a fine, rapacious sequence in which good appetite is not allowed to indulge itself without some ceremony and the attention of the church.

There is a picture of the fortress at Hastings being built, another of a house being set on fire, from which a disconsolate woman leads her small son. It was evidently William's policy not merely to live off the surrounding country, but deliberately to waste it in order to provoke Harold to attack him where he stood, with the sea behind him and his ships close at hand to provide at need a way of retreat. Despite the planned audacity of his invasion, William was more cautious than Harold in his arrangements for battle.

But now another difficulty obtrudes: a difficulty that was fore-

shadowed in the last chapter. Stamford Bridge was fought on the
25th September, duke William landed at Pevensey on the 28th,
and the battle of Hastings was fought on the 14th October. As
well as the difficulty of estimating numbers there is the difficulty
of measuring movement against time. Harold had to march from
York to London, a distance of one hundred and ninety miles, and
could not have begun his march immediately after the battle. If
one allows him a minimum of two days' rest, and assumes that
he and his few hundred horsemen could find re-mounts and march
twenty-five miles a day, then by the evening of the 2nd October
he would be within sixty-five miles of London. Pevensey is as far
again on the other side, and news of the Norman landing may not
have reached London till the 30th. A messenger, riding north to
look for Harold, might have met him on the 2nd, and Harold could
have reached London three days later.

He had five days there, from the 6th to the 11th, when he
marched again, and during that time he may well have had to meet,
argue with, and convince the magnates of the city and its neighbouring shires—perhaps a rump of the Witan—that immediate battle must be offered to the invaders. It was not a decision with
which everyone can have agreed, for clearly there was argument
—or room for argument—in favour of a contrary policy. A policy
of delay, of avoiding battle, and finally compelling William—ex-
asperated and weakened by delay—to attempt a hazardous attack
on London. Harold, moreover, had to assemble an army for the
counter-offensive, and though an army was certainly created—for
he led it to Hastings—there is no certain knowledge of how it
came into being.

The explanation, however, may be that Harold, before marching
north to Stamford Bridge, had commanded the assembly of a second army to reinforce him should his attack on the Norwegians
fail. On his hurried march to York he had had no time to mobilise
all his available strength, but the remainder could be brought in
after he had left. So when, on their lathered horses, Harold and his
brothers and their few hundred housecarls came back to London,
the levies from the more distant and scattered parts of the home
counties and the south-east of England were gathered in or near
the city; and many of them probably needed arms and equipment.
If, within five days, Harold could win the support of London for

his bold policy, and so equip the levies from a hundred scattered hamlets that they became a marching and a fighting army, he was a commander of exceptional ability and a politician of remarkable authority. And so, quite obviously, he was; but he was not a good strategist.

Leaving the city on the 11th, he marched his pre-assembled army to the ridge at Battle, seven miles from Hastings. His impetuous haste strongly suggests that he hoped to repeat the tactics which had been successful at Stamford Bridge, and take the enemy by surprise. But, on the other hand, the ground where the English rested on the night of the 13th had been well chosen, and was eminently suitable for a defensive battle. The ridge rose north-west of Telham Hill like a small island of firm ground, with a fairly narrow approach from the south, and on either side the protection of bog or marsh. The sides of the ridge were steep enough to discourage cavalry, and to the rear the ground was sufficiently broken to prevent encirclement. The extreme haste of the southward march is counter-balanced by the prudence and sagacity with which Harold chose a site so difficult to attack, and the key to a puzzling situation may be that his intention was to fortify his island and challenge William to assault it: he lay athwart the way to London, and the challenge could hardly have been refused. Freemen, indeed, declares that he strengthened his position with a ditch and an elaborate palisade, but that he could not have done—he had no time to do it—for he arrived on the ridge late at night, and in the morning the Norman army was the first to move, and moved before Harold was ready for it.

Harold in his hurry had had no time to put out a defensive screen, and his approach had been observed by William's scouts. They rode back to Hastings with their news, and all night the Norman army stood to arms. It marched at dawn to Telham Hill, and an advance guard reported Harold's position. The English had slept late, and William had ample time to array his army for the attack. Here again one must try to estimate his numbers, and in the seventeen days since his landing at Pevensey he had certainly suffered the casualties to which an army is subject: casualties from sickness, drunkenness, and temporary desertion to enjoy the pleasures of fraternisation with local inhabitants. To guard his ships and garrison his defensive works at Hastings he must have left some two or three thousand men, and his strength on the field may well have been no more than eight thousand.

Much ingenuity has gone into calculation of Harold's numbers, and Major-General J. F. C. Fuller, an able soldier and a distinguished military historian, reduced the English army to either 6300 or 7500 by his assumption that the so-called shield-wall which the army presented consisted of interlocking shields, and that the ground on which so solid a line could have stood measured no more than six hundred yards. He saw Harold's army as a phalanx of either ten or twelve ranks drawn up behind a continuous wall or rampart of adjacent shields. But he may have interpreted too literally a good visual phrase, and the ground available to a slightly looser but still closely coherent defence extends to nearly a thousand yards. There would be room, then, for a much more numerous array, and when one considers the course of the battle, the known or half-known events of the battle, it seems reasonable to suppose that Harold's army was larger than William's by an appreciable fraction. For William's army was more efficient, and armed with such modern additions as archers and cavalry, yet Harold's army, relying on an old-fashioned faith in infantry, was able to resist the Norman attack for the better part of a long day. And if it can be accepted that Harold's army was largely pre-assembled —that he had ordered its mobilisation before he marched to York —there is no hindrance to the supposition that he may have opposed ten thousand men to William's eight thousand.

The story, from a Norman source, that the English had spent the night in revelry, drinking and singing, while the invaders were piously confessing their sins and praying, need not be taken seriously, though perhaps there is a shadow of truth in the suggestion that the armies were very differently occupied. From very early in the morning the Normans must have been forming up for an approach march of six or seven miles that brought them, by nine o'clock, to the top of Telham Hill, from where, on the ridge in front of them, they could see their enemy. If the English were not yet in battle array their late rising may have been due to 'ale in a Saxon rumkin' as well as to the weariness of their march from London. The ridge on which they stood was bare, untenanted till the army came, and marked only by a single apple-tree, grey with age. No buildings foretold the village of Battle that was to grow round the minster which William endowed, but among the crowd of men on the hill where Battle Abbey was to rise two standards flaunted their colour: the Dragon of Wessex and Harold's own flag, called the Fighting Man.

The Norman army advanced in three main groups. In the centre was duke William with his own Normans where the papal banner gave to the invasion some faint suggestion of a crusade, and his necklet of holy relics proclaimed his faith in the virtue of his war. On his left were the Bretons, on his right the volunteers and mercenaries. Archers and light infantry were in the van, the more heavily armed infantry followed, and the armoured knights, on uncovered horses, brought up the rear.

There was, it is said, a fantastic prelude to the battle in which a warlike minstrel called Taillefer rode forward from the Norman host, singing songs of Roland and his paladins, and throwing his sword in the air to catch it with a dexterity that matched bravado. There is no need to disbelieve this tale, for in a much later and more grievous war, that some still call the Kaiser's war, there were occasions when Highland troops went over the top with their pipers playing—and English county regiments under a fox-hunting colonel were taunted on with the shrill call of a hunting-horn—even occasions when, irreverent of such grim names as Loos, Bapaume, and Sanctuary Wood, an impious soldiery dribbled foot-balls into No Man's Land. Let Taillefer be accepted, for his bravado led him to his death; and there is veracity in that conclusion.

The battle began with an exchange of missiles. There were archers on both sides, but the English bow was not yet the formidable weapon which dominated the fields of Cressy and Agincourt, and the English bowmen were not organised as a separate arm of the service: the Tapestry has a picture of archers occupying a gap in the shield-wall. At the start of the battle the Norman archers were ineffective—the English shields were apparently too thick to be pierced—and the exchange of heavier weapons, of throwing spears and stone-headed clubs, was inconclusive. The shield-wall remained intact, and William sent in his cavalry.

What followed, however, was not a massed cavalry charge, but repeated assault by individual knights, or groups of knights, on the English line. From the evidence of the Tapestry some rode with their lances couched, others carried them high, to throw like javelins or use in a downward stabbing thrust. The main English weapon was the axe, and a terrible weapon it must have been in the hands of big men who stood on rising ground: the tall stature of the English is noted by a Norman chronicler, and the artist of the Tapestry shows a giant of a man sinking his axe into the head of a horse. The English had adopted the axe from their neighbours in the Danelaw, and in this savage tussle they had the better of Norman spear and sword. The Norman cavalry failed to breach the shield-wall, and some turned away, others fled. Confusion spread, and retreat became general.

In the vivid pictures of the Tapestry can be seen the dire chaos of this phase of the battle. The dead are already thick on the ground, horses and men go down, and the fury of the fighting— or so it seems—may be the prelude of utter rout. But William's brother, the warlike bishop Odo, brandishes his mace and rallies the bewildered young men: *'Odo episcopus baculum tenens confortat pueros.'* William himself comes to the rescue, for a rumour was spreading that he had been killed, and to disprove it he lifts up his helmet to show his face. 'Here he is,' shouts Eustace of Boulogne, and the Normans reform for a new attack.

But the English threw away their advantage. They might have advanced en masse, but did not. They could have held their unbroken line, and did not. Many of them were tempted by the sight of a running enemy to break out in pursuit, and when the Normans rallied they had the advantage which, until then, had been so fiercely denied them. Now the English were vulnerable, the battle spread beyond the human fortress on the hill, and isolated groups of foot-soldiers were no match for charging horsemen.

Here the real, intrinsic weakness of Anglo-Saxon England was symbolically revealed. Its society was conservative but incoherent. Too conservative in military usage to have found for itself, or adapted from others, the mobile strength of horsed soldiers or the fire-power of organised bowmen, it lacked the absolute and continuous discipline which might have justified its faith in heavy infantry and a stationary defence. And, as events were soon to show, its throne was as vulnerable as the shield-wall. When a few defected there was no continuing loyalty or habit of unity to defend it.

The Norman front was restored, the general assault renewed,

and now—or so it seems—duke William had such command of his mounted men that he could order them to simulate the flight that previously had been enforced. Twice, it is said, they made a pretence of retreat, and again drew English hot-heads from their security on the hill. Again the battle spread and scattered, and again the English paid the price of recklessness. But still, under their banners of the Dragon and the Fighting Man, the hard core of the army—the superb and splendid housecarls—stood defiant and still, as it seemed, impregnable.

On both sides the losses must have been grievous, but now all were so inflamed by the lust of battle that neither side faltered, and as the westering sun went down, the savagery of that stubborn fight was undiminished. What altered it, and determined its end, was duke William's better command of his motley army, and his perception, in the thick of battle, of how to use his better arms to force a decision. With his episcopal and pugnacious brother he had fought as closely as any of his knights, as closely as Harold Godwineson and his brave brothers. In some fierce foray of the Normans—some wild and insistent attack on the centre of the shield-wall—both Gyrth and Leofwine had fallen, and three times the horse he rode had been killed between duke William's legs. The general and great men of that battle fought as far forward as their troopers or their stubborn infantry, and still exercised command. But the duke's commandments were the more effective, his perception of a possible new tactic keener.

In the chaos of battle and the fog of war he gathered his archers and instructed his cavalry. Let his mounted men maintain their pressure on what was left of the English shield-wall, and let his archers be grouped at a certain distance and ordered to shoot high in the air so that their dropping shafts could come down behind the wall.—He made, that is, his archers lob arrows that would fall like mortar-bombs beyond the defences which direct attack could not breach.—And these tactics were successful.

Harold fell with an arrow in his eye, the shield-wall collapsed, and a furious sortie of Norman knights reached the dying king and killed him. But the battle went on. Resistance was hopeless now, but a fury of intransigence still possessed the remnant English, and as darkness gathered there was a last tumult of bravery where, on broken ground, an indomitable heroism insisted on a fight *à outrance*.

The Normans were left in possession of the ridge, and duke William, it is said, compelled his people to clear the ground, where the killed and wounded most thickly lay, and set up a tent in which, at the dead centre of battle, he could celebrate his victory with a feast that good bishop Odo would bless with the grace of God.

Had the battle gone otherwise it is probable that Harold would have done the same. The prevalent faith in God was only dismembered by His several protagonists' claim to a monopoly of His favour.

Chapter XVI

CORONATION

K ITES and ravens, crows and buzzards—all the carrion birds in that corner of England—had gathered by morning on the battlefield. The artist of the Bayeux Tapestry confected for his picture-history a decorative border on which, among various grotesque inventions, birds appear to be following the invasion fleet, and then the mounted knights on their way to battle, as if in anticipation of their destined feast. But kites and crows were not the only beneficiaries, for the Tapestry also shows dead men, in a litter of death, being stripped of their clothes by human predators.

The Tapestry, indeed, finds room not only for depiction of a triumph, but for a narrow, formalised view of a scene commanding infinite pity and a flawed wonder at the tenacity of human hope, the heroic persistence of human intention. Proof that men will give their lives for the satisfaction of someone else's cause is like a window lighting some of the darker—though perhaps the richer—parts of humanity; and bishop Odo may be envied a simplicity of heart that let him swing a mace as naturally as if it were a crosier. He, presumably, could see the multitude of the dead as mere evidence of God's will: some had been His instruments, others His victims. But Odo's brother may have counted them with a different calculation.

In a battle that was fought with such manifest fury, and lasted the better part of a day—from soon after nine o'clock in the morning till the darkening twilight of an October evening—the Norman losses, though less than the Saxon dead, must have been very great. And duke William, though he had won the crucial battle of his campaign, had still to devise means for the conquest of England. It is not unreasonable to suppose that the army he had brought to battle had lost nearly a quarter of its strength, and perhaps more. The wound inflicted by an English axe must usually have been fatal, and those who survived—in the uninfected air of the eleventh century perhaps many did recover from seemingly mortal injury —were crippled for life. William had to face a large task with an army already much reduced.

He had, however, the gratifying assurance that he need make no preparation for battle with Harald Hardrada. Before Harold Godwineson's arrival he had been told by an English landowner of Norman birth—who, however, warned him to retire before the unassailable strength of the English army—that the Norwegian king had been killed, his army defeated; and from prisoners he had doubtless had confirmation of such comforting news. But he had still to make himself king of England, and within a few weeks his army was to suffer further diminution.

For a few days, it appears, he expected to receive the formal submission of a defeated country. He returned to Hastings and waited for the arrival of Englishmen prepared to offer their allegiance and become his new subjects. But none came. In London, indeed, there was no thought of surrender, but debate about who should succeed to the throne. Harold had left three sons, but they were young, possibly illegitimate, and certainly ineligible. His brothers Gyrth and Leofwine were dead. The brother-earls Edwin and Morcar had now arrived in London, but it was unlikely that Wessex and the south would accept either of them. The choice fell on Edgar the Atheling, grandson of Edmund Ironside, who with his sister Margaret—later queen in Scotland—were the last of Cerdic's line. Edgar was recognised as king, but not crowned. Edwin and Morcar supported his nomination but gave him no further help. They withdrew to the north and England, though not yet ready to submit, was no longer united in resistance.

After five days William left Hastings and began his circuitous march on London. At Romney some stragglers from his army— or perhaps the complement of a lost ship—had been killed, and for this misdemeanour he took so savage a revenge that Dover surrendered immediately, though its castle could have been defended. He spent eight days in Dover, and his army began to be troubled by dysentery. Before reaching Canterbury he received its submission, and from other parts of Kent men now came to do him homage. But in or near Canterbury William fell sick, and lay for a whole month. In primitive conditions of life—such conditions as an invading army had then to live in—dysentery was a recurrent menace, and beyond control when it occurred. Dysentery had saved Paris and defeated Ragnar Lodbrok's great army in 845. It seems certain that William's army was now temporarily disabled, and it is impossible to suppose there was no mortality. His loss from disease may have been considerable.

During this time of inactivity Winchester was surrendered by Edith, widow of the Confessor, but no word of submission came from London, and the strength of London to resist could not be taken lightly. Somewhere in the Thames, moreover, there was the remnant of Harold Godwineson's fleet. William's command of the Channel might still have been contested, and despite much local success his position was now, perhaps, more hazardous than it had been at Pevensey. Now, in a foreign country and weakened by disease, he faced the same potential dangers as in the past had confronted viking leaders when they struck inland and left the safety of their ships behind. If the English had found a resolute leader, either in London or the west country, he might still have been defeated. But despite the great achievements of the royal house of Wessex, England had found no cohesion or habit of cohesion. Harold by his own strength had riveted a front of unity upon it, but when Harold died the front broke apart, and because no one could command a general support—or even, as it seems, a strong and assured local support—there was no one to stand in the invaders' way.

William recovered from his illness, and his army resumed its march. At the south end of London Bridge there was a skirmish between the Norman advance-guard and the Atheling's troops who had ventured a sortie. The English were driven back, and Southwark set on fire. But William wisely made no attempt to cross the Thames and take London by storm. His better plan was to take it whole, by terror and isolation, and now his march lay along the right bank of the Thames. Burning and harrying through Surrey, Hampshire, and Berkshire, he came to Wallingford, forty-six miles by road from London, where the river could be crossed by ford or bridge. At Wallingford archbishop Stigand, leader of the Atheling's party, came and swore allegiance; and swore away what strength the uncrowned king of England may have had.

Now on the other side of the Thames William turned north-eastward, under the slope of the Chiltern hills, and marched to Berkhamsted, where England—in so far as anyone could speak for England—formally submitted. To him came the Atheling, the earls Edwin and Morcar, Aldred, archbishop of York, the bishops of Worcester and Hereford, and London's leading citizens, to pledge their loyalty and, it would seem, to offer him the crown. They gave hostages for their good behaviour, and William, says the Anglo-Saxon Chronicle, promised to be 'a gracious liege-lord.' He still thought it necessary, however, to terrorise the countryside, and as he marched the remaining five-and-twenty miles his soldiers pillaged as they went. It is difficult, indeed, to see how they could have fed themselves without pillaging, and what is more remarkable than Norman brutality is the fact that a marching army of considerable size could live on the country in the month of December when herds had been reduced to the minimum of beasts for which there was winter-keep. But England was a rich country, and the natural riches that had attracted so many adventurers now fed the latest and most successful of them as he advanced to its throne. With what strength he marched on London is not known, but he must have left garrisons of appreciable size at Wallingford, Canterbury, and perhaps elsewhere, as well as at Hastings.

Outside the walls of London there may have been a little unorganised resistance—accounts vary about that—but there was no serious opposition and he entered his new capital a few days before Christmas. A little more than two months after his victory at Hastings he was king-elect of the country which Alfred the Great had defended in nine pitched battles, but in 1066 no Alfred or Edmund Ironside arose to gather about him the embattled shires. In more ways than one, England needed a king, and now William had fortified the Confessor's nomination by victory in a campaign that had come to an end for lack of opponents.

England needed a king, and though William spoke with a foreign tongue, that was no innovation. It was only thirty years since the death of a foreign king whose rule had prospered in a climate of general assent. Cnut of Denmark had done well by England, and William of Normandy had the initial advantage over him in being able to claim that his accession was *de jure* as well as *de facto*. Already, it may be, the brief rule of Harold Godwineson had begun to look like a mere interlude: not rule so much as interregnum.

William was crowned on Christmas day in Westminster where Harold had been crowned less than twelve months before. Of his new kingdom he had seen only those parts through which he had marched, and his manifest authority reached no farther west than Winchester, no farther north than Berkhamsted. But the two archbishops, Stigand of Canterbury and Aldred of York, escorted him to his seat below the high altar, and to a congregation of two nations he was presented by Aldred of York in English, by Geoffrey, bishop of Coutances, in French. The presentation was loudly acclaimed, and the new king was received with a great shout of 'Yea, yea, King William!' So noisy was the demonstration of welcome and approval that the Norman soldiers guarding the approaches to the abbey were alarmed by the clamour within, and thought rebellion had begun. To suppress or contain it, they set fire to the neighbouring houses.

However inopportune, this was pure atavism. Their Norse ancestors had often used fire to suppress a cornered enemy, and at a moment of what seemed to be emergent danger—in a foreign city whose inhabitants may have shown more hostility than their leaders dared reveal—the Normans reverted to an ancient but familiar practice, and within the abbey the cold December light turned lurid with the flame of burning houses, the pious tones of the officiating clergy were lost in the roar of the encircling fire.

The congregation fled. Norman and English, noble and simple, hurried out in terror or to fight the flames, to look to their own property or for the chance of plunder. Few remained within save the new king and the clergy at the altar. Freeman, the nineteenth century historian, quotes the *Historia Ecclesiastica* of Orderic Vitalis: '*Soli praesules, et pauci clerici cum monachis, nimium trepidantes ante aram perstiterunt, et officium consecrationis super regem vehementer trementem vix peregerunt.*'— 'Only the leading persons, with a few clergy and monks, stood firmly before the altar, (though) immoderately agitated, and with difficulty continued to direct the office of consecration above the violently trembling king.'

In an age so vulnerable to religious dread, the sudden explosion of seeming anger, the light and the leap of flames at the very moment of consecration—when Aldred, not the suspect Stigand, was pouring the holy oil—must have struck even William's robust heart with superstitious fear. He, the agent of a church dedicated to reform, had come to his enthronement across a battlefield drenched with blood, and while he waited for the anointing oil that would endue him with a more than human authority—with God's grace and a divine right to rule—the house of his saintly cousin was lighted with a terrible radiance that, for a long minute, he may well have thought to be the declaration of God's wrath against a usurper. But the ceremony continued, the sceptre was put into his hand, the crown upon his brow; and outside the abbey panic subsided, the fires were quenched, or subsided into smouldering ash.

England had a new king; it had also had a fortunate escape. If Harald Hardrada and Tostig had won both their battles, it would have been riven asunder, but William's ruthless government would hold it together and nurture, under alien rule, the identity which so long had sought expression and so often been repressed. As duke of Normandy he commanded his aristocracy with a strength dependent on common assent, and acknowledged the church's dominion with some assurance that he was essential to its maintenance. He led an ordered polity, and an enforced order—governed by effective administration and safeguarded by law—was what England required, and what William could bring to it. But before order could be imposed he would have to undertake swift and fierce campaigns in the west and the north; he would have to fight to give England what it needed.

Chapter XVII

PACIFICATION

To oppose an armed invader is the virtuous exercise of a patriotic and public spirit; to obstruct a duly crowned and anointed king is mere rebellion. The Christmas ceremony in Westminster Abbey had immensely reinforced the authority of William and his Norman host, and for the first few months of 1067 England lived in a quiet but sullen acceptance of his rule. That the temper of London was not warm and welcoming may be inferred from two facts: he immediately gave orders for the building of a fortress from which it would be possible to curb the citizens' high spirits; and he withdrew his army to an encampment secure from interference but convenient for action should action be required.

The fortress was initially of the simple type common in Normandy at that time: a mound of earth was encircled by a ditch and guarded by tall ramparts within which a wooden tower was raised; at a later date this primitive structure was replaced by solid masonry and became the Tower of London. The site to which he withdrew his army was at Barking in Essex, north of the river and some seven miles east of London. It was easier to maintain discipline there, and his soldiers would not be subject to the recurrent temptations of loot and rape, which a city so freely offers.

To William at Barking came again the magnates of London to promise obedience and receive assurance of his goodwill. Some had already made their submission at Berkhamsted, others saw their king for the first time. Tostig's former lieutenant, Copsi—he who brought him reinforcements from Orkney—was among those who submitted, with several others from Northumbria. They gave hostages as security for their pledged allegiance, and many who had favoured Harold Godwineson had to pay heavily

England—
Castles built during
William's reign

CLYDE R.

TWEED R.

Newcastle-on-Tyne

TYNE R.

Gateshead

Carlisle

Durham

TEES R.

NORTH

N

York

OUSE R.

HUMBER R.

NORTH SEA

Torksey

Lincoln

Chester

Nottingham

TRENT R.

Stafford

Leicester

Stamford

Norwich

Shrewsbury

SEVERN R.

Warwick

WELLAND R.

Ely

Thetford

Worcester

AVON R.

Huntingdon

OUSE R.

Cambridge

Gloucester

Oxford

Wallingford

THAMES R.

London

Windsor

Rochester

Bristol

Winchester

Porchester

Arundel

Lewes

Canterbury

Dover

Eastbourne

Exeter

Wareham

Tintagel

ENGLISH CHANNEL

Miles

0   50   100

palacios

to retain or redeem their estates. The lands of those who had fought against the king were confiscated and granted to his Norman followers.

These initial stages in the redistribution of landed properties evoked no marked or open opposition, and early in March William counted it safe to return and see to the affairs of his duchy. England was left in charge of his Norman nobility—chief among them, William fitz Osbern and bishop Odo—and the king, accompanied by many hostages of high rank, rode to the Sussex coast and embarked at Pevensey. The sea was kind, and his Norman subjects greeted him with enthusiasm. The people of Rouen ran out to meet him and marvel at the splendour of his march. Among the hostages William had taken were the earls Edwin and Morcar, Waltheof from Northumbria, the Atheling and Stigand the archbishop: to the Normans they must have looked like the captives of a Roman triumph.

Easter was celebrated at Fécamp, and William's triumphal progress, made the more magnificent by a parade of gold and silver trophies of victory, was hallowed by lavish gifts to the church. The monastery at Fécamp was enriched, as were Holy Trinity in Rouen, the abbey of St. Mary at Dives, and the monastery at Jumièges; which, then or later, got Hayling Island for its endowment. The king's piety may have been assisted by the identification of his interests with those of the Norman church, and by the curious relationship with God that his coronation gave him; but otherwise there is no reason for doubting its reality. It was obviously prudent, however, to fortify goodwill in the powerful prelates of Normandy when affairs in France seemed a little unsettled; his acquisition of a kingdom had certainly not won him the favour of the French court.

In England there were now signs of imminent unrest. There was no single great eruption, but here and there, as in country where thermal springs are active, the surface broke and local resentment exploded. Bishop Odo's headquarters were in Dover, William fitz Osbern's in Norwich. In the south-east there was armed revolt, aided from abroad, which had the advantage of Odo's absence; he was somewhere north of the Thames, dealing with a small uprising there. On the Welsh border there was a little local war, and before the year was out there came rumours of a new attack by Denmark.

In Herefordshire there was a man known as Edric the Wild—in an old chronicle he is more splendidly called Edricus Silvaticus—who was a nephew of the abominable Edric Streona whom Cnut sent to his death for treachery. Edric may have submitted to the new king at Barking, but if he did, he quickly changed his mind, and now in alliance with two Welsh princes, Bleddyn and Riwallon—who owed their power to Harold Godwineson—he wasted Herefordshire as far as the river Lugg, and is said to have carried off a vast booty. With his allies and his booty he retired beyond the border and waited for new opportunity.

In Kent, where the rebels had the advantage of bishop Odo's absence on a punitive expedition, they got the assistance of Eustace, count of Boulogne, who had fought on the Norman side at Hastings and then returned to his own country. Earlier in life Eustace had quarrelled with earl Godwine; since the battle he had fallen out with William; and now, with the promise of English allies, he landed and tried to seize Dover castle. The garrison was strong enough to defeat him, and he retired to his ships and re-crossed the Channel before bishop Odo could reach the coast. The Kentish revolt occurred in the autumn of 1067.

Later in the year the regents were alarmed by news of the Danish king's preparation for attack. Sweyn Estrithson's mother was a sister of Cnut the Great, and after the death of Harthacnut his claim to the Danish throne had been obscured by the aggression of Magnus of Norway. After Magnus's death he had for long been at war with Harald Hardrada; he had appealed, but in vain, to England for help, and had fought unaided for Denmark's independence till an arranged peace secured it in 1064. As the inheritor, by blood and force of arms, of one part of Cnut's empire, it may have seemed to him that he had a claim to its farther half, and he might well have joined the other contestants for the Confessor's throne in 1066 when Tostig went and asked him for assistance. Now, it appears, he was encouraged to press his claim by invitation from East Anglia, where families of his race were numerous and men had been as bitterly alienated by fitz Osbern's harsh rule as the men of Kent by bishop Odo's. Sweyn was a nephew of Gyda, wife of earl Godwine; cousin, therefore, of Gyrth, earl of East Anglia, who died at Hastings. There may have been those—English as well as Danes—who recognised a tie of sentiment.

When news of the widespread unrest, and now a threat from over sea, reached William in Normandy is not known, but early in December he returned to England, and almost immediately had to deal with new insurgents. Exeter was in revolt, Exeter had strengthened its walls, and the men of Devon had formed a confederacy of neighbouring towns that openly defied the king. They would neither give him their allegiance, they said, nor let him inside their gates. They were prepared to pay to the crown their usual taxes, but they would yield nothing else.

William led a combined army into Devon—English and Normans marching together for the first time—and his approach so daunted the Devon thanes and the leading citizens of Exeter that they, or some of them, came out to pledge their fealty and save their possessions. But the townspeople refused to surrender and stoutly defended themselves for eighteen days. Then, as it appears, some part of the wall collapsed, in consequence of mining, and the town yielded. It was neither plundered nor punished for its resistance, but to balance a free pardon a castle was built within its walls and a garrison left there.

Gyda, earl Godwine's widow, had been in Exeter, but escaped before it surrendered. With her, it seems, were some of her grandchildren, including three illegitimate sons of king Harold. They found a comfortless refuge on Steep Holm and Flat Holm in the Bristol Channel, and then a better retreat in Dublin. The Irish Norsemen were willing to give them limited help, but it brought them no appreciable success. It is evident that William's occupation of Exeter, and perhaps some punitive expeditions beyond it, established his power throughout the south-west; for when, later in the year, the sons of Harold and their Irish auxiliaries attacked Bristol, they were driven off, and a little while later were defeated in Somerset. To Robert, count of Mortain, the king's half-brother, was granted the larger part of Cornwall.

William's victory in the south-west gave him some leisure and the opportunity to make arrangements for the coronation of the duchess Matilda. She crossed the Channel and came to London at Whitsuntide, and was duly crowned queen of England. But much of England had still to be subdued, and in summer the north erupted.

The Atheling had fled to Scotland, where he was warmly welcomed by king Malcolm. With Edgar were his mother and his sister Margaret, who became Malcolm's wife with remarkable consequences for Scotland. Also in retreat to the north were Edwin and Morcar; Edwin, it is said, having been disappointed in his expectation of marrying one of William's daughters. In Northumbria a miniature war of succession had already been fought and lost: doubly lost indeed, for both contestants had been killed. One of them was Copsi, formerly Tostig's lieutenant, who after his submission at Barking had been given the northern earldom and had encountered local opposition, of the most indignant sort, from a surviving representative of the house which had anciently ruled Northumbria. Copsi lived in his earldom for a few weeks only. Then, on a bank of the Tyne, he was killed by Oswulf, of the ancient house; and some months later, in a wayside brawl, Oswulf was killed. Cospatric, Oswulf's cousin, then acquired the earldom by consent of the king, and doubtless by a substantial payment, but was so ill-advised as to offer his support to the Atheling when that young man returned to Scotland.

William's response was quick and masterful. He marched first to Warwick, and built a castle there. That was enough to overawe Edwin and Morcar. Then to Nottingham and another castle, which convinced many in the dissident north that defiance would be too expensive. William entered York without opposition, raised a third castle on the mound where Clifford's Tower stands, and after negotiation with Malcolm of Scotland persuaded him that active support of the Atheling would be injudicious. William then returned to the south, leaving as the record of his march new castles at Lincoln, Huntingdon, and Cambridge.

To the troubled north he sent Robert de Comines, one of his Normans, with the title of earl and an army to enforce a proper respect. But Robert had neither William's faculty of inspiring fear nor the shrewd caution that underlay his audacity. In Durham, or some little distance from it, Robert ignored the bishop's warning that an insurgent army was prepared to resist his authority. He entered the town, and in the darkness of an early morning, at the end of January 1069, the angry men of the

Danelaw surrounded it and again reverted to an ancestral habit and the northern devotion to fire which the troopers who guarded Westminster Abbey at William's coronation had revealed. They attacked and slew the men of Robert's little army in the narrow streets of Durham, and gathering about the good bishop's house, where Robert de Comines was sleeping, they burnt it.

This spirited action was followed by an English attack—an attack, that is, by the men of the Danelaw—on the city of York, whose commander, appointed by king William, was killed, and whose people, by persuasion, compulsion, or a natural instinct for intransigence, promptly declared for Edgar the Atheling. In the newly built castle a loyal garrison resisted and held it for the king, to whom they were able to send an appeal for help.

William returned to York, and marched so fast that he took the rebels by surprise, scattered them, and relieved the castle. The town and its people suffered heavy punishment, and in the space of eight days a second castle was raised, this one on the right bank of the Ouse. The king returned to the south, to Winchester, and William fitz Osbern was left in command of York. He, it appears, had to undertake other punitive measures, but Durham, very strangely, escaped retribution for the killing of Robert de Comines. There is a legend that it was saved by the intervention of St. Cuthbert, but it is permissible to believe that the king, who had come so swiftly to the rescue of York, had then been in an equal hurry to leave it: it was about this time that queen Matilda returned to Normandy with the authority of a crown to impress the people, and for personal reasons or reasons of state it may well be that William wanted to see her before she went. After his departure from the north it was probably native caution, rather than the voice of St. Cuthbert, which persuaded fitz Osbern to leave Durham unharmed.

In June two of Harold's sons appeared off the coast of North Devon with a fleet of some sixty ships, and sailed into the mouth of the Taw. They had again recruited strength in Ireland, but they lacked the ability to use it for a political purpose. Their company scattered to plunder, and may have assaulted Exeter. If so, the attack was beaten off and presently the rampaging invaders were defeated with great slaughter. The sons of Harold escaped, but are not heard of again.

The Danish attack, so long expected, was announced by a great show of naval strength off the coast of Kent. The fleet may have numbered about two hundred and forty ships: almost as many, perhaps, as sailed with Harald Hardrada. But the army it carried had no commander as forceful and determined as the great Norwegian. King Sweyn remained at home, and the fleet was led, probably with divided counsel, by his sons Harald and Cnut, and his brother Biorn: two grand-nephews and a nephew, it may be noted, of Godwine's wife Gyda. There had possibly been a plan to synchronise this attack with the Irish invasion, so lately defeated, that Harold Godwineson's illegitimate sons incompetently led. An offensive on two fronts, in which were united most of the surviving members of the house of Godwine, might have embarrassed William if the invaders had had a general of aggressive genius and a co-ordinating faculty that also amounted to genius; though genius itself would have been strained to accommodate and reconcile the rival claims and differing temper of continental Danes, Irish Norse, and an English cousinry of dubious origin. King Sweyn's attempted invasion, though foreseen for some considerable time, had not induced William to build a defensive fleet. There were no naval engagements as the Danes sailed up the east coast of England; no naval defence, in the southwest, against Irish attack. William built castles throughout England, but no warships; and the ships immortalised on the Bayeux Tapestry were never re-commissioned for any memorable enterprise.

When the Danes attacked Dover William was hunting in the Forest of Dean, west of the Severn. The attack was repulsed, as was another on Sandwich. Then the fleet headed north, but raiding-parties put ashore in East Anglia were defeated. Early in September the Danes entered the Humber—just three years had elapsed since Harald Hardrada's sails had coloured the great estuary—and an insurgent English army was there to greet it. The north had risen again, under Edgar the Atheling, Cospatric, and Waltheof, the son of old Siward of Northumbria. Invaders and insurgents marched on York together, and Aldred the archbishop, who had crowned both Harold and William, died within its walls a little while before disaster shrouded them. It does not seem extravagant to suppose that his death was hastened by the prospect of war renewed and the vengeance it would invite.

What followed is by no means clear, but it seems that the Norman garrisons, distrusting the strength of their newly built castles, tried to increase their security by burning the nearby houses: the intended effect being to deny the attackers a covered approach, and to give the defenders the advantage of a wide field of fire. Their leaders, William Malet and Gilbert of Ghent, had lately sent messengers to tell the king they could hold out for a year, if need be—so says Orderic Vitalis—but the unexpected magnitude of the rising must have taken them by surprise and induced a decision that panic discoloured. The flames of the burning houses spread to other parts of the city, and menaced, perhaps, the wooden castles. By miscalculation, or some mishap that enforced their move, the garrisons came out into the open, through burning streets, and possibly made a stand outside the city walls. There is a story that Waltheof the Northumbrian, a mighty man, stood by a gap in the wall and dealt sudden death with his Danish axe. The historian William of Malmesbury tells of Waltheof—mighty of shoulder, broad of chest, tall and strong as an oak—lopping off heads as the Normans made their desperate sortie; and however that may be—whether they fought in the streets, or under the walls, or in open country beyond—the numerous garrison was cut to pieces.

The Danes and their English allies won a considerable victory, and did not know how to take advantage of it. The Danes, with their booty, retired to their ships; and many of the English, with theirs, dispersed and went home. The Danish fleet sailed over to the south shore of the Humber, and fortified an island from which they could move at will in a friendly countryside; for the villagers of north Lincolnshire had still a warm memory of Danish ancestors though their knowledge of the Danish tongue had diminished. Farther north the situation was complicated by the uncertain attitude of Malcolm, king of Scots. His court had been the refuge of English fugitives from William's oppression, and by 1069, it is probable, he was married to Margaret, the Atheling's sister. He certainly favoured the Atheling's party, but his savage depredations in the north of England were apparently an expression of private hostility to Cospatric when Cospatric was again given the earldom of Northumbria. Malcolm's sympathy with Edgar, his brother-in-law, may well have been limited by the knowledge—which he must have acquired by 1069—that Edgar had no policy other than to harbour resentment, and a character so weak that his policy was unlikely to change.

Even without Malcolm's active intervention, the stability of all England appeared to be in jeopardy. News of the Danish invasion had re-awakened a sleeping animosity to Norman rule in many parts of the country. There was revolt in Devon and Cornwall, which wasted its strength in a hopeless attack on Exeter. There was revolt in Somerset and Dorset, which the soldierly bishop of Coutances suppressed; but he had to summon troops from Salisbury, Winchester, and London to master the rebels. In Mercia there was a more serious rising—not revolt, but a new declaration of continuing independence—when Edric the Wild and the Welsh princes who were his allies came over the border and carried their war as far north as Cheshire, as far east as Stafford. The castles which William had built hindered their advance, and the castle of Shrewsbury resisted an attack in force. But Edric and the Welsh were too strong for any local force to defeat.

William had marched north when news reached him of the calamity at York, and at word of his approach the Danes re-embarked and crossed over to the north side of the Humber. In their ships they were, if not impregnable, at least immune from any counter-attack that William could easily devise; for he lacked a navy. With castles and cavalry he could master landward dissidents, but a king of England who had no fleet was at sorry disadvantage against a maritime power.

The menace of Edric and the Welsh gave him an excuse for leaving an insoluble problem—he left it to his half-brother, Roger of Mortain, and his cousin, Robert of Eu—and marched from north Lincolnshire to Stafford, where again he revealed his mastery on land and easily defeated his opponents. He set out on a return march to the Humber, but in Nottingham heard that the Danes were now threatening York. He headed north, but the river Aire, which meets the Ouse north-west of its entry into the Humber, delayed his progress. The bridge by which he meant to cross it, near Pontefract, had been demolished; the Danes held the farther bank; and at that time of year—it was not long before

Christmas—the river was running high. For three weeks William looked for a possible crossing place before he found an undefended ford—or a ford that could be crossed against a scanty rear-guard—and from the northern bank of the Aire set out to devastate the country west and north of York. That was done so thoroughly that seventeen years later, when the Domesday survey was made, the land showed no sign of recovery. Having totally desolated a wide area, he left the wilderness he had created to spend Christmas in the northern capital.

The Danes had again retired to their ships, and because William had no means of reaching them or dislodging them, he was compelled to buy their promise of peace and formally give them permission to remain in the shelter of the Humber till winter was over. But if, perforce, he was lenient with the shipboard Danes, he still showed no mercy to their landward cousins of the northern Danelaw. Punitive forces went out from York to harry and destroy the neighbouring country. The brutality of the punishment he ordered was extreme even by the standards of warfare in the eleventh century, and because in other places, and at other times, William was not wantonly cruel—often, indeed, he was fairly tolerant—some reason must be sought for his uncommonly savage treatment of Yorkshire. That he had been frightened is fairly obvious: not, of course, frightened for his own safety, but put in deeper fear for the security of the realm he had so narrowly won. Less obvious, but perhaps as true, was an ancestral stirring in his mind of the almost cousinly relationship between himself and the insurgent north. That part of England had been fought over, conquered, and settled, by men of his own kind, if not of his own blood, and the quarrel he pursued had all the bitterness of a family dispute. The presence, moreover, of a Danish fleet in English waters, in the shelter of the Humber —a fleet that, to his fury, he could not touch—may have raised resentment almost to the pitch of insanity. Fury frustrated on the one hand turned to unleash itself on the other with a double impetus, and the wilderness that he made in Yorkshire remains the darkest stain on William's memory.

At this time, indeed, he had no mercy on himself or his own men. He was statesman enough to accept the submission of Waltheof and Cospatric, and in the exigencies of the time—in a

situation where there was no one else to whom he could entrust
the defence of the north—to show confidence in the sincerity of
their submission; for they both got back their earldoms. But
there was to be no respite for enemies still undefeated, and having
harried Teesdale in the dark cold of mid-winter the king set off on
a return march to York that faced all the horrors of an exception-
ally vicious January. Snow in which the horses foundered, a
blizzard in which William and six companions were lost and be-
nighted—these are among the details of a dreadful journey that
Orderic Vitalis has preserved—and when they arrived in York
there was little comfort there, for almost immediately the army
had to march again.

The supporters of Edric the Wild and the Welsh princes, whose
army he had defeated at Stafford, were still contumacious, still a
menace to his peace. Their main strength was now in Cheshire,
and between York and the Cheshire plain are the Pennine hills.
They are hills, it is true, of no great height, but even to-day that
countryside, though subdued by civilization, can wear in February a daunting aspect; and nine hundred years ago a winter march
across the rough backbone of England was a formidable undertaking. Too formidable, thought some of William's troops, and
threatened mutiny.

A year before he had dismissed most of his mercenaries, but he
may have found it necessary to re-engage them, or engage others,
for Orderic Vitalis says the mutineers were men from Anjou,
Maine, and Brittany. William listened to their complaints, and
with casual assurance ignored them. He said, in effect, 'Let those
who are faithful, those who are strong, come with me. About the
others it matters very little.' The march began, and the mutineers, rather than be left behind, glumly followed. The hard-
ships they anticipated were realised, horses were lost in swollen
streams, hill-lands were bitter cold and valley floors a treacherous
marsh, but at last the rigours of the journey were overcome. They
went down into the Cheshire plain and approached the old Roman
City of the Legions.

Yet again his resolution, the speed of his movement and the
fear of his name, were enough to dispel opposition. There was
no organised resistance. He entered Chester, built a castle there,
and another at Stafford. Then he returned to the milder south,

dismissed his mercenaries, and was in Winchester before Easter.

One may—indeed one must—deplore the savage temper that William showed in Yorkshire and the farther north, but even the most bitter disapproval of his reprisals there cannot obscure or deny the adamantine resolution which characterised the whole campaign, or the brilliant discipline by which he compelled his army to move at speed through appalling weather. As a soldier in the field he demands the utmost respect, and the strategy of his march and incessant castle-building are no less admirable. To these abilities must be added the machinery, now invisible, by which he fed and maintained his army. On a forced march there can have been no opportunity for sporadic looting; nor, in a Teesdale blizzard or the swampy bottoms of the Pennines, would soldiers be much inclined to wander far in search of rations. His army must have been at least partially supplied before it set out for York or Teesdale or Chester; the foundation of his discipline, the backbone of his strategy, was administration, and all three— discipline, strategy, administration—were in service to a defined purpose.

From this distance in time one may well feel that William had now earned the reward of a little season of peace; but that William so deluded himself is unlikely. The Danish fleet was still in the Humber, and his impotence at sea was made startlingly manifest when, in the spring of 1070, king Sweyn came over to join his snugly anchored ships. From the Humber they sailed south to the Wash, where a Danish force landed and established itself on the Isle of Ely; which was truly an island before the Cambridgeshire fens were drained. Danish blood ran strongly in those parts, and the invaders were joined by many dissident Eng- lishmen, chief of whom was Hereward, a thane of Lincoln- shire, who as the last great champion of English resistance was to achieve the sort of fame which, for its peculiar merit, wears its legend like a halo that both illumines and obscures the truth.

Nothing certain is known of Hereward's background or of his early life; though speculation has been busy. He breaks suddenly into history in company with a mixed force of Danish seamen and English rebels who are on their way from the fen-girt Isle of Ely to plunder the abbey and monastery at nearby Peterborough. A new abbot had lately been appointed, Turold by name, who is said to have been of militant rather than monkish habit. According to the Peterborough Chronicle he commanded a company of a hundred and sixty French soldiers when he set out for his new charge, but Hereward arrived before he did, and the abbey was thoroughly plundered, the town and monastery set on fire. The river Nene was navigable, the raiders were ship-borne, and with a great cargo of booty they returned to the Danish fleet or their island stronghold. One sick monk, a burnt-out monastery, and an empty church were all that abbot Turold found when he rode in.

In the summer of that year, William came to an arrangement with the Danish king by which Sweyn agreed to remove his fleet from English waters, his men from Ely. Sweyn, it is evident, was unprepared for serious war on land, and William, incapable of war at sea, paid to be rid of him. His English predecessors had often paid Danegeld, and now William followed an old example. But he had not bought the Isle of Ely.

Hereward took over its defence, and for some time remained undisturbed in its possession. His position grew stronger, indeed, as outlaws, rebels, and masterless men came to join him. In the spring of 1071 no less a person than earl Morcar arrived, perhaps with other magnates; but Morcar, whom the chroniclers appear to make inseparable from his brother Edwin, was now deprived of that companionship. The brothers had finally quarrelled with the king, or fled before his hostility became explicit; and Edwin, as it appears, had been killed by his own people.

At last William was moved, or found time, to mount a watery offensive against the island rebels. From such a position they could never have menaced the security of his kingdom, but they were a nuisance, and a growing nuisance, and it was necessary to deal with them. A fleet of boats was assembled, the island was besieged, and there are stories of building, with prodigious labour, a causeway across the marshes. What certainly happened is that most of the insurgents surrendered, and were treated leniently—Morcar was sent to open imprisonment in Normandy—but Hereward and some others escaped, and Hereward vanishes into the mists of legend. One story gives him a rich wife, another describes his heroic death in battle; but a third more soberly discovers him, in Domesday Book, as a contented tenant under a Norman lord.

Of greater importance than disorder in the fenland were events in Normandy or its neighbours, and on the Scottish border. For some years Maine had acknowledged Norman rule, but there had lately been a major revolt in Le Mans; and the death of William's brother-in-law, Baldwin VI of Flanders, opened the way to a domestic struggle in which William suffered a grievous loss. William fitz Osbern, the most powerful of his magnates— except for his half-brothers—had gone to Normandy when danger threatened in Maine, and when the dowager of Flanders pleaded for his help, he rode lightheartedly to her assistance, and was killed in battle at Cassel.

The effect on Scotland of William's northern campaigns had obviously been disturbing. Malcolm had spent much of his youth at the court of Edward the Confessor, and his own court, so long the resort of English fugitives, now had, as its strong-minded queen, the Atheling's sister Margaret. As the consolidation of William's conquered English kingdom became apparent, there must have been some disquiet in the neighbouring realm whose southern frontier on the Tweed had been established only half a century before. On several occasions during a long reign Malcolm showed himself sensitive about the security of his frontier, and by devastating raids attempted to create beyond it a no-man's-land which might be an obstacle to invasion. At the time of William's first campaign in the north he prudently decided not to intervene, and Orderic Vitalis, commenting on this, found a flattering explanation for his inactivity: 'For the Scottish nation, although harsh in battle, yet loves ease and quiet; wishes not to be disturbed by neighbouring kingdoms, being intent upon the study of the Christian religion rather than of arms.'

But immediately after William's second offensive, and the harrying of Yorkshire, Malcolm led a merciless punitive raid into Durham and Cleveland, while Cospatric, restored to his earldom —Cospatric who, while under the shadow of William's wrath, had found shelter in Scotland—counter-attacked in parts of Cumbria, about the Solway, which were under Malcolm's rule. If the chronicler Symeon of Durham can be trusted, Malcolm's devastation was no less cruelly thorough than William's; and William's estimate of the threat to northern England was such that he decided to launch a preventive campaign against Scotland.

He had first to visit his duchy, where presumably there was concern about its changed relations with Maine and Flanders; and bishop Odo was with him there. Before Easter 1072, he was in England again, and with his customary speed he made ready for a bold and unusual assault on his northern neighbour. He had, by now, built or acquired some ships, and while his fleet, of unknown size, sailed north along the east coast as far as the Tay, and into the Firth of Tay, his horsemen rode through Durham and Lothian to Stirling Bridge, and under the Ochill hills to Abernethy, near the south bank of the Firth. There Malcolm, having avoided battle, met him in a mood which justified that pleasant opinion of the Scots which Orderic Vitalis so obligingly recorded.

Common sense dominated their meeting, and Malcolm prudently agreed to give hostages, do homage to William, and become 'his man.' That was common form on such occasions—Harold Godwineson had sworn as much—and it is doubtful if an oath of allegiance, exacted by advantage, had any more substance than the extravagant promises made on the eve of an election by the leaders of political parties in a modern democracy. But when Malcolm recognised the new ruler of England, he accepted, as a corollary to recognition, his obligation to disavow the Atheling; and Edgar had to leave his court. The bloodless campaign had achieved a useful result; and then William had to return to Normandy.

Chapter XVIII

THE NORMAN CASTLES

THE military innovations that first facilitated and then maintained William's conquest of England were the mounted knight and the moated castle; and both were imported from France.

It is difficult to visualise the architectural clothing of England in Anglo-Saxon times, but there were probably no public buildings other than churches, which were relatively numerous, and except for a minority of churches there can have been few stone buildings. When William started to raise his castles—though, in the beginning, they were hastily built of wood—they became bases for the exercise of a new sort of power, and to a startled countryside must have been structures of a menacing novelty.

It appears that the church brought in continental masons, to work in Kent and Northumbria, in the seventh and eighth centuries, when the early kings in England had no capital cities but in all probability moved seasonally and slowly, with a numerous retinue, from one to another of their royal houses, which had to be maintained and supplied by their neighbouring subjects. The principal part of a royal house was the great hall, timber-built, that might be furnished and decorated, as in the tale of Beowulf, with barbaric splendour. Recent excavation at Yeavering in Northumberland has uncovered the ground-plan of such a hall, with lesser buildings grouped about it, and a nearby palisaded fort, that dates from the seventh century; and at Cheddar in Somerset discovery has been made of a similar building, apparently of the ninth century, that was 78 feet long by 18 feet in width, a two-storeyed timber hall, again with subsidiary smaller buildings. It is natural, at this date, to suppose that life in such buildings, even though inhabited by royalty, must have been insanitary and uncomfortable—cold and over-crowded, full of smoke and the inspissated odour of humanity—but from very early times there survives evidence of a magnificence in the decoration of life that cannot have consorted with total squalor. The poem about Beowulf, the treasure of Sutton Hoo, and the Lindisfarne Gospels are not the work of a people devoid of imagination, manual skill, and a taste for elegance, and the domestic building of the upper classes may have had both comfort and dignity, though its walls were timber and its roof was thatch. But only to churches was given the permanence of stone.

In the first half of the eighth century the Venerable Bede repeated the statement of a monk called Gildas, who wrote in the sixth century, that there were twenty-eight walled cities in Britain; and there is early evidence of the forced labour demanded even from monasteries for the repair and maintenance of city walls and bridges. But even before the great destruction of the Danish wars, and the general dilapidation of the country, civic defences had been neglected; the walls of York were in decay when the Danes took it in 866, though parts of them remained until the Conqueror's time if the story of Waltheof and his axe is true. There is nowhere surviving evidence of domestic mason-work, and the fact that even in the largest towns houses were built of wood is shown by the ease with which Norman troopers, during the coronation of their king in Westminster Abbey, set its surroundings on fire. In the country people lived under thatch within walls of wood or wattle and daub—the vast majority within small villages of wattle and daub that they shared with their animals—and the wealthier had learnt to raise a house to two storeys by means of timber arches.

It was Alfred the Great, who died in 899, who first built defensive works in a systematic way, and thirty-one of his fortresses are named. His son Edward, and Edward's redoubtable sister, the Lady of the Mercians, were also energetic fortress-builders. It would probably be more accurate, however, to call these structures defended localities, for though in some of them Alfred made use of Roman masonry, others appear to have been little more than earthen dykes that enclosed a natural stronghold. According to bishop Asser, who wrote a life of Alfred, he used both stone and wood in the construction of his royal halls, built and restored towns, and from Roman sites took dressed stone for his building. Roman domestic building, of which there must have been a great deal, disappeared so completely that it is difficult to avoid a suspicion that the early Angles and Saxons shared a superstitious horror of stone walls, and believed that only from the forest's growth could a respectable house be built.

After the introduction of continental masons, churches in increasing numbers were built of stone. Ecclesiastical masons in Saxon crypts fabricated arches on columns that owed a little to Roman practice, and raised strange towers that copied the design of older wooden towers. Alfred built churches and monasteries, and so did Cnut. Then, on the eve of the Conquest, Edward the Confessor's abbey dwarfed all others: it was built of large square blocks of a darkly coloured stone, and set an example for the great Romanesque churches of later years. It must have seemed to advertise the fact that only for churches and city walls, and perhaps a kingly residence here and there, might stone-masons be employed; and only church towers raised their roofs above the common mean, until the Normans came and built their castles. The very first was raised on the Welsh border by a Norman knight in the Confessor's service; but William proclaimed his belief in defensive works by fortifying his bridgehead immediately after landing at Pevensey.

There, in the old Roman fort, he built an inner rampart, and when he moved his troops and his fleet to Hastings he built another to close and guard the peninsula on which the town then stood. After the battle he retired within his defences to rest his troops and await developments. When he saw that no development was likely—that no offers of submission were coming in— he marched to Dover and there, without a blow being struck, the castle surrendered to him. It is said to have been a castle of great strength, but perhaps it had been sited against direct attack from the sea, for in the eight days that he remained in Dover, William added to its defences. So, before marching on London, he made safe his communications with Normandy.

After his coronation he withdrew to Barking in Essex while, as William of Poitiers wrote, '*firmamenta quaedam in urbe contra mobilitatem ingentis ac feri populi perficerentur.*'—'while certain strongholds in the town were completed against the fickleness of the huge and fierce population.'—The Londoners had already ac-

quired a dangerous reputation, and to overawe a volatile and warlike people, three strongholds were thought necessary, of which
two were in the western parts of the city, and the more famous,
which later became the White Tower, in the south-east where it
could command the approaches from the east, both by land and
water, and control shipping in the Thames.

Exeter was captured in 1068, and the king himself 'chose a spot
within the walls for the erection of a castle.' That began a year
of extraordinary activity, for already the north was in revolt,
and as William marched rapidly to suppress it he began his
systematic planting of castles where they could most effectively
command important roads and control or intimidate the populace. On his northward march he found sites at Warwick, Nottingham, and York; on his way south again at Lincoln, Huntingdon,
and Cambridge; and in each place he left a garrison for the
great wooden tower that was raised by forced labour.

In 1069 York rebelled, and he built a second castle on the right
bank of the Ouse. The Danes destroyed them both, and both
were rebuilt before the end of 1069. In 1070 castles rose at
Chester and Stafford; in 1071 at Ely, after the revolt of Hereward the Wake had been crushed; at Durham in 1072, after
William's return from Scotland. He built castles at Rockingham
in Northamptonshire, at Corfe in Dorset, at Shrewsbury, Canterbury, Gloucester, Rochester, Wallingford, Windsor, and Winchester. His barons built castles at Oxford, Worcester, Newcastle-
upon-Tyne; and for the defence of the Sussex coast others were
raised at Arundel, Bramber, Lewes, Pevensey, and Hastings. The
military occupation of England was made evident to all, and
the towers of Saxon churches were given fierce neighbours.

The original castles consisted of motte and bailey, wooden
tower and palisades. The motte was a big, flat-topped, artificial
mound of rammed earth, perhaps a hundred feet or more in
diameter, which could be raised by forced labour within a few
days. It was surrounded by a ditch filled with water if a river
ran near, and surmounted by a wooden tower for whose building
carpenters were important.—Forced labour was paid for, and
men could hold land, as tenants, in return for their services as
carpenters, masons, and ditchers.—The bailey was a kidney-
shaped enclosure on one side of the castle—and sometimes on

either side—designed for the shelter of horses and cattle; it gave access to the motte, and both motte and bailey were enclosed by wooden palisades. In the Confessor's time work on national defences, such as they were, had been compulsory; under the Conqueror compulsion was maintained, work was more arduous, and the people were 'sorely oppressed.'

For some two hundred years the Norman and Angevin kings of England gave primary attention to the building, improvement, and maintenance of their castles, and the replacement of wooden structures by stone walls began about a dozen years after the Conquest. The church was the home of all the talents, and the most celebrated of the castle-architects was a priest called Gandulf, the son of Norman parents in the Vexin, who had made a pilgrimage to Jerusalem and served and studied in the great monastery of Bec when Lanfranc was its prior. With Lanfranc he came to Canterbury, and in 1077 William appointed him to the see of Rochester. But his most memorable work was to design the White Tower—or, perhaps, to oversee and finance its building—and then to construct, at Colchester, an even larger keep.

The White Tower, in the complex known as the Tower of London, was a rectangular keep, three storeys high, with walls 15 feet thick at the base. It was built, not on a motte, but on level ground. It included a great hall, measuring 95 by 40 feet, and at the south-east corner a chapel surprisingly large—60 by 35 feet—and of major architectural interest. The aisles meet in the apse, above which is a half-dome, and the chapel is barrel-vaulted. The upper floors of the keep are divided into rooms of unequal size—a main room and an ante-room—and though the building was primarily intended as a fortress, it was also a residence. The doorway, accessible by a removable wooden stair, was on the first floor, and the tower stood within an angle of the old Roman city wall. New defensive walls were added by William Rufus, the tower later became famous as a prison for royal persons, and in the latter part of the seventeenth century its appearance was much altered by Sir Christopher Wren.

At Colchester a greater keep was built to a design closely resembling that of the White Tower, and probably by the same architect. It measures 150 feet by 110, and has Roman foundations. East Anglia was still vulnerable to Danish aggression—the many waterways of the Essex coast were a permanent invitation to sea-borne attack—and in recognition of its dangerous position the keep at Colchester was the largest of William's defensive works. The castle which he had originally sited within the city walls of Exeter was later re-built in stone by Baldwin de Meules. These three were the only stone castles that are definitely known to have been raised during the Conqueror's reign.

They were impregnable to all weapons and means of assault known to soldiers of the eleventh century, and as buildings they were architectural novelties without obvious or known predecessors, unless an ancestral pattern existed in the fortified palaces of the Carolingian kings of France.

In their habit of life the Norman kings were perhaps as mobile as the petty kings of Anglo-Saxon England—at Easter William wore his crown in Winchester, at Whitsuntide in Westminster, at Christmas in Gloucester—and to house not only a royal retinue, but an assembly of local magnates, large accommodation was required, and to military building succeeded domestic works on a kingly scale. The Conqueror built a hall at Winchester which was later burnt, and William Rufus built his vast hall at Westminster whose dimensions, of 240 feet by 67, exceeded those of any other building in Europe.

When William died the conquest of England was complete, but the pattern of conquest was steadily and progressively strengthened as timber-walled castles were replaced by solid mason-work. Some of the new castles were built by Norman and Angevin kings, some by their barons; but none could be built without royal permission, and those that were built to excessive strength invited the requisition, by the monarch, to which all were liable. Almost every great estate, of the sort known as 'honours,' had its castle. They dominated towns—much urban building, of a humble sort, was flattened to make room for them —and over all the country they stood as the symbols of royal authority and military power. England wore its castles as badges of the feudal system to which it was subject.

Chapter XIX

THE KING IN HIS DUCHY

B<small>Y</small> the normal accidents and processes of life—because of death and the fact that young men grow up, and new ambitions emerge—the duchy of Normandy was less happily situated than it had been in 1066. Baldwin V of Flanders—William's father-in-law and regent in France during the minority of Philip I—had made Normandy secure from French attack; but Baldwin died in 1067. His son, Baldwin VI, maintained good relations with the duchy, and as fellow-guardians for his heir named Philip of France and William's great vassal, William fitz Osbern. But Baldwin VI died in 1070, and revolt broke out against his widow, Richildis. She appealed for help to France and fitz Osbern. He came at speed to her assistance—he hoped to marry her—but near Cassel was killed, with the boy who was his ward, in battle against Robert le Frison, brother of Baldwin VI, who quickly won all Flanders. The English king was unwilling to recognise him, Robert was unable to forgive fitz Osbern's hostility. Flanders and Normandy were no longer on friendly terms.

In Maine the situation was more complicated. William's eldest son, Robert, was nominally count of Maine, but still a minor. The revolt in Le Mans, which briefly brought William back to his duchy in 1069, had released local antagonisms and provoked a parochial war in which William's seneschal and Norman knights had been expelled. The war subsided, before the end of 1070, when a dominating position was temporarily secured by Geoffrey of Mayenne, a border baron, and his mistress, Gersendis, the sister of a count of Maine who had died some twenty years before. But Geoffrey's rule lacked stability, and a year or two later he was thrown out by Fulk le Rechin—Fulk the Cross-grained—count of Anjou, whom the people of Le Mans had invited to help them. Fulk was a nephew of Geoffrey Martel,

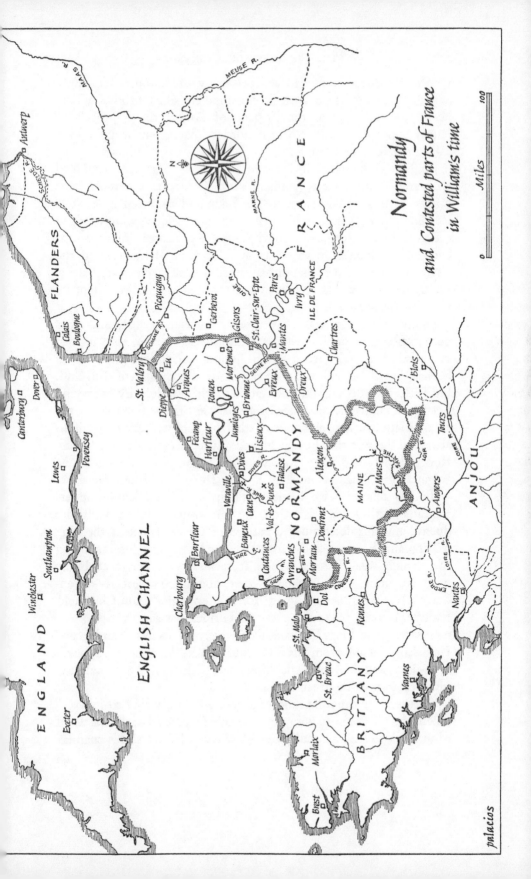

palacios

ENGLAND

Canterbury
Dover
Pevensey
Lewes
Southampton
Winchester
Exeter

ENGLISH CHANNEL

FLANDERS

Antwerp
SCHELDE R.
Calais
Boulogne

MEUSE R.
MAAS R.
MARNE R.
OISE R.

FRANCE

Paris
Mantes
Ivry
ILE DE FRANCE
Chartres
Dreux
Blois
Tours
LOIR R.
Angers
LOIRE R.

St. Clair-sur-Epte
Gisors
Gerberoi
Picquigny
SOMME R.
St. Valéry
Eu
Arques
Dieppe
Fécamp
Harfleur
Rouen
SEINE R.
Jumièges
Brionne
Lisieux
Évreux
Mortemer

NORMANDY

Varaville
DIVES R.
Dives
Caen
ORNE R.
Falaise
Val-ès-Dunes
Bayeux
VIRE R.
Barfleur
Cherbourg
Coutances
SIÈNE R.
Avranches
Mortain
Domfront
Alençon
Le Mans
SARTHE R.
MAINE

St. Malo
Dol
COUESNON R.
Rennes
BRITTANY
St. Brieuc
Morlaix
Brest
Vannes
ERDRE R.
LOIRE R.
Nantes
ANJOU

N

Normandy
and Contested parts of France
in William's time

Miles
0   100

who had reduced Maine to a dependency of Anjou, which Fulk had acquired by war against an incompetent elder brother whom he imprisoned. It was the menace of Anjou—the approach of Angevin power to the Norman border—that again brought king William over the Channel.

English troops were in his army, and before a bleak land had recovered from winter, William invaded Maine. He took some border fortresses, laid siege to Le Mans and captured it. Fulk le Rechin was not among his prisoners, but Maine acknowledged the return of Norman authority, and by Easter William was back in his duchy, on the coast not far from the mouth of the Dives where he had gathered his invasion fleet seven years before. An immediate danger had been averted, but the political climate was far from genial.

Philip of France was now twenty or twenty-one, and it is permissible to suppose that a traditional distrust of his Norman vassal had been reinforced by the jealous resentment with which he had heard of William's elevation to the throne of England. He had renewed an old association with Flanders by marrying Bertha of Hainault, the sister of Robert le Frison; but the temper of association had changed from that of Baldwin's time. As if to advertise the fact that he and Flanders were no friends of William, Robert le Frison had given asylum to Edgar the Atheling when Edgar, by William's insistence, was forced to leave Scotland.

To his alliance with Flanders Philip added a friendly understanding with Fulk of Anjou, on the other side of William's duchy; and this determined a pattern of events that kept the king of England in Normandy for the greater part of his remaining life, which was fourteen years. It seems, moreover, that Philip tried to employ the Atheling—that unavailing creature—as another ally, or perhaps his agent; for in the Anglo-Saxon Chronicle, under the year 1074, there is this curious passage:

'In this year king William went over sea to Normandy; and child Edgar came from Flanders into Scotland, on St. Grimbald's mass-day: and Malcolm the king and (Edgar's) sister Margaret received him with great worship.

'At the same time the king of France, Philip, wrote to him and asked him to come to him, and he would give him the castle of Montreuil, so that he could thereafter do evil daily to his enemies.

'So then Malcolm the king and (Edgar's) sister Margaret gave him and all his men great gifts and many precious things, of skins covered with purple, and of fur-robes of martin and miniver and ermine skins; and of fine raiment, and golden vessels and silvern: and conducted him and all his sailors with great worship from his domain.

'But on their journey it evilly befell them, when they were out at sea, that very rough weather came upon them, and the raging sea and the strong wind cast them on the shore; so that all their ships burst asunder, and they themselves came with difficulty to land; and very nearly all their precious things were lost. And some of his men also were taken by Frenchmen. And he himself and his best men went back again to Scotland, some wretchedly walking on foot, and some miserably riding.

'Then the king Malcolm advised him to send to king William across the sea, and crave his protection; and so also he did. And the king granted it him, and sent for him.

'And again Malcolm the king and (Edgar's) sister gave him and all his men innumerable gifts, and very honourably sent him again from their domain.

'And the sheriff of York came to meet him at Durham, and went all the way with him, and caused food and fodder to be found for him at every castle at which they arrived, until they came over sea to the king. And then king William received him with great worship. And then (Edgar) was at his court there, and took such rights as he allotted him.'

That is to say, the French king proposed to establish Edgar at Montreuil, in what is now the Pas de Calais, where English opponents to William's rule might conveniently gather. Edgar's persistent ill-luck—or perhaps ineptitude—prevented his acceptance of the French invitation, and Malcolm, having had second thoughts, advised him to surrender. William, rather than let him remain mischievously free, offered him hospitality and took him into protective custody with a daily allowance to sweeten it. The plan—or perhaps it should be called a plot—to give the Atheling a French domicile as a focus for malcontents had failed ludicrously; but graver danger was coming to a head in Brittany, and sedition was brewing in England itself.

The Breton lords, many of whom had fought for William in

1066, cherished an old habit of independence, and were impatient of authority. One of the most powerful was Ralf de Gael, the son of a distinguished official in the Confessor's court called Ralf the Staller. The father had served William as well as Edward, and Ralf the son had inherited not only the Breton barony of Gael but the English earldom of Norfolk. Among the many Bretons who had followed the Conqueror to England, Ralf de Gael had friends and dependents who would obey him; but why he, who in his second country was now Ralf of Norfolk, should wish to lead them in rebellion against his king is wholly a mystery. That a feudal relationship could breed jealousy and resentment is obvious enough; that Breton lords were unruly of temper may be accepted; but such generalities cannot explain what followed, though they may well be predisposing causes.

A marriage had been arranged between Ralf of Norfolk and Emma, the sister of Roger, earl of Hereford, who was a son of king William's great auxiliary—now dead—William fitz Osbern; and, as the Chronicle laconically observes:

> 'There was that bride-ale
> That was many men's bale.'

For the wedding-feast at Exning, near Newmarket, was occasion for the planning of revolt, and a notable ally was found in Waltheof, son of Siward of Northumbria; Waltheof, the burly champion who had fought with such muscular valour under the walls of York, but later had submitted to the king and now, high in his favour, was earl of Huntingdon. Why Waltheof conspired against his king lies in the obscurity that hides Ralf of Norfolk's motive. Roger of Hereford, whose conduct may have been injudicious, appears to have been under a ban of excommunication, imposed by archbishop Lanfranc, but subject to withdrawal should Roger's behaviour improve; of itself that seems hardly a cause for armed rebellion.

The monk Orderic Vitalis reports that wild speeches were made against the king—he does not say they were delivered at the wedding feast, but others imply they were—in which William was taunted with his bastardy, accused of many acts of criminal vengeance, denounced for the injustice of his invasion, blamed for his failure to recompense those who had helped him most, and vilified for acts that had made him an object of general hatred. There were those who declared that the English were a peaceful race, fonder of ale than battle, but even they, to avenge their kinsmen's blood, would unite against such a king; and others pointed out that now was the time to turn against him when he, overwhelmed with care and distraught by discord on the frontiers of his duchy, was oversea and few believed he would ever return to England.

If the story of the drunken wedding is true, the revolt may indeed have been hatched by the furious, ale-fed warmth of men who had eaten too much, drunk too much, and had too much power and wanted more. The wedding-feast at Exning seems not unlike the notorious funeral-feast or grave-ale at which Sweyn Forkbeard and the Jomsburg vikings drank too much and made braggart pledges for which, in the sobriety of morning, reluctant honour compelled respect. That may have been the temper engendered by the bride-ale of Ralf of Norfolk and Emma, the sister of Roger of Hereford. If so, it was an atavistic temper, and in the absence of any known reason for rebellion atavism can perhaps be accepted as the motivating force of conspiracy—aided, of course, by a strictly contemporary appreciation of the opportunities of reward that William's absence appeared to make possible. But caution suggested the advisability of strengthening the conspiracy with help from abroad, and Ralf sent emissaries to Denmark. Sweyn Estrithson was dead, and his two sons, Harald and Cnut, were both contenders for the crown. Cnut, the loser, welcomed the distraction of foreign adventure, and presently sailed for England with a fleet of two hundred ships. But the dispute with his brother had wasted time, and before he arrived the rebellion had been crushed.

The conspirators had underestimated the strength of the king's party and the ability of his viceroy. In charge of his kingdom he had left Lanfranc, archbishop of Canterbury since 1070, when the often-excommunicated Stigand had been deposed. By birth a Lombard, Lanfranc was a lawyer by early training, and diplomat as well as theologian and scholar; he had for long been William's intimate counsellor. He persuaded the king that there was no need for him to leave Normandy, and justified self-confidence by the measures he took to frustrate the rebels.

An army raised by Norman barons and English prelates—Wulfstan, bishop of Worcester, and Ethelwig, abbot of Evesham—held Roger of Hereford west of the Severn; while another army under Norman lords and churchmen—the bishops Odo of Bayeux and Geoffrey of Coutances, William of Warenne and others—met Ralf of Norfolk near Cambridge and forced him to retreat. He fell back on Norwich castle, which his newly-wed wife held against long besiegement and let him escape to Brittany. Waltheof, in the meantime, had listened to good advice from archbishop Lanfranc, deserted his fellow-conspirators, and gone over to Normandy to offer his submission to the king. When Cnut of Denmark appeared off the east coast there was no rebel army to welcome him, and he had to content himself with some pillaging in Norfolk and Yorkshire.

At Christmas 1075, William came back to England and two of the traitors were brought up for trial. Ralf of Norfolk was condemned in absence to outlawry and the confiscation of his lands. His gallant wife, having surrendered Norwich castle on terms, had been allowed to join him in Brittany. The others were less fortunate. Roger of Hereford had his lands confiscated and was condemned to imprisonment for life; Waltheof, after long delay, was condemned to death. He, who had taken no active part in the rebellion, is said by Orderic Vitalis to have been 'accused by the denunciation of his wife Judith because he was cognisant of the aforesaid treason and a promoter (of it).' His wife Judith was the Conqueror's niece, and Waltheof had clearly chosen less wisely than Ralf of Norfolk. Judith may have had her own reasons for appearing in person against her husband, but why the king insisted on Waltheof's death is by no means clear. It was not until the 31st May, 1076, that he was beheaded, and his execution—on St. Giles' Hill by Winchester—may have been determined by his breed: he was an Englishman of the Danelaw, the last of the English earls, and so the last who might have led a native rising.

Long before his death the king was in Normandy again, for though rebellion in England had been extinguished promptly, and with little difficulty, the outlawed Ralf of Norfolk had taken advantage of the distracted state of Brittany to ally himself with another Breton lord and occupy the castle of Dol, between St.

Malo and Mont St. Michel, near the southwestern corner of the
frontier of Normandy. There they were reinforced by troops
from Fulk le Rechin's county of Anjou. William advanced to
besiege the castle, and failed to take it. But Philip of France saw
an opportunity to humiliate his ducal neighbour, his kingly rival,
and with a large army came to the relief of Dol. William was
defeated, and with great material loss had to withdraw.

Now his enemies went over to the offensive, and while Fulk
made war on Norman adherents in Maine, the French king
strengthened his position in the debatable land where William,
ten years later, was to essay a last offensive and ride to his death.
That was in the Vexin, between Normandy's eastern boundary
and the river Oise. At the beginning of the century the duchy
had extended its frontier as far as the river Epte, and beyond it
the count of Vexin Français, though he held his land of the
French king, acknowledged the duke as his over-lord. The line
of the counts of Vexin Français became virtually extinct in 1077,
when the last of them entered a monastery, and before William
had recovered from his defeat at Dol, king Philip annexed the
territory, and Mantes, its capital on the Seine, became a French
outpost. Treaties of peace were patched up between the two
kings, and between William and Fulk le Rechin; and by both of
them William lost prestige, though his possessions remained intact.

About this time he suffered also from that domestic malady to
which almost every sovereign, of his or any age, was subject.
Robert, his eldest son, rebelled. William, in a happy married life,
had fathered a family of four sons and five or six daughters, of
whom two sons—William Rufus and Henry I—succeeded in turn
to the throne of England, and a daughter, Adela, became the
mother of the calamitous king Stephen. Robert, the oldest of the
family, had been formally recognised as heir to the duchy, and
during his father's repeated absence had grown accustomed to
the exercise of authority within it. He was a popular young man
with no apparent vices but extravagance and lack of judgment.
He had inherited his family's bravery and spirit of adventure, he
was a good talker and light of heart. In the circumstances of his
life, with a father who had had to spend so much time abroad, it
is remarkable that Robert's loyalty endured so long; for when the

breach occurred, in 1077 or 1078, he was twenty-four or twenty-five, and he had a host of friends who owed no friendship to William.

His demand for independence and full authority in Normandy and Maine—in effect, for the realisation of his inheritance—seems not unreasonable, and did not immediately provoke William's displeasure. It did, however, create bad blood between him and his surviving brothers, William and Henry. Their dissension infected their followers, and when fighting broke out the king, very properly and impartially, suppressed it. Robert's vanity was wounded, he left his father's court, and encouraged by a multitude of sympathisers tried to storm Rouen. The castle withstood the attack, and the king gave orders for the rebels' arrest. But Robert and many of his companions fled the country and found, a little way beyond its frontiers, places of refuge that could become points of attack.

The leading insurgents were young men of consequence: the heirs or younger sons of the great families who had helped to conquer England and were now governing it. The revolt wears a look of youthful impatience with a warlike, statesman-like, older generation which, it is probable, had become domineering and full of rectitude in consequence of its great achievements and vast increase of wealth. But whatever excuse may be made for it, the revolt was monstrously ill-advised and led to William's deepest humiliation.

His enemies were quick to take advantage of it, and Robert's willingness to accept their aid against his father alienates the sympathy that a display of wild impetuosity—had it gone no further—might well have retained. He went to the court of Flanders, took help from Philip of France, and with an army reinforced by French knights, by troops from Brittany, Anjou, and Normandy itself, he occupied, by the French king's permission, the castle of Gerberoi near Beauvais—midway between Paris and Amiens—and awaited his father's attack.

William laid siege to the castle, and for three weeks in the dark cold of January 1079, was held at bay. Then the rebels made a sortie, and in the ensuing battle William was unhorsed and wounded. One of his new English subjects saved his life, but William's old gift of mastery on the field had deserted him, and

Robert with his Angevin and French supporters was left the victor. Or, to be more accurate, the apparent victor; for he who had gained the most was the French king. The union of Normandy and England, which no French king could accept with equanimity, had been shaken and perhaps permanently weakened.

There were those among the Norman barons who saw the need for reconciliation, and William was obliged, though reluctantly, to make peace with his son and confirm his right of succession to the duchy. But though his empire was physically divided, in another respect it was indivisible; for apparent weakness in one quarter invited assault in another. Because William had suffered defeat at Gerberoi, forty miles north of Paris, Malcolm of Scotland crossed the Tweed and plundered eighty miles of England as far as the river Tees. Norman rule in the north of England had never been very secure, despite the punishment that Yorkshire had suffered, and rebellion again broke out.

After Waltheof joined the conspiracy hatched at the bride-ale of Ralf of Norfolk, his Northumbrian earldom was rashly given to Walcher, bishop of Durham, a cleric born in Lorraine. He was a good bishop who had been on good terms with Waltheof, and was devoutly interested in the monasticism which had once brought such glory to the north. But his gifts were less suited for the government of a rough and ever turbulent northern province, and his attempted policy of placating the native aristocracy, but leaving administration to one of his own relatives, only resulted in a head-on collision of opposing interests in which the Northumbrian leader was killed. To prove himself innocent of collaboration Walcher called for a meeting of all concerned at Gateshead on the Tyne. The Northumbrians came armed for the occasion and drove Walcher and his followers into a convenient church which, in a well-proved and traditional manner, they set on fire. Then they advanced on Durham and besieged the castle. They failed to capture it, but Malcolm of Scotland took advantage of disturbance to launch another raid into England.

The warrior bishop of Bayeux retaliated with a punitive expedition, and the heir of Normandy, to prove perfect reconciliation with his father, crossed over into England and invaded Scotland with an army of considerable strength. The result of that expedition is doubtful. According to the Abingdon Chronicle

Malcolm met the invaders in Lothian, gave hostages for peace, and acknowledged the subjection of 'the principality of Scotland' to the kingdom of England; but Symeon of Durham, who detested the Scots, painted all their actions in the most lurid colours, and never failed to rejoice in a triumph over them, merely says that 'William sent his son Robert to Scotland against Malcolm. But when he had come to Falkirk he returned without accomplishing anything, and founded a New Castle upon the river Tyne.' The new castle, however, was a recognition of the ever-present danger from a kingdom that still had expansive tendencies, and whose English queen, the energetic and saintly Margaret, can have had no affection for king William.

The Conqueror was on the defensive now, and lamentably it appears that his great qualities—his vigour, his imagination, his faculty of instant control in good fortune or adversity—were fast diminishing. In 1080 he was no more than fifty-two or fifty-three, but from youth his exertions had been immense and continuous, and now the warrior's frame that had let him wield his mace in the front of battle against Harold Godwineson was beginning to put on weight, and the mind that had planned and energised the long struggle for preservation of his duchy, and then the conquest of England, was losing its vision and growing short-tempered, tetchy, and suspicious.

When Robert began his march into Scotland, William was in his kingdom, but had to leave it to meet a new attack by the malignant Fulk of Anjou. He, with support from Brittany, took the fortress of La Flèche in the south of Maine, and though William commanded an army of both Norman and English troops he was constrained to make peace, and later to negotiate with open revolt in Maine. More serious, and certainly more indicative of William's failing strength—his strength of mind, that is—was his quarrel, in 1082, with his half-brother Odo, bishop of Bayeux, and since 1067 earl of Kent. Odo, who had fought so valiantly for him, and supported him so faithfully, was now suspected of private ambition. He wanted, it was said, to make himself pope. He had thought of engaging as a soldier under the emperor Henry IV. And William came over to England and put him in prison. Whatever the truth may have been—and the likelihood is that Herlève's younger son was showing the same sort of impatience with his brother's waning faculties as Robert had evinced—there is little doubt that if William had retained the elasticity, the mental quickness, of his early manhood, he could have found some compromise with so doughty an adherent, so loyal and serviceable a friend. But the Conqueror's mind was darkening, he could find no recourse but insensate action, and the hardened autocracy that committed Odo to prison was probably the cause of Robert's new rebellion.

Robert now openly opposed his father, and either took shelter with the king of France or enjoyed, within the realm of France, a licensed freedom to recruit opponents to Normandy. The loneliness of the Conqueror became apparent, and his solitude was embittered when, about the end of 1083, his queen Matilda died, to whom he had been devoted and, contrary to the habit of his time, strangely faithful.

A review of his latter years in Normandy cannot fail to be melancholy, but how untrue would be a review that confined itself to the duchy! Even there he was not defeated, for he kept his duchy against increasing enmity, and his defence of an empire —for Normandy and England can be so regarded—was maintained against the hostility of Scotland and Denmark, of Fulk le Rechin and Philip of France, and the recurrent insubordination of the Danelaw and Anglo-Norman barons. To hold those disparate lands together was a truly remarkable achievement, but not the achievement on which William's fame and honour were substantially built. To appreciate that foundation one must return and look at his work—and the work of his devoted clerks and lieutenants—in England, the great prize he won against the competition of the Scandinavian north.

Chapter XX

THE NORMAN STATE

THE Conqueror ruled England for twenty-one years, and by the end of that time the government of the land, both secular and clerical, was, with a couple of exceptions, in the hands of men who, a generation before, had been foreigners. There had been revolution as well as conquest, and a small, powerful, and coherent military caste had been created which held its lands of the king by virtue of a precisely defined service to him. The great nobles had their own tenants who held of their feudal lords by a similar obligation, but with the all-important addition that they owed their basic loyalty not to earl or abbot, but to the monarch. This revolutionary re-shaping of society had been an unmitigated disaster to the old nobility of England, to the thanes and all their class, whose privilege and authority had been swept away; yet paradoxically it had not destroyed the fundamental institutions of English government, but rather re-defined and strengthened them.

In the beginning it had not been William's intention to destroy native authority completely. With some confidence, indeed, one can say that so drastic a change had come about against his will. Though he had won his throne in battle, he wished to appear as king by right of inheritance—as the Confessor's kinsman and nominated heir—and at his coronation in the Confessor's abbey the great assembly had twice been asked, in English and in French, if they accepted him as their lord. The fact of acceptance —of general acknowledgment—would have been made manifest by a framework of government in which there was room for both English and Normans, and his earliest councils were attended by the earls Edwin and Morcar, by Waltheof who had been given an earldom in the midlands, by English churchmen and officials who had served the Confessor's court; while the north was still ruled by native magnates. Had England accepted its Conqueror as complacently as he hoped, the Witan of its Saxon kings might have continued in being though dominated by a Norman majority. But all England muttered its resentment, many parts of England broke into angry rebellion, and the façade of peaceful union had to be demolished to make way for the grim face of a military structure.

If William was to keep his throne, and his Norman nobles were to keep their English lands, the transformation was necessary. There were Scots in the north, Welsh in the west, there might be another Hereward in the fens, or sullen prelates in Devon; and watching the open frontiers of the duchy of Normandy were the greedily expectant eyes of Flemings, Angevins, and Philip of France. So William divided his conquered kingdom between his imported nobles, organised them for war, and laid such duties on them as to ensure, beyond question, his own absolute rule.

Here and there in Saxon England there had been lands held in return for certain services—with a premonition, as it were, of feudalism—but the Norman revolution imposed a general system of military tenure, and feudalism emerged as tenancy by knight-service: a Norman noble who became an English landowner accepted an obligation to provide a certain number of fully accoutred, trained, mounted men, called knights, whenever the king should require them. It has been estimated[1] that the number of knights who were thus held available was at least 4000, but may have been greater; while the number of barons who by contract had to supply them can hardly have been more than 180. The church was also feudalised and had to accept a comparable obligation: Canterbury, Winchester, and Lincoln had to find 60 knights apiece, other bishops 40, and the church's whole contribution amounted to 780.

These knights were not, as knights later became, men distinguished by admission to some order of knighthood, such as the Templars or Teutonic Knights, or Edward III's Knights of the Garter. They were members of the retinue or military household of a baron, or bishop, or abbot, and as the English countryside grew more peaceful, and the need to keep them in a state of

[1] Sir Frank Stenton, *Anglo-Saxon England.*

immediate readiness receded, they were commonly granted fiefs within the great fiefs of the lord to whose household they gave their service. This subsidiary distribution of land and responsibility followed no given plan, and a knight's fee—his holding, that is— had no constant size. There were those who accepted holdings for their own service, and others who had to find several trained and mounted men. The rigidity of the Conqueror's general plan allowed a great deal of local elasticity, and this may be accounted as a compromise, either deliberate or casual, with English method. A new class was thus gradually created, which in its upper ranks filled the place of vanished Saxon thanes and might claim to be a minor aristocracy; while its less able or less fortunate members enjoyed a tenancy sufficient for their maintenance and the responsibility of their engagement.

It is obvious, of course, that William did not rely solely on his feudal knights to fill the ranks when an army was mobilised. He led English troops against an English uprising, and took English forces into his duchy; he retained, that is, the right of Saxon monarchs to summon all able-bodied men for defence of the realm. But that right seems to have been discreetly exercised, and when in 1085 the country was in danger of Danish invasion —when Cnut, the son of Sweyn Estrithson, led his unavailing fleet into English waters—William came over from Normandy with an army, both horse and foot, of exceptional size, most of whom must have been mercenaries. When the east coast was menaced—though the menace did not materialise—he clearly thought it safer to rely on paid troops from abroad than on the mobilisation of a warlike peasantry who might still be inclined to friendship with the invaders.

Of how the peasantry fared under Norman occupation there is little record. It is safe to assume that it suffered less than the thanes and their class, for the thanes could be replaced by suitably enfeoffed Norman knights, but there were no substitutes for tillers of the soil. It is unlikely that their lot was materially bettered—save, perhaps, for some additional security—but it is equally improbable that they were subject to wanton violence, depredation, and injustice. Laws were strict, and therefore respected; and behind the law there was a powerful church as well as a responsible aristocracy.

Much has been made of the savage enforcement of laws devised for the protection of game, and there is no disputing the fact that William, in his creation of the New Forest, drove out the inhabitants of many villages for the better protection of hart and hind; though the extent of his clearances is not known. In theory, apparently, his right to do that was derived from the fact that as king he was constantly burdened with the cares of his realm, the preservation of its peace, and was therefore entitled to make provision for his recreation; while in practice there was none to prevent him. There had been royal forests and forest laws before the Conquest, but William's extravagant love of hunting, at the expense of his people, was bitterly resented; and as the royal passion was perpetuated, resentment grew as time went on, for under his successors, Henry II and his sons, the royal forests were extended until there were woodlands sacred to the beasts of chase and warren in thirty-three counties.

The forest laws, though not of alien birth, acquired a foreign look by extension and the rigour of their application; but in general the processes of law followed an established English habit. The administrative divisions of the country were maintained, the shires continued to be shires, and the sub-divisions called hundreds also survived. Within the shires and hundreds the local courts of Saxon origin were confirmed in their ancient authority, and under different masters an old tradition continued in service to a new king. Before the Conquest there had been, in every shire, a reeve or sheriff appointed by the king to maintain his law and secure his interests; his function was enlarged until, in effect, the sheriff's duty was the execution of justice and the collection of taxes. Under William he presided over the shire court, and even within the borders of a great earldom represented the greater dominion of the monarch. In the course of time the Norman sheriffs usually became considerable landowners.

The English earldoms were not preserved. Under the Confessor the land had been distracted by the rivalry of a few almost independent nobles whose power had been too extensive for the well-being of any king, however strong; and William did not make the mistake of perpetuating conditions which invited anarchy. After Harold's death at Hastings the earldom of Wessex disappeared. After the death or disgrace of Edwin and Morcar the great earldoms of Mercia and Northumbria vanished. A diminished Northumbria survived, but only for a little while; and the last of the English earldoms went out of existence when Waltheof died under the executioner's sword near Winchester.

New and much smaller earldoms were created for protection of the kingdom against the danger of military attack: Odo of Bayeux became earl of Kent, William fitz Osbern earl of Hereford, Ralf de Gael of Norfolk, and the earldoms of Chester and Shrewsbury guarded the Welsh frontier. But few of these new creations endured. The Norman earldoms of Kent and Norfolk lapsed after the king's dispute with his brother Odo and the rebellion of Ralf of Norfolk; and the earl of Hereford went to prison. The old order had become obsolete, and to replace it the Norman sheriffs—in the justice-seat of Saxon reeves—exercised increasing power, but exercised it for defined purposes and within limited areas.

Before the end of the reign the principal officials of the royal household were all French, and under the guise of domestic appointment controlled the administration of the kingdom. Again there was definition of function, as opposed to the looser or less specific constitution of the Confessor's court. The church also acquired a more closely ordered regimen. With the church in Normandy William's association had been intimate and authoritative—the Norman church was governed by the aristocracy of Normandy—and in England he accepted his ecclesiastical obligations in return for the church's acknowledgment of his kingly rights. Stigand, the often excommunicated archbishop of Canterbury, was replaced by the resolute, sagacious genius of Lanfranc, whose over-all authority was, by the king's influence, established when Thomas, archbishop of York—previously a canon of Bayeux—unwillingly pledged obedience to Lanfranc as primate of all England. Lanfranc's primacy was later ratified by an English ecclesiastical council at the instigation of Pope Gregory VII, who as archdeacon Hildebrand had once promoted William's claim to the English throne. English bishops and English abbots were in like manner succeeded by Norman prelates who, as the king's tenants, had to render unto Caesar the service of twenty, forty, or sixty properly accoutred knights as well as profess, expound, and inculcate the Christian doctrine in which they and the king and all his subjects not merely proclaimed their belief, but accepted as revelation of God's purpose and the nature of the world in which they lived.

Without diminution of his faith in its teaching, William made the church, both in Normandy and England, part and parcel of his political system, and while many of his bishops became admirable administrators, the spirit and purpose of monastic life revived under the stimulus of Lanfranc, the great statesman, who may have remained a monk at heart. The strength of William's position in the church was remarkably demonstrated when, after 1079, pope Gregory attempted to assert his authority in threefold fashion, and was thrice rebuffed. He tried to compel the prelates of William's church to attend his council in Rome; he tried to curtail the power of the archbishop of Rouen; he tried to convince William, as king of England, of his duty to swear fealty to the papacy—and all three demands were refused without loss of papal favour. The king's authority was unimpaired.

The heart of his power, in England, was the *curia regis:* his domestic senate. To promulgate its edicts the Great Council of the realm was summoned at fairly regular intervals—usually at Christmas, Easter, and Whitsuntide—and at these meetings the king's authority was emphasised, or advertised, by the splendour of his retinue, the magnificence of royal entertainment. To pay for that splendour William had the revenue of crown lands and the taxes which were rigorously collected according to the several systems of assessment which had been established by Saxon monarchs. Taxation was heavy, but impartial. If peasants had reason for complaint, the newly ennobled magnates had cause to count the cost of their advancement, for their assessment in terms of knight-service was heavier by far than the customary rate in France. But they recognised a community of interest with the king, and maintained his law as much for their own advantage as for his.

They had won the realm of England, but their prize was still subject to foreign menace, and they knew the value of their conquest. They accepted their burdens, of loyalty and the labours of administration, because they shared with their stern monarch both a common cause and the rewards it had brought.

Chapter XXI

DOMESDAY BOOK

As claimant to the kingdom and as king of England William had a military career brilliant in achievement and ruthless in device. The feudal revolution that he instigated was remarkable for the speed and totality of the transition from a somewhat inchoate form of society to a disciplined and purposive order. But the civil enquiry into the economic constitution of life in England, which produced the 'description' known as the Domesday Survey, is perhaps his most memorable activity, if only because the vast labour of his clerks—their elegant penmanship and the answers to their relentless questioning—are still whole and visible.

A battle may be decisive of history, but its emotions die within a generation and its dispositions are soon forgotten. Norman castles crumble, or lose their outline under later addition, and feudalism's harsh structure has long since vanished. What remains intact from the two decades of William's momentous rule is the scrupulous survey of the kingdom's resources contained in Great Domesday Book, a folio of 760 pages, and Little Domesday Book, a large octavo of 900 pages. The former covers the greater part of the kingdom, the latter the counties of Norfolk, Suffolk, and Essex. The four northern counties of Northumberland, Cumberland, Westmorland, and Durham were excluded from the census; their exclusion is a cold and shocking tribute to the thoroughness with which William, and Malcolm of Scotland, had wasted their blackened villages and exhausted fields.

The proposal to essay an economic census was discussed and determined at the Christmas assembly of the Great Council of the realm in 1085; and in the Anglo-Saxon Chronicle a passage of great interest describes the circumstances in which the decision was taken, relates the instructions given to the king's commissioners, and suggests the existence of a financial crisis that made the undertaking a matter of urgency. A translation of the passage reads as follows:

'A.D.MLXXXV. In this year men declared, and for sooth said, that Cnut, king of Denmark, son of King Sweyn, was bound hitherward, and would win this land with the aid of Robert, count of Flanders; because Cnut had Robert's daughter to wife. When Wm., king of England, who was then living in Normandy —because he owned both England and Normandy—was informed of this, he went into England with so large an army of horsemen and foot, from France and from Brittany, as never before had sought this land, so that men wondered how this land could feed all that army. But the king caused the army to be distributed throughout all this land among his vassals; and they fed the army, each according to the measure of his land. And men had great affliction this year; and the king caused the land about the sea to be laid waste, so that if his foes should land, they might not have whereon they might so readily seize. But when the king was informed in sooth that his foes were hindered, and could not further their expedition, he let some of the army go to their own land; and some he held in this land over the winter. Then at midwinter the king was at Gloucester with his Witan, and there held his court five days; and afterwards the archbishop and clergy had a synod three days. . . .

'After this the king had a great council, and very deep speech with his Witan about this land, how it was peopled, or by what men; then sent his men over all England, into every shire, and caused to be ascertained how many hundred hides were in the shire, or what land the king himself had, and cattle within the land, and what dues he ought to have, in twelve months, from the shire. Also he caused to be written how much land his archbishops had, and his suffragan bishops, and his abbots, and his earls; and—though I may narrate somewhat prolixly—what or how much each man had who was a holder of land in England, in land, or in cattle, and how much money it might be worth. So very narrowly he caused it to be traced out, that there was not one single hide, nor one yard of land, nor even—it is shame to tell, though it seemed to him no shame to do—an ox, nor a cow, nor a swine, was left, that was not set down in his writ. And all the writings were brought to him afterwards.'

The commissioners, *legati regis*, were instructed to enquire—from the sworn testimony of sheriffs, lords of every manor, presbyters of every church, the reeves of every hundred, the bailiffs and six villeins of every village—into the accepted name of the place under investigation, its owner in the time of king Edward, its present owner, the number of hides in the whole manor and in the demesne—a hide or ploughland was one hundred and twenty acres—the number of villeins and other inhabitants, the extent of meadow and pasture, the number of mills and fish-ponds, its present value, its value when bestowed upon its present owner, and its value in the time of king Edward. It appears, moreover, that the answers given to the commissioners were subject to further scrutiny. In the chronicle of a monk called Marianus Scotus it is said there was rigorous checking of the returns of the first inquisitors, and men were sent into districts where, as strangers, they had to criticise the 'description'—it is Marianus who first uses that word as a label for Domesday—given by their predecessors. Marianus, like the Anglo-Saxon chronicler, refers with apparent disapproval to the inclusion of domestic animals in the census: the sturdy belief that an Englishman's home is his castle, though not explicit in the eleventh century, was evidently inherent, and a free man's rightful privacy was invaded when investigators came to count his pigs and sheep.

In Cambridgeshire juries were empanelled to give evidence. The jury system, a Norman introduction, was used in the shire-courts, but whether testimony of this sort was widely taken for the survey, or required only in certain parts of the country, is not known. There is also doubt as to the precise status of the several sorts of rural inhabitants named in Domesday. At the bottom of the scale are the *servi*, or serfs; but a serf may have been a man without any legal rights, a mere chattel, or a man who was not wholly free. Whatever its definition, slavery of a sort existed at the time of the Conquest, and quickly disappeared thereafter, though whether by edict of the church or secular power is not known. At the top of the scale, in a village census, was the *villanus*, who was a free landholder who acknowledged certain obligations in respect of his holding; and who, if he had the wit and ability to enlarge his holding to five hides, might enjoy the status of a thane. Between *villanus* and *servus* there were, in descending order, *bordarii, cotarii,* and *buri* or *coliberti,* of whom the two first named were cottars and labourers distinguished by their differing dependence on the land they worked and the labour they supplied: the *bordarius,* that is, had rather more land, the *cotarius* spent more time working for his master. The *coliberti,* only a little removed from the *servi,* had no possessions of their own but were life-rented, so to speak, in a couple of oxen, a few sheep, seed-corn, and household utensils which, on their death, reverted to their lord.

Of higher rank than the *villani*—their superior privilege lay in their greater independence—were those called 'freemen' and 'sokemen'; whose status declined under Norman rule. What may be called the upper middle classes of rural society lost power and wealth, and the jurisdiction that the mere fact of tenure had given to Saxon squires—their sonorous right to 'sake and soke, toll, team, and infangenetheof'—passed to their Norman successors; who would translate the burly phrase as the right to convene a court, to take payment on a sale of goods and settle disputed claims, and to sentence a local thief caught in possession of stolen goods. But if the middle classes suffered, the number of slaves diminished rapidly, and the institution of slavery was discountenanced.

The reference in the Anglo-Saxon Chronicle to the great army of mercenaries that William brought into England—so many of them 'that men wondered how this land could feed all that army' —reflects, almost certainly, the fact that more money was needed and a serious investigation was required to discover what sources were open to further taxation. That the king, as a practical monarch with an orderly mind, wanted to know all he could be told about the social structure and economic constitution of his realm may be readily admitted; but the circumstances of the time put a new pressure on natural curiosity, and demanded immediate answer. Nothing in his reign more clearly shows the clear-thinking, constructive mentality of those who, in the *curia regis,* instigated policy, and the administrative efficiency of those who, throughout the country, set it to work, than the rapid compilation of a survey which has no equal in the mediaeval world; but it must be admitted that Domesday will disappoint those who go to it in the hope of finding an account of the life-and-times of Norman England as vivid, for example, as the Bayeux Tapestry. It is dry, factual, and truly expository only to a mediaeval accountant.

Each county is separately described, but the picture is confused by the fact that properties within the county are dealt with under the names of tenants-in-chief, though the lands belonging to a tenant might be widely scattered. Here, for example, is a fragment—in translation—of the description of Kent, opening in Dover:

'Dover in the time of King Edward used to pay 18 pounds, of which money King Edward had two-thirds and Earl Godwin the (other) third. [This was one moiety.] And against this the canons of St. Martin had another moiety. The burgesses supplied to the king once in the year 20 ships for 15 days, and in each ship were 21 men. This they did because he had remitted to them the sac and soc. Whenever the king's messengers came there they paid 3 pence for the passage of a horse in the winter and 2 pence in the summer, the burgesses finding a steersman and one other helper; if more help was needed it was obtained out of (the steersman's) pay. In the interval between the feast of St. Michael and that of St. Andrew the town was under the king's peace. If any one broke it the king's reeve took for the breach a fine from all in common. A permanent settler in the town paid customary dues to the king and was exempted from toll throughout England. All these customs were in force there at the time when King William came into England. Just after he came into England the town was burnt down, and therefore a right valuation could not be made of what it was worth when the bishop of Bayeux received it. It is now valued at 40 pounds, and yet the reeve pays there from 54 pounds, to the king 24 pounds at 20 to the ore, to the Earl 30 pounds by tale.'

More typical is the methodical description of certain lands 'in Bewsborough Hundred':

'Ralf de St. Sansone holds 1 manor as a prebend. It is called Charlton, and it is assessed at 1 sulung. There he has three villeins and 4 bordars with 1 plough. In all it is worth 70 shillings; in the time of King Edward it was worth 100 shillings. Lewin held it as a prebend.

'In the same vill William son of Oger holds 1 sulung, and there he has 1 villein and 7 bordars with half a plough and 1 mill worth 40 shillings. There a certain Frenchman has one plough. The same William holds 1 church in Dover of the bishop and pays him 11 shillings. The canons claim this. This is in all worth 6 pounds; it was worth 12 pounds *T.R.E.* Sired held it.

'In Buckland Alwi holds 1 sulung, and there he has 6 villeins and 10 bordars with 1½ ploughs. In all it is worth 4 pounds; it was worth *T.R.E.* 100 shillings. The same Alwi held it as a prebend.'

That is sufficient to show that Domesday was not intended for the general reader, though the general reader need not know the precise dimensions of a sulung—a measure of land—to observe that many lands and properties showed a sad decline in value from *T.R.E.* (the time of king Edward) in consequence of war and the dislocation of society. There are items of greater interest—or minor yet illuminating interest—but they have to be sought and gleaned. It is, for example, agreeable to learn that in the small county of Middlesex woods of oak and beech grew to the gates of London. William fitz Stephen, a Canterbury monk who lived in the reign of Henry II, wrote of London—perhaps a hundred years after Domesday—'Close by lies an immense forest, in which are densely wooded thickets, the coverts of game, red and fallow deer, boars and wild bulls.' Worth noting also is the fact, attested by fitz Stephen, that the Norman forest laws were not so regally and cruelly exclusive as is often thought; for according to him: 'Many citizens do take delight in birds, as sparrow-hawks, gos-hawks etc., and in dogs to sport in the woody coverts, for they were privileged to hunt in Middlesex, in Hertfordshire, in all the Chilterns, and in Kent as low down as Crag Water.'—'Two nests of hawks in the wood' is an item that may occur in the survey.

Woodland was of great value, and always included in the survey of a manor. In addition to fuel and timber for building, the forest-floor, rich in acorns and beech mast, gave autumn feeding, called pannage, to large herds of swine; and a forest was commonly measured by the number of swine it would graze. In

Middlesex there were no fewer than 20,000, including 2000 in Harrow, 500 in Tottenham, 200 in Westminster, another 200 in Kensington. Of the twenty-eight vineyards mentioned in Domesday, six were in Middlesex; a high proportion which may not be unconnected with the ownership of the county, the greater part of which was in the hands of the bishop of London and the abbot of Westminster.

Unique and of immense value though it is, one cannot read a page of Domesday without wishing, however vainly, that it had been written with a more human fullness: with some regard for the frustrated interest of posterity, as well as for the grasping hands of the tax-gatherer.

Chapter XXII

DEATH OF A KING

THE Danish attack in 1069, when Sweyn Estrithson was king, had been led by his sons Harald and Cnut, and Osbern, his brother. The great fleet of two hundred and forty ships reached the Humber, the men of the northern Danelaw rose in rebellion to join the invaders, Norman garrisons were defeated, and York fell. Six years later, when Sweyn was dead, Cnut commanded the fleet which sailed—but sailed too late—to join forces with the rebel earls Ralf of Norfolk, Roger of Hereford, and Waltheof. Between Cnut and his brother Harald there had been conflict for the crown, and Harald, who was tolerant at home and disinclined for war abroad, had won the succession by popular favour. But in 1081 Cnut succeeded Harald, and from the Danish throne revived his family claim to the throne of England. One may assume that he was moved, not so much by the faint legitimacy of his claim, as by the viking spirit and a still lively hope of the great prize west over sea.

He established an alliance with count Robert of Flanders, whose sister Adela he had married, and with Olaf the Quiet, king of Norway. Olaf had sailed with his father, Harald Hardrada, on the voyage that came to an end at Stamford Bridge. He and the two young Orkney earls had remained with their ships when Harald went into battle, and Harold of England had mercifully given them their freedom. Olaf had ruled Norway peacefully— a fair-haired, genial man, talkative and merry in drink—and once had told his people, 'Your freedom is my happiness'; in his reign they had grown rich and taken to new fashions in dress and fine clothes. But he was friendly with Cnut of Denmark, and listened, a little doubtfully, when Cnut proposed an alliance against England. He remembered his father's ill-fortune and had no wish to go into war himself, but he gave Cnut a well-found fleet of sixty ships. The naval strength of the coalition—if the combined fleets were to sail—would be overwhelming.

That was the threat which brought William out of Normandy with the great mercenary army of horse and foot that raised, in the mind of him who wrote the relevant paragraph in the Anglo-Saxon Chronicle, a doubt of England's capacity to feed it; and prompted the Domesday survey of the kingdom. William's fear for the safety of his realm was realistic—this was the third time that Cnut had made ready to fight for it—but one cannot exclude a suspicion that anxiety over-rode his judgment; or, perhaps more accurately, that if his judgment had been as sound as twenty years before, his anxiety would have been less acute and his defensive preparation less prodigal. His foreign army strained the resources of England, and he caused widespread grief by laying waste much coastal land to deny the invaders the produce of easy foraging. There is nothing to indicate that he could not have mobilised the usual defensive levies, though he may have doubted the loyalty of the East Anglian militia when opposed to Danes. However that may be, his mercenaries gave him an uncommonly large and mobile force: a force that would to-day be called a mass of manoeuvre. With so great a strength of horse and foot for rapid counter-attack, the devastation of seaside areas seems evidence of a prudence at fever-pitch that was quite foreign to the habit of his youth, and unjustified by sober calculation of the danger.

The danger did not, in fact, materialise; and it is, of course, very easy to be judicious about an error nine hundred years old. But in his decision to hire so numerous an army, and then desolate a frontier strip, the element of extravagance is fairly obvious; and his relief when he heard of Cnut's defeat must have been sharply discounted by the bills he had to pay.—Cnut was defeated by rebellion at home. The powerful fleet he had assembled in the Limfjord in Jutland was dispersed, and before increasing hostility the king had to flee. He was killed in a church at Odensee, and by some strange mutation his viking spirit is said to have acquired in the grave a saintly quality that brought pilgrims to his tomb and wrought miracles above it. He was duly canonised.

William was less fortunate. His kingly authority was re-affirmed, but his death was unhallowed. After his Great Council at

Gloucester, where the Domesday survey was ordered, he went to Winchester at Easter, to Westminster at Whitsuntide, and there, at a service taken by Lanfranc, knighted Henry, the youngest of his three surviving sons: Henry who would rule as Henry I of England after the death of his brother William Rufus. Then, at Lammas time, the beginning of August, an extraordinary council of the realm assembled at Salisbury. It was a gathering, not only of his usual councillors, but—says the Anglo-Saxon Chronicle—of all landowners of any importance throughout the whole country. Orderic Vitalis, indeed, declares the number of those attending to have been 60,000; and that figure, though swollen far beyond belief, can perhaps be accepted as an estimate of the importance of the meeting, if not of its actual size. It was a unique occasion, and at first glance seems to indicate doubt or uncertainty in William's mind about the loyalty of some of those he had summoned; for, in the words of the Chronicle, they were required to submit to him and take oaths of allegiance, swearing fealty to him against all others.

There has been much argument about the purpose and constitution of this assembly. In one sense, of course, its purpose was obvious: a general declaration was elicited of loyalty to the king that took precedence over a man's nearer loyalty to his immediate feudal superior. But why was such an oath desired, or thought necessary? That the king had smelt a little draught of treachery, either among his tenants-in-chief or their tenants, may be the easiest answer, but it is not the only one. It may be that the feudal principle, so recently introduced into England, needed definition: it was, perhaps, academically desirable that the primacy of the king's claim to his subjects' allegiance should be emphasised. Or, on the other hand, the Salisbury assembly and the Salisbury oath may be yet another indication of William's aging mind and an agitated determination to set his house in order. The intemperate arrest of his doughty brother Odo, his extravagant preparation against Danish attack, the hurried, intensive scrutiny of Domesday Book, and now this insistence on a general re-iteration of his acceptance as England's undoubted king—were they symptoms of a premature senility and the anxieties of a mind obsessed by the fear that his great achievement was still in jeopardy? He was nearing sixty, his soldierly strength had become a bloated corpulence, but his mind was still active, still indomitable; his mind, however, was in a hurry, and to achieve haste it demanded extreme measures. His royal authority must be established beyond doubt, the safety of his realm assured, and in the restless pertinacity of his last years he would suffer neither tardiness nor restraint.

Little or nothing is known of his activities in the later months of 1086. He is said to have been in the Isle of Wight, he is reported to have been exigent in the collection of new taxes; and that is the bare record of his last autumn—so often the sweetest season of the year—in his obedient realm of England. He was in Normandy again before Christmas, and he still had time, it seems, to show a paternal care for his church. The abbey of Westminster got his attention about this time, and a nunnery in Rouen benefited from his interest. But dominating his mind was the ever-present need of military defence against the enemies who still threatened the frontiers of his duchy.

The Vexin, that troubled strip, was again debatable land. In the south a timely marriage had extended the possessions of Roger of Beaumont, on whose allegiance he could rely, and when French troops from Mantes made a foray into Normandy William demanded the cession of all that was called the Vexin Français. Philip refused, and William boldly attacked with the apparent intention of occupying by force the disputed territory. Having crossed the Epte, he advanced on Mantes. A French garrison came out to offer battle, and as if to recall the quick decision and fierce movement of his early campaigns in England, William met the advancing enemy before they were ready, and routed them. They fled into the town with the Normans at their heels, and with horrible brutality Mantes was sacked. An old Norse weapon came into play again, the conquered town was set on fire and utterly destroyed. Now Mantes, on the Seine, is only thirty miles from Paris, and it has lately been suggested[1] that its cruel and deliberate destruction may have been designed, not merely as a warning that William of Normandy would tolerate no further inroads on the Vexin, but as a threat to Paris itself.

On one side of his duchy there was a hostile Flanders, on the other a predatory Anjou, and between them Philip of France. In

[1] David Douglas, *William the Conqueror.*

the haste of his premature old age, and with the savage intention of a man who has little time to achieve his final purpose, it may well be that William—with England secure behind him—had resolved on the audacity of a frontal attack against the French king, whose defeat, if it could be achieved, would discourage the envious ambitions of Anjou and Flanders. To give William credit for so bold a purpose is, indeed, no more than a wondering admission that in his anxious mind there still lived an imaginative fragment of the military genius that had carried him to greatness. But the age of his unwieldy body denied him the reward that a persistent spirit might have won, for as he rode through the blackened streets of Mantes he pitched forward and lay helpless on his charger.

His horse, rearing in fright at the fall of a blazing timber, may have thrown its ponderous rider onto the iron peak of the mediaeval saddle with heavy impact; or perhaps an inflamed and overladen intestine perforated. The king collapsed, in violent pain, and the advance was halted. From Mantes, in the heat of August, William was carried to Rouen again, but the noise of its busy streets would not let him rest, and from there he was taken to the priory of Saint Gervais on the low hills west of the city. Two churchmen, reputed to be good doctors, attended him, but it soon became apparent that he was beyond their help; and then, says the monk Orderic Vitalis, those who were the enemies of peace were glad, and looked forward to seizing at will their neighbours' goods; but others, who treasured peace, dreaded the death of him who had kept the peace.

By the king's bedside were his sons William Rufus and Henry, his brother Roger, count of Mortain, the archbishop of Rouen, and the great men of his household; but his brother Odo lay in prison in Rouen, Lanfranc was in England, and Robert, William's eldest son, was with the king of France. To him, the rebel, William gave reluctant forgiveness. He neither hid his anger nor concealed his belief that Robert was little suited to the government of a brave and headstrong race. The Normans needed the control of a firm hand, as did Robert himself. But he had promised Normandy to his eldest son, and the barons of the duchy pleaded for peace between them and the fulfilment of his promise. So Robert was forgiven, and the duchy committed to him.

It was an edifying death-bed, dominated by piety and penitence, and Orderic Vitalis has recorded at great length the long agony of the king. His piety is not to be doubted, for in that century piety was as common to the minds of men as violence to their hands, and penitence was often passionate. Warfare had filled much of William's life, and he remembered the cruelty of his wars, the rape of England, the desolation of Yorkshire and the north, and the burning of Mantes. Many thousands had been done to death by his will, towns had been plundered, hunger had followed the bloody progress of war. For all this he repented, and ordered a lavish distribution of alms to purge his guilt. The ruined churches of Mantes were to be re-built, many churches in England got rich gifts, money must be given to the poor. And his prisoners were to be set free—all but the son of Herlève, the bishop of Bayeux.

Against this bitter discrimination his barons strongly protested. Foremost among them, Roger of Mortain pleaded for his brother's release. William was still obdurate. If Odo were pardoned he would bring trouble to the realm and ruin to thousands.—William on his death-bed seems still to be defending his hotheaded imprisonment of the bishop.—But none of those about him shared his pretended fear, they offered pledges for Odo's good behaviour, and by sheer persistence persuaded the weary, dying king to give him freedom; and Odo left his prison in time to attend his brother's funeral.

Robert had been provided for—Robert had got Normandy— but disposal must be made of England, and though William wanted his son William Rufus to succeed him, he was now aware—or so says Orderic Vitalis—that England was his not by the hereditary right of blood, but by the guilty blood of a battlefield. He had no right to bequeath a kingdom so acquired to any but God himself. So to William Rufus he gave his sceptre, sword, and crown, and prayed that God would lend substance to them by His gift of England. Thus, with God's goodwill, was provision made for William Rufus, and in anticipation of God's complaisance the dying Conqueror gave him a letter addressed to Lanfranc, in which his disposal of the kingdom was confirmed, and bade William go at once to his inheritance. William Rufus obeyed him promptly, and was on his way to England when he heard of his father's death.

There remained Henry, the Conqueror's youngest son, who is said to have asked, with apparent impatience, 'And what do you give me, my father?' 'Five thousand pounds of silver from my treasury,' said the Conqueror. 'But what use is treasure to me, if I have nowhere to live?' asked Henry. 'Be patient, my son, and trust in the Lord,' replied his father. Whereupon Henry left as promptly as his brother, to count his legacy and find a place of safety for it.

The Conqueror, who had already made his last confession, received the sacrament from the hands of the archbishop of Rouen. He slept quietly, and at dawn on Thursday the 9th September he woke to the sound of a great bell ringing. 'Why does it ring?' he asked. 'For prime in the church of Our Lady,' he was told. Then the Conqueror lifted his hands in prayer and said, 'To our Lady Mary, the holy Mother of God, I commend myself that by her prayers she may reconcile me to her dear Son our Lord Jesus Christ.' And so, if the good monk Orderic Vitalis can be trusted, his soul passed into peace.

But there was no peace in the death-chamber. The king was dead, and his death had dispelled the mystical authority that even a dying king exhaled; and confusion remained. The magnates who had watched his bed mounted and rode off. Their houses and possessions, no longer protected by the king's peace, had to be guarded against the lawless forces that even a brief anarchy might release. And when their lords had gone, the lesser people about the place began to plunder the bed-chamber. They took what they could carry—arms and silver, bed-linen and the royal furniture—and left the king's body half naked on the floor. In the streets of Rouen there was panic, as if a foreign army were at its gates, and people sought hiding-places for their valuables and meditated flight. Nothing shows more clearly the power of the Conqueror, over the minds of men as well as their bodies, than the fear that followed his death; his rule had been strict and often harsh, but his rule had given peace and law to his own people, and his death was like the collapse of the ramparts within which they had lived.

His death-chamber had been pillaged, his funeral was threatened by the flight of his household. The archbishop gave orders for his body to be carried to the monastery of St. Stephen in Caen, but no one, it seemed, had remained to prepare and take it there. Then a Norman gentleman called Herluin, otherwise obscure, came to the rescue of his dead king, and the body was put aboard a boat on the Seine, and from the mouth of the river carried to the out-skirts of Caen. There a pious host of mourners waited, but the procession was interrupted by an outbreak of fire in one of the houses of the town. The fire spread quickly, the mourners scattered to fight the flames, and only a few monks attended the bier, singing the office of the dead as they walked. Fire had alarmed the congregation at William's coronation in Westminster Abbey; fire dispersed the mourners at his funeral.

But in the church there was a great assembly of Norman clergy, bishops and abbots, and the magnates of the duchy. The Conqueror's son Henry was there, and the bishop of Lisieux preached a funerary sermon in which the Conqueror's great deeds were extolled, prayers demanded for his soul, and forgiveness was asked for any wrong that any there might have suffered from the king.

At that a knight called Ascelin, a native of Caen, got up and stood upon a stone, from which he told the astonished congregation that the ground on which the church was built had belonged to his father, and that William had taken it by force. He laid claim to the land, and in the name of God forbade them to bury the body of a thief in his earth or within the bounds of his inheritance.

There was consternation in the church, but when Ascelin and others were questioned his neighbours said the charge was true, and Ascelin was summoned to hurried consultation with prince Henry and the several bishops who were present. He was given sixty shillings for William's grave, and promised the full price of his father's estate. He accepted the offer, and the bier was carried to the altar, before which lay a stone coffin.

And now the king's poor swollen body suffered its last indignity. The coffin was too small, and when those who carried him tried to force his unwieldy substance into a room too narrow for it, his body burst and filled the church with a stench of fearful corruption; and the service was concluded with improper haste.

A little while later reparation was made for the clumsy horror of his burial, but his resting-place was not destined for peace. His son William, king of England, ordered to be built for him a splendid, richly ornamented shrine, within which the stone coffin stood on columns of white marble, and in letters of gold an epitaph composed by Thomas, archbishop of York, proclaimed the scope and vigour of the Conqueror's achievements. Early in the sixteenth century the tomb was opened, the body examined, and buried again. Forty years later, when Catholics and Calvinists became savage political parties and devastated France with their religious wars, the church was wrecked by Calvinists, the shrine destroyed, and the Conqueror's bones—all but one long thigh-bone—were exhumed and scattered. The church was rebuilt, and the thigh-bone buried again. The furious revolutionaries of 1793 demolished its new tomb, but in the next century a plain stone slab was inscribed with the Conqueror's name to mark his burial place. In the prolonged and bitter fighting of 1944 much of Caen was destroyed, but the abbey church of St. Etienne, the Abbaye aux Hommes, survived. It was a British army that provoked the worst and loudest of the battles that Caen had suffered, but the men from the Conqueror's own kingdom were not guilty of disturbing yet again his remnant bone.

Nothing that can now be said about him will disturb his place in history. He was one who created history—he created a nation—and the shaping of a kingdom and its destiny is not done without hurt and violence. The Norman Conquest re-made England, and re-made it in a form which did not destroy its Anglo-Saxon origin but gave to an exhausted Saxon polity a new vigour, a new regimen, a sternly directed new purpose which proved capable, through years of tormented trial, of extraordinary growth. The Conquest was inspired by William himself. He fought for his duchy of Normandy, he made of Normandy a power that could undertake the invasion of England, and with a viking's disregard of risk —but with a civilised thoroughness of preparation—he crossed the narrow sea and gave desperate battle to Harold Godwineson. The conception of conquest was his; its strategy and tactics were his; and therefore its enormous sequence must acknowledge an origin in his heroic mind. Much of the history of Europe—perhaps of the world—was dictated by the brilliant and ruthless son of duke Robert and Herlève the tanner's daughter.

Of the man himself one has some knowledge by report, more perhaps by inference. He was tall beyond the average, burly beyond the mean, a soldier who could fight and defend himself in the front of battle as well as he could determine the place of battle and drive an army into battle with speed and resolution. He had the physical abilities of a primitive hero, and a harsh, guttural voice to shout his commands above the din of battle. But his mind was a visionary's mind, though nowadays his vision may be suspect. He wanted power, he wanted an empire, and to achieve his end he established a rule of law by extreme violence, and used his natural piety to enlist and dominate a powerful church. As a man he is not to be judged by contemporary standards, but against a mediaeval scale he is a giant who dominated his age and could shock even a mediaeval critic by the excesses of his temper.

Where he saw a politic or strategic need for brutality, his brutality was extreme. His circuitous march on London was characterised by cruel plunder of the countryside, but London yielded to his demonstration of power, there was no street-fighting, and the city was spared. The devastation of Yorkshire and the north was unforgivable, in a human context, but in the cold logic of politics it was necessary to his purpose: the forces at his command were limited in number, limited in their power of movement, and the north of England with its Norse or Danish population offered a standing invitation to Scots or Scandinavian trouble-makers. No excuse can be found for the burning of Mantes; but William had grown old, his duchy on the landward side was girt by enemies, and for an old man in a hurry, terror was the obvious weapon. He never shrank from brutality when brutality was the logical policy; but in a time when wantonness was common, he was not wantonly brutal.

He was, on the contrary, often tolerant, and he could be kind. Those who rebelled against him, when rebellion was a terrible threat to a precarious monarchy, were not summarily executed when they fell into his hands; only Waltheof can be exalted to a doubtful martyrdom, and Waltheof, who had been forgiven once, was beheaded after months of hesitation, at the end of which time some compelling reason for his death may have emerged that history—or rather a lack of history—has hidden from our knowledge. To Edgar the Atheling William showed patience, sympathy, and lastly an astonishing generosity. It is difficult to share his sympathy, for the surviving evidence of Edgar's behaviour seems to show him as a tiresome person, always ready to take advantage of a policy inimical to William—always prepared to fish in troubled waters—but without initiative, strength, or purpose of his own. His sister Margaret, the redoubtable and finally canonised queen of

Scots, had inherited all the thrust and imagination of the family stock, and to Edgar had been left nothing, one imagines, but a vacuous amiability that could turn, as in a lunar phase of his reflecting character, to mischief, spite, and spleen. But William was long-suffering—perhaps, with his deep respect for the royalty of England, he felt a superstitious regard for the Atheling's kingly blood—and when, at about the time of his lamentable quarrel with his brother Odo, Edgar asked leave to go to southern Italy, with no fewer than two hundred soldiers to attend him, William let him go.

It is worth the mention that during the Conqueror's reign in England the Byzantine emperor's Varangian Guard in Constantinople got many warlike recruits of Saxon blood. They were, it may be assumed, young men who had been deprived of their patrimony by Norman incomers. They were unwilling to live in England with a diminished status, or as servitors of a foreign ascendancy. They preferred a life of mercenary adventure in the east. And William, with a statesman's tolerance, did not hinder them. The Atheling was not the only man permitted to show dissatisfaction and leave a country that had not, as he thought, given him his deserts. He had been preceded by many others, unnamed and unknown, who had gone to profitable employment, or their death, by William's bounty.

The Conqueror's domestic life set an example of uncommon virtue; for according to all accounts he was happy with his wife and faithful to her. It is by no means improbable that the declining judgment manifest in his last years—or, to put it more charitably, the apparent loss of an heroic equanimity—was a consequence of her death in 1083, which must have aggravated the solitude he felt in the isolation of power among his watchful enemies. That he was capable of a strong family affection is suggested by the favour shown to his son William; no one else, so far as is known, felt any fondness for William Rufus.

Except in his wife, of whom little is known, it is improbable that the Conqueror inspired much love; but certainly he inspired a useful fear. For most of his life he was temperate in habit, and detested drunkenness; but as he became excessively corpulent, it seems likely that he ate more heartily in his later years, and if, as William of Jumièges wrote, 'he rarely drank more than thrice after his meal,' he may have drunk from larger beakers. He was lavish in his gifts to the church, ostentatious in the splendour of his court, and inordinate in his demand for money. In this he may have shown his continuing heritage of Norse blood, for the viking hero was typically rapacious with one hand, generous with the other. The sagas are full of greedy, overbearing men whose lust for plunder is equalled only by a prodigal hospitality. Common, too, is a vast respect for law—or, at least, for a display of legality—and a constant readiness to resort to force if the law fails to oblige; in this also the Conqueror's life reflects the ethos of the sagas. What set him apart from the masterful warrior-kings of Scandinavia was a larger achievement to which he gave the previously unknown quality of endurance; and like Charlemagne before him he had acquired a Latin culture to improve the gifts of ancestry.

That culture, with all its practical applications, he brought to England, and because William, like a Colossus, overstrode the English Channel, England finally came into association with the central and classical tradition of Europe, not with the eccentric and predatory north whose kings had striven so hard to win it.

THE DISTANT FAILURES

T HE Norse achievement cannot fully or fairly be assessed without some consideration of two historic failures, and a scrutiny of the circumstances in which the farthest and most fantastic of Norse or Norman ventures met defeat. Beyond the Atlantic an unknown continent was discovered, and in the midst of the Mediterranean the island of Sicily was conquered; but on both continent and island the impact of the foreigners was unsubstantial, their tenure of new or conquered territory short-lived.

According to the saga of Eric the Red, the American continent was first observed by Norse seamen who had sailed from Norway to Iceland and then, by accident, went farther. The owner and master of the ship was called Bearne, who appears to have entertained a quite uncommon affection for Heriulf, his father. It was to spend the winter with his father that he went to Iceland, but when he reached there he learnt that Heriulf had gone with Eric the Red to Greenland. Eric, who had previously explored the south-west coast of Greenland, led some five hundred colonists there in 986. Bearne, that dutiful son, decided to sail west in search of his father, and after three days with a fair breeze ran into fog and northerly winds, and for many days saw no sun. When the sky cleared and they got a sight of the sun they hoisted sail again, and made westing till they saw land ahead. It was low-lying, wooded, and here and there rose to small hillocks. They turned north, and for two days sailed without sight of land till they came to a flat, well-wooded shore. Bearne, still looking for Greenland, turned away and for three days sailed before a south-west wind that carried them to a mountainous island whose hillsides were streaked with glaciers. Again they turned away, and running with a reefed sail before a strong westerly, came on the fourth day to Greenland.

There Bearne found his father, and lived with him till the old man died.

Bearne then sailed east to Norway, where he told earl Ericson of the great earl Hakon of Lade—of his discoveries, and endured some criticism for his lack of curiosity and his failure to explore the new lands. He returned to Greenland, where there was talk of the possibilities of exploration. Leif, the son of Eric the Red, bought Bearne's ship and mustered a crew of thirty-five men. He asked his father to lead the expedition, but Eric said he was too old, and the ship put to sea under Leif's command. He and his crew sailed west, and their first landfall was the mountainous island streaked with glaciers. They went ashore and found it an inhospitable place where no grass grew. They called it Slate Land and sailed away—the saga does not mention their bearing, but it must have been southerly—till they came to a low-lying land with white beaches. They called it Mark Land, and sailing again, now before a north-east wind, came after two days to an island where the grass was drenched with dew, and moved into a shallow sound between islands and the land-mass. On the flood tide they rowed into a river that led them to a lake, and on the lake-shore built a house. It was good land, rich in pasture, and in both lake and river there was abundance of bigger salmon then they had ever seen before.

They built a stockade round their house, and prepared to spend the winter in pleasant surroundings. Leif divided his company into two parties, who took turns to explore the nearby country. The most remarkable discovery was made by a small, clever, but unhappy-looking man called Tyrke, a German, who had been Leif's foster-father. He came in one evening with the news that he had found vines, and grapes growing on them. After that they gathered enough grapes to fill the ship's small-boat, and cut vines to take back to Greenland: a cargo unlikely to bring them profit. The winter-months passed without the discomfort of frost—or so it is said, though what may be meant is that the lake, the river, and the inland sea were not all frozen solid—and the days were noticeably longer than in Iceland or Greenland. When spring came, Leif and his crew put to sea again, from the country they called Wineland, and sailed till they saw the cliffs of Greenland under its ice-cap.

The date of Leif's momentous voyage is uncertain; a year as

early as 1000 has been suggested, but it was probably in 999 that he went out from Norway to Greenland as Olaf Tryggvison's appointed missionary—Greenland was still heathen—and it is unlikely that the new colony was by then sufficiently well organised to man an expedition to the west. For various reasons a much later date is preferable, and more credibly the year of discovery was 1025.

A second voyage—according to Eric's saga—was less fortunate. Led by Leif's brother Thorwald, the adventurers came into conflict with Eskimo—or *Scraelings*, as the saga calls them—in their oomiaks, or skin-boats; and after the Greenlanders had killed eight of them, a vast number returned, and Thorwald was mortally wounded by an arrow. A third voyage was led by Thorfinn Carlsemne, a Norwegian who came to Greenland, apparently to settle, and after a winter there married a woman called Gudrid, whom death had deprived of two previous husbands. Encouraged to go farther, Carlsemne mustered a ship's company of sixty men and five women, and with cattle aboard he and his wife sailed westward with the intention of colonising the land where Leif had spent a winter. They found the house that Leif had built, and the grape-bearing vines; their cattle had plenty of pasture, and a whale, driven ashore, gave them sufficiency of meat. They spent a peaceful winter, but with summer the Scraelings came. They were frightened by the bellowing of the Greenlanders' bull, but returned to trade sable and other furs for milk; they asked for weapons, but Carlsemne refused and they took milk instead. They left the settlers in peace, but Carlsemne built a new stockade round the house, and within it Gudrid gave birth to a man-child, and he, the first of another race to be born in the new land, was called Snorre.

At the beginning of the second winter the Scraelings returned, now in large numbers, and one of them, trying to steal weapons, was killed by one of Carlsemne's servants. The others fled, leaving behind the furs they had brought for barter. They came again, prepared for battle, and many more were killed. One of them, finding an axe, examined it with curiosity, and as for experiment struck his neighbour. His neighbour fell dead, and then a big man, the chief of the Scraelings, picked up the axe, looked thoughtfully at it, and flung it into the sea. The Scraelings fled into the woods, and the Greenlanders enjoyed another quiet winter.

In the spring, however, Carlsemne decided to sail east again, and it may well be that his reason lay in a prudent calculation that his strength was insufficient to meet the challenge of so large a land where his potential enemies were so numerous. On the other hand—for Carlsemne was a trader, not a warrior—it may be that he was tempted to find a market for the rich cargo of furs he had accumulated: he sailed to Norway, sold his wares, and bought an estate in Iceland where his family prospered.

If the saga can be trusted—which at this point is extremely doubtful—there followed a fourth voyage, of which the instigator was Freydis, a daughter of Eric the Red. In the summer when Carlsemne left Wineland, it is said that two Icelanders, brothers called Helge and Finbow, came to Greenland and were persuaded by Freydis to join her in a new venture. She in her ship would sail with thirty men and some women, the brothers with a like company; but Freydis broke the compact by embarking thirty-five men. Their voyage was uneventful, and their navigation good enough to find again the house that Leif had built. But no sooner had they landed than dissension began, and so much ill-will was fomented by Freydis—whose husband, Thorward, was slavishly devoted to her—that the brothers and all their followers were killed, not by Scraelings, but by their fellow-adventurers who fell upon them while they slept. After which Freydis and her husband returned to Greenland and lived in dishonour for the remainder of their lives.

That story of a fourth voyage wears a very artificial complexion. Almost certainly it is fictitious, but it may well be the fabulous enlargement of some incidents in Carlsemne's expedition. His voyage earned a saga of its own which expands the story told in the saga of Eric the Red—agrees substantially but not in detail with it—and adds some picturesque items. It is said, in Carlsemne's saga, that three ships sailed from Greenland, manned by a hundred and forty men, and with them were women and cattle. Two of the women were Gudrid, Carlsemne's wife, and Freydis, Eric's daughter; and commanding one of the ships was Thorward, the husband of Freydis. Their course took them first to Slate Land, then to Mark Land, and from there to a land where long firths ran far inshore. Two very strange members of Carl-semne's crew were Highland Scots, a man and his wife, whom Olaf Tryggvison had given to Leif Ericson: they were valuable because, like all Highland Scots of that time—or such was their reputation—they were fleet-footed as a deer. In one of the long firths the ships lay to their anchors, and the Scots were put ashore with orders to run southward, spy out the land, and return within three days; and when they came back one carried a bunch of grapes, the other an ear of wild wheat.

The ships sailed south as far as a firth guarded by an island on which birds had laid so thickly that it was hardly possible to set foot between their eggs; and somewhere on the shore of the firth, within sight of mountains, the colonists disembarked their stores and cattle and made a settlement. They had a hard and hungry winter, though their cattle found good pasture, and the meat of a whale that came ashore made them ill. But when spring came they caught an abundance of fish and found birds' eggs in plenty. A few of them, discontented, put to sea under command of a man called Thorhall Huntsman, and were storm-driven, says the saga, as far as Ireland; but Carlsemne and the main body sailed south and after a long time came to the mouth of a river that ran into the sea behind a group of islands. Only at high water could they sail into the river, but on its banks they found self-sown wheat and vines, there were brooks full of fish, and wild beasts in the woods. There for the first time they saw the Scraelings—small, ugly men, with ugly hair, big eyes, and broad cheek-bones—but had no conversation with them.

After a quiet and comfortable winter the Scraelings came again, in great numbers, and settled down to trade. What they wanted—apart from weapons, which Carlsemne would not give them—was red cloth; but the market was interrupted, as in the other story, by the bellowing of the Greenlanders' bull. The frightened Scraelings did not return for three weeks, but when they did come again there was a multitude of them, in a solid stream of boats, and they were howling for battle. They were armed with slings and some strange engine that flung large missiles. The Greenland-ers were driven back towards the houses they had built, and there was a hard fight in which Freydis played a decisive part.

She came out of her house and spoke scornfully to the retreating men, but had to follow them as they withdrew into a wood. She was heavily pregnant, and walked slowly. The Scraelings ran towards her, and Freydis, stooping to a dead man—killed by a stone stuck fast in his forehead—picked up his sword and prepared to defend herself. She pulled her breasts out of her shift and slapped the bright sword on them, and at that astonishing spectacle the Scraelings took fright, as they had when the bull bellowed, and fled to their boats.

Now the Greenlanders began to think that the new land, though full of riches, was too dangerous to live in. They journeyed to and fro, with apparent restlessness; tempers were frayed, their spirits low, and the men who had no wives quarrelled with their married companions. There was a rumour that Freydis, whose husband was Thorward when they left Greenland, was living with a man called Bearne; and that redoubtable and shameless woman may indeed have caused much dissension and started gossip enough to furnish the tale, in Eric's saga, of a disastrous fourth voyage. During their three years in the New World the Greenlanders did not always live in one community, and from their physical separation could have emerged stories that, to a later generation, seemed quite unconnected. It is probable, therefore, that Carlsemne's expedition was the last attempt to make a settlement in the west, and when he sailed away the Norsemen looked back, for the last time, at Wineland the Good. His ship was the only one that returned; for Thorhall Huntsman had deserted, and on the homeward voyage Bearne was carried far to the south where in warm water the ship-worm, or teredo, ate deep into the hull of his vessel and sank her; but half his company, in the ship's boat, are said to have escaped and been carried by westerly winds to Ireland.

It is quite obvious that Wineland was infinitely richer in natural resources that either Iceland or Greenland. Present knowledge leaves no doubt about that, and from the voyagers' own stories it is clear that they themselves appreciated the wealth of the unknown continent of which they had seen no more than a fragment. Why, then, was no further attempt made to explore and exploit it?

In the first place, the bare facts of geography imposed difficulties. From Bergen in Norway to Reykjavik in Iceland was more than 900 miles; from Reykjavik to Cape Farewell at the southern corner of Greenland about 800; from the south-west of Greenland to Nantucket Island, close on 2000 miles. The obvious base from which to mount an expedition was Greenland, but Greenland was itself an outpost of Norse colonisation where a scattered population numbered, at most, about three thousand people. From its own resources Greenland could never have equipped a colonial venture much larger than that which Thorfinn Carlsemne led, or more clearly capable of dealing with the recurrent danger of angry Eskimo. It is fairly evident that the Greenlanders were not warriors, but traders, fishermen, and cultivators of their narrow fields below the ice-cap; the demands of their environment were such as to leave them no surplus of heroic spirit to inspire a reckless penetration of unknown country.

It is true, of course, that news of the discovery reached Norway, and for many years after the voyages of Leif and Carlsemne there must have been, in all parts of the northern world, much talk of the land that lay beyond the westering sun. There is a passage in the Icelandic Book of Settlements that refers to what may be called gossip about it in the court of earl Thorfinn of Orkney, who died a year or two before 1066. And whoever talked with any seriousness of Wineland would have had to think of the enormous difficulties of organising, in Norway, an expedition which would have to provision itself, and find fodder for cattle, for an Atlantic voyage broken after 900 miles in Iceland; after another 800 in Greenland; and that would then, after scanty replenishment, have to face the long haul to its ultimate harbour. There was, in fact, no feasible way of planting a colony large enough to protect itself, except by first establishing in Greenland a parent-colony equipped not only with the necessary material for settlement, but with an adequate company of fighting-men.

In the second place—second to geographical difficulty—there was an historical obstacle. The time of the discovery was inopportune. Carlsemne's adventure probably came to an end about 1030, when Olaf of Norway—he who was later called St. Olaf —was killed at the battle of Stiklestad, fighting to regain the country from which he had been expelled; and when his son Magnus the Good succeeded him a few years later, the prospect of extending his kingdom over Denmark promised a nearer reward than distant exploration. Thirty years later Harald Hardrada might conceivably have had the strength, the moral influence, to lead a great expedition into the west; but Harald had the throne of England in view.

Had Wineland been discovered thirty or forty years earlier—if, some years before 1000, positive and detailed news of its riches had reached the Scandinavian homelands—there were two men, then living, of sufficient stature to essay its settlement. One was Sweyn Forkbeard of Denmark, though he, being a Dane, would have had to pay dearly for the use of Iceland as a staging-area; and the other was Olaf Tryggvison. If Olaf, that passionate and warlike missionary, had been seized with the idea of planting a great militant Christian colony on rich soil beyond the western ocean, he with his towering strength and fierce sense of purpose might have overcome all difficulties—to him the Scraelings would have been the least of them—and the history of the world would have taken a different turn. But Leif Ericson's discovery came too late for that.

The attempt on Wineland failed because Norway and its outposts had not strength enough to meet the physical difficulties of such distant voyaging, and because, in the circumstances of the time, there was no one then living, with the necessary authority of birth and intellect—and unencumbered by other plans—to lead men against those difficulties. Greenland itself lay too far away for life to be maintained, and when history proved as inimical as geography, the Greenlanders died. By 1500 its only human inhabitants were the Eskimo.

The opposite failure, of the venture into Sicily, was opposite in many respects, and can only be called a failure because its brilliant success was so short-lived. The conquest of Sicily in no way resembles the Norman conquest of England, but it was comparable with the Norse forays into Wineland because—in so far as it was Norman—it was due to the effort of a few individuals. The Norse in Wineland, however, were daunted by the huge emptiness of the new lands; the Normans in Sicily were suffocated by the multitude who came to share the riches they had won.

The Normans who first sought opportunities for military service in southern Italy were soldiers of fortune in a land so fragmented as to make war profitable. Sicily was in the hands of the Moslems, the power of the Lombard dukes of Benevento was broken, the provinces abandoned by the Lombards were weakly ruled by the Byzantine emperor's Greek governors. In the beginning the Normans served either Greeks or Lombards, but when Sergius, duke of Naples, entrusted the fortress of Aversa to an adventurer called Rainulf in 1030, he gave them an opportunity to fight for their own advantage; and the sons of Tancred of Hauteville rode in to enrich themselves and bequeath to history a few scintillating paragraphs. Tancred was a member of the lesser nobility of Coutances in the Cotentin peninsula, and may well be compared with the half-legendary Ragnar Lodbrok, in that his historical importance was asserted by his several remarkable sons.

William and Drogo were the first to arrive, and their determined effort to win Apulia from the Greeks brought in two more of the family, Humfrey and the outstanding Robert Guiscard: Robert the Ingenious or Independent. He fought successfully against the pope, and later won papal approval. Roger, his youngest brother, joined him, and they continued their war against the Greeks of southern Italy. To Robert were granted, by pope Nicholas II, Apulia, Calabria, and Sicily—though Sicily was not yet conquered—and he agreed to maintain the cause of Rome and pay rent for his dukedom.

In 1061 he and Roger invaded Sicily and took Messina. The Arab princes of Sicily were almost independent of their nominal suzerain, the sultan of Tunis, and among their subjects were many Greek Christians. While Robert Guiscard maintained his offensive against the Greeks of the mainland—and waged war on the Byzantine empire—Roger continued his slow but progressive conquest of the island. He captured Palermo in 1072, and was invested by his brother as count of Sicily. In 1086 Syracuse surrendered to him, and five years later his conquest was complete. He ruled the island with almost undisputed authority through Norman, French, and Italian vassals, and as apostolic legate was master of its church. He created Latin bishoprics and made the archbishopric of Palermo a Catholic see, but the Greek churches continued to enjoy freedom of worship in their own style, and the Moslems retained their mosques and their freedom to trade. From the Moslems he enlisted the infantry of his army, but the peace and prosperity of the island drew to it so many Lombards and other Italians that the Latin element prevailed, and the conquest of Sicily marked the decline of Arab power in the Mediterranean.

Geoffrey Malaterra, a contemporary historian, wrote of count Roger that in his youth he was 'of the greatest beauty, of lofty stature, of graceful shape, most eloquent in speech and cool in counsel. He was far-seeing, pleasant, and merry with all his men; strong and brave, and furious in battle.' Malaterra has left a general description of the Normans as he saw them. They were, he says, very astute, given to revenge, and capable of holding their own lands cheaply when there was hope of winning better. They were eager for gain and dominion, good at imitation; they could be lavish as well as greedy. Their leaders, indeed, were extremely bountiful because of their delight in good reputation.—'*Principes vero delectatione bonae famae largissimi.*'—They knew how to flatter, they were eloquent, but as a race utterly violent—'*effrenatissima*'—unless held firmly down by law. They could endure labour, hunger, and cold; they took pleasure in hunting, horses, and the weapons of war. And it was because they themselves had come from the north that they called their land Normandy.

It is a remarkable description, for it could have been written, with equal truth, about the original Norse settlers in France and about the viking invaders of England. The Sicilian adventurers had polished their speech, their traditional gift for intricate versifying had become a more purposive eloquence, but their violence, their endurance, their avid desire of fame, and the alternation between generosity and rapacity—these were the characteristics of every Norse warrior of repute in the heroic age of the great propulsion. Their faculty of imitation had given them a light disguise, but their nature was so little altered that the Latinity of Geoffrey Malaterra brings to mind the Horatian tag: '*Caelum non animum mutant qui trans mare currunt.*'—'They change their sky, not their souls, who run across the sea.'

Roger, the Great Count, died at the age of seventy in 1101, and was succeeded by his son Roger II, born of his third wife, who when he came of age exposed a truly Norman ambition. He resolved to unite all the Norman possessions in Italy—all the lands won by the wandering sons of Tancred of Hauteville— and after nearly twenty years of intrigue and war got his opportunity when schism in Rome elected two popes, and Roger supported Anacletus II, by whose bull he was crowned king of Sicily in 1130.

War followed, and for ten years Roger of Sicily fought against a coalition, formed by the party of the true pope, Innocent II, that was joined by Louis VI of France, Henry I of England, and the emperor Lothair. Twice he was defeated by his brother-in-law Ranulf, but the Moslem infantry whom his father had enlisted were formidable warriors, and after the death of Ranulf and the withdrawal of the emperor, Roger was master of the field, and pitilessly he subdued the last of the rebels. Anacletus died in 1138, and Roger demanded confirmation of his title from Innocent II. The pope's reply was to march south with a large army, which was ambushed on the Garigliano; and the pope acknowledged his defeat by investing Roger as king of Sicily, duke of Apulia, and prince of Capua.

Now one of the great kings in Europe, Roger turned his ambitious eye to the sea, and his admirals made Sicily the greatest maritime power in the Mediterranean. Chief of them was George of Antioch, who conquered much of the African coast from Tripoli to Cape Bon, and in the second crusade gave Roger the means to renew Robert Guiscard's old hostility to the Greek empire. George of Antioch sailed to Corinth, sacked Thebes, and from the waterfront of Constantinople fired into the palace windows. The emperor Manuel was not seriously perturbed by his attack, and a few years later, in 1154, Roger's ambitions were confounded by death.

He was not, like his uncle Robert, a great warrior, though he had the appearance of one, being tall and powerfully built, fair-haired and full-bearded, with a harsh voice and the face—so it is curiously said—of a lion. But he was a sovereign who combined a marvellous audacity and great powers of diplomacy with intellectual interests that drew to his court the scholars of many races; and like all the Normans he was splendidly tolerant of all creeds and nationalities and their languages.

It was, in part, that tolerance which led to the disappearance, as Normans, of the conquering incomers. They were too few in number to establish a dominant caste, and with Norman adaptability they accepted the conditions of their environment. They could not become Sicilians, as the Normans in England became Englishmen, because Sicily was a confusion of races, of Arabs and Greeks and Jews and Lombards, and tolerance gave no impulse to amalgamation. They did, however, give Sicily a political structure, a financial system, and an administration which distinguished it by an efficiency very rare in Europe of the twelfth century.

Roger was succeeded by William I, called the Bad, who suppressed rebellion with great severity, and by William II, called the Good, who married Joan, the daughter of Henry II of England. He defended his kingdom against Byzantium and the emperor Frederick Barbarossa, he attempted the conquest of Constantinople, and maintained the internal peace of his kingdom. But after his death the succession was disputed, violence returned, and the brief dynasty was over-thrown by the emperor Henry VI. The Norman adventure was concluded, but the memorials to its short period of splendour and achievement remain in the churches and palaces that Roger and his successors built.

The Norman passion for architecture flourished riotously in Sicily, and Romanesque happily absorbed both Byzantine and Moslem forms. Court architecture preferred the Moslem models, and in Palermo there are palaces in which Roman arch and classic column blend with Byzantine mosaics and Moslem domes. In the Palatine chapel in Palermo, built by Roger II between 1132 and 1143, there are slender Byzantine marble columns, and under pointed Moslem arches dedicated to St. Peter the colour of Byzantine mosaics. S. Cataldo looks nothing like a church, beneath Moslem domes, but the Mediterranean sun makes it acceptable. The cathedral at Cefalù, begun by Roger II, has a magnificent front in which towers like minarets enclose a columned porch with pointed arches, behind which are Norman arches; and the Romanesque sanctuary is superbly decorated with Byzantine mosaics. In the cathedral of Sta Maria la Nuova, which has been called the climax of Sicilian Romanesque architecture, the plan is Romanesque but the decoration Byzantine and Moslem. To the solid achievements of Norman adventure—martial and clerical and administrative—must be added, in Sicily, a superb and exuberant fantasy, that cannot be divorced from a light-hearted delight in living, and looks very odd indeed against a background of rapacious, warlike knights and sea-darkened vikings. It demonstrates yet again, however, the extraordinary adaptability of Norse and Norman, and, of course, the benignity of the Mediterranean.

But the Mediterranean, like North America, was too far from the homeland of adventure for its plantations to flourish. In the latter its colony perished of inanition, in the former, of superfluity. In Sicily the Normans did not make a desert and call it peace, but created an oasis and let it become over-crowded; and the conquerors were lost in the throng. It was in England that the Norse propulsion, which found its ultimate and formative strength in the Norman conquest, had its greatest and most lasting success, because England had been shaped for the process by both history and geography. It lay close enough to the continent of Europe to make invasion—and the replenishment of invasion—possible in practice, and the consanguinity of its people was such that when the Normans became Englishmen they did not lose in an alien mass their essential Norman quality.

BIBLIOGRAPHY

The Venerable Bede's *Historia Ecclesiastica*, trans. J. A. Giles, takes
English history as far as 726.
The Anglo-Saxon Chronicle, 494–1154. There is a new and excellent
translation, edit. Professor Dorothy Whitelock, which contains
versions of the several mss.

Early English chronicles subsidiary to, or complementary of, the
A. S. Chronicle are:
Asser's *Life of King Alfred*, trans. L. C. Jane. Asser was a Welsh
monk, later bishop of Sherborne, who apparently wrote his *Life*
in 893.
Florence of Worcester was a collector and editor of earlier material,
and died in 1118. Trans. J. Stevenson in *The Church Histories of
England*.
Simeon of Durham wrote, after 1104, a history of the kings and
another of the church in Durham, trans. J. Stevenson.
William of Malmesbury wrote in the twelfth century *Gesta Regum
Anglorum and Historia Novella*, trans. J. A. Giles.
Henry of Huntingdon: His *Historia Anglorum* stops in 1154. Trans.
T. Forester.

The principal Norse originals are:
Heimskringla, by Snorri Sturluson. A collection of sagas of the
Norwegian kings, trans. Wm. Morris and E. Magnusson, who
add very informative indexes and genealogies.
Njal's Saga, trans. as *The Story of Burnt Njal*, by George Webbe
Dasent.
Egil's Saga, trans. E. R. Eddison.
Orkneyinga Saga, trans. A. B. Taylor.
Origines Islandicae, by Gudbrand Vigfusson and F. York Powell;
translations of important sagas and such early Icelandic writing
as the Book of Settlements; with copious notes.

Corpus Poeticum Boreale, by Vigfusson and Powell.
Gesta Danorum, by Saxo Grammaticus, trans. (in part) Oliver Elton.

Irish annals include the *Annals of Ulster, of Innisfallen, of Tigernach, of Clonmacnois,* the *Book of Leinster,* and *The Wars of the Irish with the Foreigners;* and translations of those parts of them which relate to events in Britain can be found in the two indispensable volumes of A. O. Anderson's *Early Sources of Scottish History.*

Some French originals are the chronicles of Richer, a monk of Rheims, the only authority for the end of the Carolingian period; Flodoard, also of Rheims, who died in 996; Dudo of St. Quentin, who died before 1043 and whose account of the early Scandinavian settlement in France is not reliable.
William of Poitiers wrote *Gesta Willelmi ducis Normannorum et regis Angliae.*
William of Jumièges wrote *Historia Normannorum* (851–1087), partly based on Dudo, partly trans. Stevenson.
Robert Wace wrote *Roman de Rou,* in which there is a very romantic account of the battle of Hastings, and presented it to Henry II.
Orderic Vitalis, a monk of English birth who lived in Normandy, wrote *Historia Ecclesiastica,* trans. T. Forester, which is useful for the history of England after the Conquest.
The relevant portions of the above works are to be found, very largely, in the footnotes of E. A. Freeman's *The Norman Conquest.*

E. A. Freeman was a Victorian scholar who published *The Norman Conquest* in five substantial volumes between 1870 and 1876. His opinions may not all be so generally acceptable today as they were some ninety years ago, but he was scrupulously careful to quote in very generous footnotes and long appendices the authorities on whom he built his narrative, and these additions to his own magisterial pages make a delightful anthology of prime sources. For this reason Freeman is invaluable.

Of the works of modern scholars Sir Frank Stenton's *Anglo-Saxon England* is a first necessity, and the recently published *William the Conqueror* by Professor David C. Douglas, the leading authority on Anglo-Norman history, is equally essential.

Domesday Book and Beyond, by F. W. Maitland.
Scottish Annals from English Chronicles, ed. A. O. Anderson.

Decisive Battles of the Western World, by J. F. C. Fuller. (For the battle of Hastings.)

The Fifteen Decisive Battles of the World, by Sir Edward Creasey. (This contains a translation of Wace's romantic description of the battle in his *Roman de Rou.*)

An Introduction to the Viking History of Western Europe, by Haakon Shetelig.

The Vikings, by A. Mawer.

A History of the Vikings, by T. D. Kendrick.

Several articles (esp. by E. A. Freeman) in the Eleventh Edition of the Encyclopaedia Britannica.

Several chapters by W. J. Corbett in Vols. II, III, and V of the *Cambridge Medieval History.*

Various passages in the *Victoria County Histories.*

The King's Works, H. M. Stationery Office, from which most of the material in Ch. XVIII is derived.

The Bayeux Tapestry: There are several 'editions,' of which the most compendious is by Sir Eric Maclagan.

It may be noted that, as a tailpiece to his *William the Conqueror,* Professor David Douglas adds 'A Select Bibliography' of Primary Sources (Chronicles and Narratives; Documents and Records) and Secondary Authorities and Works of Reference that fills twenty pages. The chronicles and books named above do no more than erect the bare authority of a skeleton.

INDEX

hAROLD:SACRAMENTVM:FECIT:

THE BRITISH ISLES IN 1066

N

ORKNEYS

HEBRIDES

LOCH NESS

SCOTLAND

IONA

L. LOMOND

Dumbarton

CLYDE R.

Edinburgh

LOTHIAN

TWEED R.

Berwick

GALLOWAY

LINDISFARNE

Bamburgh

NORTHUMBERLAND

Newcastle

Hexham

TYNE R.

Durham

ULSTER